It Takes Money, Honey

Also by Georgette Mosbacher

Feminine Force

It Takes Money, Honey

A Get-Smart Guide
to Financial Freedom

Georgette Mosbacher

with Diane Harris

ReganBooks
An Imprint of HarperCollinsPublishers

HarperCollins books may be purchased for educational, business, or sales promotional use.
For information please write: Special Markets Department, HarperCollins Publishers, Inc.,
10 East 53rd Street, New York, NY 10022.

FIRST EDITION

Designed by Elina D. Nudelman

Library of Congress Cataloging-in-Publication Data

Mosbacher, Georgette, 1947–
    It takes money, honey : a get-smart guide to financial freedom.
      p. cm
     ISBN 0-06-039236-3
     1. Finance, Personal. I. Title
  HG179.M677 1999
  332.024—dc21   98-42935

99 00 01 02 10 9 8 7 6 5 4

*First and foremost, to my mother, Dorothy Paulsin, whose good-
ness and strength of character have given me the wherewithal
to accomplish what I have in life and who remains my back-
bone to this day; and to my sisters, Melody and Lyn, and my
brother, George, whose unconditional love makes everything
possible.*

—GM

*To my mother, Eileen Harris, with deep love and gratitude: You
may not have the most money, but you surely have the biggest
heart.*

—DH

Contents

Acknowledgments

My deepest appreciation goes to my collaborator, Diane Harris. From our very first meeting, you seemed to have an intuitive understanding of what I wanted to say in this book and how I wanted to say it. Although I was familiar with the quality of your work before this, I was truly amazed by what we were able to accomplish together. I want you to know how much I appreciate your commitment to this project and what a joy it was to work with you.

I'd also like to thank my publisher and dear friend Judith Regan, who first suggested this project to me and who has been confident of the value of the message and my ability to convey it from the very start. Please know how much I value both our professional and personal relationship. Thanks as well to the staff at Regan Books who helped shepherd this project along, particularly our editors, Nancy Peske and Dana Isaacson.

Diane and I would both like to take this opportunity to express our gratitude to the team of reporters who scoured the country for the "real people" who grace the pages of this book: Barbara Burgower Hordern, our talented and tireless lead researcher, along with the equally enthusiastic and talented Nancy Chambers, Jeanhee Kim, and Hagar Scher. Thank you all for a great job! Thanks also to the terrific staff of Above and Beyond in Montclair, New Jersey, especially Irene

Rottenberg, for the many hours spent listening to our taped conversations and faithfully transcribing them.

We also want to extend our heartfelt appreciation to the dozens of very special women who shared their stories with us and helped put a human face on our advice. Thanks as well to the many financial planners and other experts who shared their wisdom with us.

On a more personal note, I am always grateful for the guidance offered by my lawyers, Ron Greenberg and Marty Michael. And a very special thanks to the friends who have stood by me during the most difficult and painful year of my life and who encouraged me to complete this book: George Votis, Jewel Jackson McCabe, Susan Glesky, Ed Rollins, Naseer Hashim, and Pat Harrison.

Last but not least, a loving thank-you to my wonderful family. You have inspired me to achieve what I have achieved, tirelessly supported my efforts, and provided me with the role models I sought to show me the way. To my mother, Dorothy Paulsin; my grandmother, Mary Bell, who died while I was working on this book; my sister Melody; my brother, George; and, most especially my younger sister, Lyn, who, in addition to being family, is my most trusted and able colleague and confidante. Thank you so much for everything.

—GM

Thank you, Georgette, for giving me the opportunity to work with you on a subject that I feel so passionately about. You *are* an extraordinary woman, it's been an extraordinary experience, and I am deeply appreciative.

I also want to underscore Georgette's sentiments about the reporters who worked with us (Barbara, Nancy, Jeanhee, Hagar—you're the best!), the women who shared their personal stories with us, and the experts and office-support staff (especially you, Irene) who helped us immeasurably in putting this book together. You are terrific, one and all, and we're more appreciative than words can say. A special thank-you as well to Judith Regan, Dana Isaacson, and Nancy Peske at Regan Books for everything you've done to make this book the best it could be. Thanks also to my agent, Phillippa Brophy, at Sterling Lord Literistic, as well as to her assistant Nikki Britton.

To my family, particularly my mother, Eileen Harris, and my sister, Beth Gentry, who offered continuing moral support (as always) and seemed to understand and forgive when I disappeared off the face of the earth to write—a very loving thank-you. My gratitude goes as well to the many dear friends who similarly encouraged me along the way.

Most of all, I want to thank my husband, Chris Tipovski, and our children, Rachel and Michael, who encouraged me from the start, put up with a lot as the process stretched on (uncomplainingly, to my amazement), and whose love inspired me along the way, as it does in all aspects of my life. I'm so grateful to have you. I love you guys.

—DH

Georgette's Financial IQ Test

*D*o you really need the financial information and advice that you'll get in this book? Answer yes or no to the following questions and find out.

1. Do you worry about your financial well-being on a regular basis?

2. Do you know how much it costs to maintain your current lifestyle within $50 of your monthly bills?

3. Do you have enough money tucked away so that you could sustain that lifestyle for at least three to six months in case of a financial emergency, such as the loss of your job or a serious illness in the family?

4. Can you give a ballpark estimate of the amount of money you owe, from your credit-card balances to your mortgage, off the top of your head?

5. Can you give a ballpark estimate of your total assets, from the equity in your home to the amounts you've accumulated in various savings and investment accounts?

6. Do you know what a mutual fund is?

7. Do you know what a stock is?

8. Do you know what a bond is?

9. Do you know which of these investments has historically earned the most over time?

10. If someone gave you $10,000 in cash, would you know the best way to invest it?

11. Are you often unable to buy or do something you really want because you simply don't have enough money?

12. Do you seek approval from your husband, boyfriend, or father before you make a sizable purchase, or do you have to ask him for the money outright?

13. If your husband dropped dead tomorrow or otherwise left you, would you know where to find the household's key financial papers, such as his life insurance policy, your joint tax returns, your bank and brokerage statements as well as the deed to your home and a copy of his will?

14. Do you ever worry about becoming a bag lady when you're older?

15. Are you living the lifestyle of your dreams?

Scoring:

Add up the point value of your answers, then check below to see what your total means.

1. Yes—0; No—1
2. Yes—1; No—0

3. Yes—1; No—0
4. Yes—1; No—0
5. Yes—1; No—0
6. Yes—1; No—0
7. Yes—1; No—0
8. Yes—1; No—0
9. Yes—1; No—0
10. Yes—1; No—0
11. Yes—0; No—1
12. Yes—0; No—1
13. Yes—1; No—0
14. Yes—0; No—1
15. Yes—1; No—0

Your Total Score: _____

What Your Score Means:

12 to 15 points: Congratulations on your financial savvy. Use this book to fill in any gaps in your knowledge and to pick up additional pointers that can enhance your financial prowess.

9 to 11 points: You've made a good start on the road to financial independence, but you still have a long way to go. Read this book thoroughly to get the direction you need to reach your destination: financial independence.

6 to 8 points: Danger! Danger! You could be headed for real trouble. You don't have a good handle on your financial situation, haven't prepared for the unexpected and constantly find your dreams undermined by a lack of cash. Make this book your new best friend and take its advice to heart.

5 points or less: You are a financial disaster waiting to happen. You are woefully unprepared for a financial emergency and have not begun to take action to turn your dreams and aspirations into reality. Read this book from cover to cover, follow the advice faithfully, and get ready to turn your financial life around once and for all.

Making Dreams Come True

I am not an extraordinary person, but I have lived an extraordinary life.

Just consider: I grew up on the edge of poverty in a tiny two-bedroom house in the small steel town of Highland, Indiana, and now live quite comfortably in a spacious Fifth Avenue apartment overlooking New York City's Central Park. My grades were not exactly spectacular in school, yet I went on to run my own multimillion-dollar cosmetics company and later to launch a successful consulting firm, which I still own and operate today. I've loved and eventually married three fascinating and highly prominent men. And over the past twenty-odd years, I've traveled around the globe countless times, hobnobbing regularly with presidents, prime ministers, CEOs, and the occasional movie star.

In short, my wildest childhood dreams have become quite gloriously true. And I am convinced that if you really put your mind to it, your dreams can come true, too.

I do not know what your specific dreams are, of course, but I can tell you nevertheless, at least in part, what it will take to achieve them because it's the very same thing that enabled me to achieve mine. As the title of this book says, it will take money, honey. That's right, money. And along with money it will take an unwavering determination to make your dreams come true.

Understand this, my friends: Every dream in life has a financial price, just as every action you take and every decision you make has an economic consequence. To get where you want to go, you must figure out what those costs are and exactly how you will pay for them. That in turn means you must seize control of your finances, find a way to earn your own money, your own way, and to save, invest, and plan for a secure future.

Now, I know that it's not considered admirable or even polite to be quite so blunt about the importance of money to our personal fulfillment. And I don't mean to suggest that money in and of itself is enough to buy happiness. But it *is* a critical part of the equation—and it's time that women stop pooh-poohing that notion. Unless you have money, you cannot put a roof over your head, feed and clothe yourself, get medical care when you are sick, or provide any of those basics for your children or any other loved one who depends on you. Just try being happy under those circumstances.

Unless you have money, you can be trapped in a rotten job or a loveless marriage or an abusive relationship. Money causes you constant anxiety if you don't have it and diminishes your self-esteem. Conversely, when you have money, you feel empowered, in control, able to take on the world.

For too long women have left their security and well-being up to someone else—usually their husbands or their fathers or their bosses or their boyfriends or some other male authority figure. Sure, that's changing, but not nearly as fast as we think and certainly not fast enough. Husbands leave or die, so do fathers and boyfriends; we may stay single by choice, or get downsized or demoted. Statistics tell us it's so. Life has too many variables. We owe it to ourselves to become secure in our own right and then to pursue our dreams, wherever they may take us.

That is exactly what I have done in my own life and what in this book I will show you how to do, too.

• • •

Some people, I know, may question my credentials in writing a personal finance book for women. After all, I'm not a financial planner or a Wall Street money manager or any other kind of professional money expert. Some may even snicker, believing that I'm financially successful now only because I've married rich men in the past. What could I possibly know about working hard for money, about budgeting and bargain hunting, about getting out of debt, about saving and investing, dollar by painstaking dollar, to build financial security?

The answer is, plenty.

I got my financial education in the school of hard knocks, and the lessons began back in Highland, not long after my seventh birthday. Until then my family had lived comfortably enough. Dad didn't exactly earn a bundle, but he made enough to allow my mother to stay home full-time with four children and enough so that we didn't constantly worry about how we'd pay the bills or where our next meal was coming from. But everything changed one rainy day in 1954, when my father was killed on impact in an automobile accident. And in a way, the whole rest of my life has been a reaction to that moment.

I will never forget the fear and panic in my mother's voice, mixed in with her grief, when she told us how different our lives were about to become. As it happened, my father hadn't had any life insurance, savings, or tangible assets, and his Social Security survivor benefits were nowhere near enough to support our family of five. So Mother sat us kids down and explained that we were going to have to move in with Grandma for a while, that she was going to have to go out to work, and that we were all going to have to pitch in around the house and help take care of ourselves. As the eldest, I was to be in charge when Mother wasn't there. She told us that, from now on, there would be many things that other kids had that we wouldn't be able to afford, and that with Mom working and Grandma working, we were just going to have to do our best and be grateful for what we had.

Mother didn't have any work experience or a college degree, so she took what jobs she could find. She worked as a cashier; she demonstrated products in a grocery store; she did clerical work at a travel agency and eventually worked her way up to being an agent. As soon as we were old enough, she encouraged us to go out and get jobs, too. I started baby-sitting at fourteen, moved on to styling hair for money, and took in ironing for pay as well. As I got older, I worked multiple jobs so that I could put myself through college, which I did, graduating with a bachelor of science degree.

I remember clearly the insecurity of those early years, how frightening it was not to know if we'd have enough money to pay the rent and gas and electricity and all of our other bills every month. I've never forgotten how it feels to live without a financial cushion, to go from paycheck to paycheck, to worry constantly about how to come up with the money to keep the household going, to be unable to pick the work that you'd like to do, but rather to be forced to take what work you can find.

Getting a college degree helped change that for me, and after I graduated, I took my degree and used it to get a job in advertising. After a couple of years I moved to Los Angeles, where, within just a few weeks of my arrival, I met my first husband, Robert Muir.

Which brings us right back to the subject of rich husbands. It is certainly true that I have been married to very wealthy men. And it is true as well that during my marriages to these men, I came to enjoy the kind of affluent lifestyle that comes only with serious money. Lovely homes, fancy cars, beautiful clothes, travel, luxury—I had them all, in abundance.

But when my first two marriages ended—the first amicably, the second bitterly—so did the financial good times. I'd signed prenuptial agreements before both that basically left me with whatever I'd brought into the marriage, which in each case was virtually nothing. I was too young and naïve at the time of my first marriage (I was just twenty-two when we wed) to realize I could ask for more. And I was too anxious to get away from what turned out to be an emotionally abusive relationship to push for more in the second. Unfortunately, my second husband was also my boss, and when I finally worked up the courage to leave him, he summarily fired me. In both divorces, the end result was the same: all I walked away with was a modest settlement that gave me just enough breathing room to find a job and a place to live, and nothing more.

Let's be frank: Except in rare and highly publicized cases (the Ivana Trumps and Lorna Wendts of the world), the days of fat divorce settlements or substantial ongoing financial support from ex-husband to ex-wife are over—if indeed they ever really existed. Marriage is not a security blanket. When the union is over, you are on your own. What you think you deserve and what the courts and your husband think you deserve are usually two different things.

And if it isn't divorce that does you in, it may be the death of a loved one who supported you financially as well as emotionally. Or you may never marry at all.

If you take only one lesson away from this book, let it be this: *THE ONLY PERSON YOU CAN DEPEND ON TO TAKE CARE OF YOU FINANCIALLY IS . . . YOU!*

When I married for the third, and what I believed would be the final, time to Robert Mosbacher, a Houston oil-company owner who later became Secretary of Commerce under President George Bush, I never again fell into the trap of believing I was rich because he was. Instead, I continued to work, building an independent, highly-paid career in the cosmetics industry, and taking other necessary steps to maintain my financial security. Eventually, I bought my own company, a potentially great but downtrodden firm called La Prairie, and restored it to profitability. When I sold the company several years later, I finally became, by most people's standards, a rich woman in my own right.

During those years, I really felt as if I were living a fairy tale. After all, I was married to the ultimate man of my dreams: kind, handsome, generous, smart, powerful and a Cabinet secretary, for goodness' sakes—I just didn't have enough superlatives to describe Robert properly in those days! I was running my own high-profile business. And I moved in circles that included some of the richest people in the country as well as the president of the United States. What an extraordinary outcome for a poor girl from Indiana.

At the very pinnacle of my success, I decided that I had to share the lessons that had made all of it possible with other women as a way of giving thanks for all that I had. And that is how this book came to be.

Now here comes the ultimate irony: Little did I know when I started writing this book that my husband, my best friend, the person I most trusted in the world and loved more than life itself, was about to betray me and I would have to put to the test yet again every bit of my own advice. For less than halfway through the research for this book, Robert coldly and without warning served me with divorce papers, shattering my fairy-tale existence in an instant. I tried to save the marriage at first, but it was not to be. Our divorce became final a few weeks before the text of this book was completed.

So here I am once again, at age fifty, in the process of rebuilding my life. The emotional pain that accompanied the breakup of my marriage has been devastating—the endless self-recrimination and despair has given me a taste of hell on earth. But while I've been laid flat emotionally, financially I am just fine. Because as you will see throughout this book, I really have learned my lesson at last. Throughout this dark period I took great comfort from the fact that even if my divorce became contentious, or I failed to win a fair settlement, I still would have the financial means to sustain my lifestyle and ensure my family's financial stability. I cannot even imagine the complete desperation I would have felt if, in the midst of coping with the end of my relationship with Robert, I also had to move out of my home and worry about how I'd continue to take care of my aging mother.

Yes, I've learned my financial lessons and I've learned them well, and when you are finished with this book, you will have learned them, too—and you'll be ready to achieve your dreams as well.

There has never been a better time historically than now for women—you, me, all of us—to take control of their financial lives.

One important reason: For the first time ever, many of us have some real money of our own to work with. Nearly 60 million women are now in the workforce, two-thirds of them full-time—that's 56 percent of the adult female population, compared with just 32 percent who were working in 1950. And while we haven't caught up to men on the wage front—women still earn only 76 cents for every dollar that a man brings home—we are making strides. From 1979 to 1995, the average working woman saw her salary rise 4 percent after adjusting for inflation, while men's wages actually dropped 15 percent. College-educated women made out even better, with a 19.5 percent rise in earnings, compared with a barely-there 0.6 percent gain for their male counterparts.

As our salaries have increased, so have our contributions to our family's financial well-being. Nearly half of all working women (48 percent, to be precise) now provide at least half of their household's income. We take pride and ownership in our new role as providers and are empowered by it. As a result, growing numbers of women are taking a more active role in their family's financial decisions. Rightly so, too.

But the change in women's attitude about money isn't confined to those who work outside the home. It encompasses all women. I believe it has to do with our growing realization of our financial vulnerability. More and more of us have encountered, either firsthand or close up, the kind of life-changing events that trigger financial action. We've seen our fathers die and our mothers struggle to cope financially, or we've lost a spouse ourselves. We've been divorced or our best friend has or a close female relative, and we've lived through or witnessed the dramatic decline in lifestyle that typically results. We've been laid off from our job or our husband has or a colleague has. And, if it hasn't happened yet, we're worried, *really worried*, that it will.

Events like those are wake-up calls.

A dramatic cultural change in attitudes about money is helping us change our personal attitudes, too. Whereas just a few years ago talking about money was still considered somewhat vulgar, today people do it all the time. Thanks to the spectacular rise of the stock market over the past few years and the proliferation of retirement-savings plans at work, money and investing are hot topics around the office water cooler and the kitchen table.

And whereas just a generation ago, it was considered somehow unfeminine for a woman to be smart about money, those days are over now. A woman who can speak intelligently about personal finance is considered sexy today—it's a trait that separates the interesting women from uninteresting women.

• • •

Tangible signs of women's changing attitudes about money are everywhere.

The results of a survey earlier this year by OppenheimerFunds, a financial-services company, quantifies the differences. Nearly two-thirds of the women surveyed claimed to be more interested in investing today than they were five years ago, and 71 percent believed they were smarter about financial planning, too.

The evidence also suggests that when women do take the investment plunge, we're every bit as good at it as men—sometimes even better. Since female-only investment clubs began, for instance, they have earned a 21 percent average annual return, compared with 15 percent for men-only groups and 18 percent for mixed-gender clubs. "The gender gap in investing is no longer between men and women; it's between women's ability and their confidence," Ronna Lichtenberg, former head of education and marketing efforts for women at Prudential Securities, told *Money* magazine just a couple of years back. "Women don't yet realize just how knowledgeable they've become."

I don't want to take anything away from the progress we've made. But I have to tell you honestly that it's not enough. Not even close.

Indeed, some two-thirds of women say that they still worry regularly about money, according to a survey last year in *Money* magazine. Fifty-eight percent of women recently surveyed by Merrill Lynch expressed anxiety about outliving their money in retirement. And 63 percent of the women in Oppenheimer's study yearned for more control when it comes to investing know-how.

We have good reason to be concerned, considering how the deck is stacked against us. After all, women tend to live longer than men, so we need a bigger nest egg to see us through our old age. But because we typically earn less than men, we end up saving less. Then too, many of us take time away from our jobs to raise children or care for an elderly relative (the average woman is out of the workforce for more than eleven years, compared with just sixteen months for men), which means we end up with smaller pension and Social Security benefits (payouts are generally based on salary and length of service). That's if we receive any benefits at all, since women are only half as likely as men to work in the kind of job that offers a retirement plan in the first place.

As if all that weren't dismal enough, we unwittingly add to our own dilemma. For one thing, we typically take a much too conservative approach to managing our money, focusing more on preserving what little we have than on making our savings grow. We still leave investing largely up to men: Only 15 percent of the women in the Oppenheimer survey, for instance, had ever purchased a stock, bond, or mutual fund on their own, independent of their husbands or other loved ones. And when we do act of our own accord, we're still typically motivated to do so by a crisis, such as the break-up of a marriage or the death of a husband, financial planners say. And a crisis is the absolute worst time, from an emotional standpoint, to learn how to handle money. Your head is just not clear at those times, and your financial results are likely to be muddled as well.

The upshot: If the present pattern continues, most women will end up with less than half the amount of money they need to maintain their lifestyle when they grow older, according to calculations by Merrill Lynch and OppenheimerFunds. And if, like the vast majority of women, you find yourself divorced or widowed or otherwise alone along the way, you're talking about a recipe for true financial disaster.

Enough is enough. Get smart about your money now and avoid the post-crisis rush.

It's easy enough to get there from here, wherever here may be for you. All you need are the steps that I'll outline in this book. Seventeen simple steps. That's all, honest.

Before you get started, though, let me explain a little bit more about what you can expect in these pages.

First, let me tell you what you *won't* find. You won't find standard, one-size-fits-all advice about how to save, spend, and invest based on some mythical Ozzie-and-Harriet-type household that no longer exists. You won't find sophisticated but confusing investment strategies designed to double your money in six months or outsmart the wizards of Wall Street or achieve any other, to my mind, absurd goal. Those kinds of techniques rarely work. And in any event, there's no sound reason to bother with them, since you do just as well with the simple stuff and often a whole lot better. You also won't find a lot of financial mumbo-jumbo here—that is, silly jargon and over-your-head explanations that lose you in the translation or make you feel just plain stupid about money. (When I do use a financial term, I've marked it clearly in italics, with a simple explanation immediately following.)

What you will find here is a handbook for real life, a financial primer that deals with the stuff that really happens to women and offers practical advice on how to handle it. Step by step, you'll learn sound, straightforward strategies to live within your means, build your savings, invest for the future, and achieve your financial goals. You'll learn how to create a financial safety net so you will never be caught short in a crisis, from the loss of your job to the loss of your husband. You'll learn about ways you can maximize your earnings and minimize your debts. And you will learn how to overcome the emotional hurdles that prevent women from making the most of their money as well as how to develop the attitude and style that are essential to achieving your goals in life.

Along the way, you'll meet a number of very special women, from all walks of life and of all ages and backgrounds, who exemplify the steps you need to take—women who overcame everyday obstacles and women who triumphed over extraordinary hardship, women who are winning small financial victories every day and women who have already achieved great wealth. (A few names have been changed, but the stories themselves are real.) They are, one and all, inspirational women, and they help show the rest of us the way to financial freedom.

In summary, as I said at the outset, this is a guide to realizing your dreams, a realistic and pragmatic manual that will show you how to live the kind of life you dream about. Not the kind of life your parents wanted for you, not the kind of life that your husband wants, not the kind of life that your friends hope to lead, but your own, very personal vision of what ultimately will bring you happiness and fulfillment.

Because life shouldn't only be about being safe. Financial security is crucial, but it's not enough. You should always be reaching for more.

Throughout my life I have always aimed for the stars. And, to my delight, I have always found them within reach. To get there I simply took the right financial steps.

Now it's your turn to take them, too.

Step 1:
Don't Live in Denial

You'd have thought that I, of all people, would have known better. After all, I'd already lived through two failed marriages, watched my mother and grandmother struggle to raise young families on their own, and served as a shoulder to cry on for countless women friends whose husbands had traded them in for younger models or otherwise left them in the lurch, emotionally and financially.

But when my call came, I was still totally unprepared. On a beautiful spring afternoon in 1996, I picked up the phone to hear my beloved husband, Robert, say, without warning, fanfare, or explanation, "Georgette, you're not going to like this, but I thought you should know that I've just filed for divorce." I was shocked, confused, panicked, paralyzed. Most of all, I tortured myself by wondering why, over and over again.

Like countless women before me, I felt like I'd been hit by a proverbial train. Until the second before he delivered his bombshell, I'd believed I had the perfect marriage, my own personal fairy tale come true. Robert and I had been married for eleven years, together for fifteen, and I was as in love with him at the end as I had been in the beginning. As clichéd as it may sound, we were friends and partners as well as lovers, and I really thought we'd be together forever. There'd been none of the telltale signs—or so I thought at the time—to let me know that our marriage was unraveling: no violent arguments, no unaccountable absences, no lipstick on his collar. But although I worked hard over the next year to put the pieces of our relationship back together again, the marriage was irretrievably broken.

Only two facts make my story different from that of any other woman who's been summarily dumped by her spouse. First, I happened to have been married to a well-known and wealthy man (Robert was Secretary of Commerce during the Bush administration, and I had gained a certain degree of notoriety myself during our years together in Washington, D.C.) So my private pain quickly became public, as gossip and society columnists speculated on the demise of my marriage, and, as a result, even more difficult to bear.

The second, and far more important in the long run, difference: While I was completely unprepared emotionally for the break-up of my marriage, I was well prepared for it financially. Although I had been married to a very rich man for more than a decade, I never once in all that time mistook his good fortune for mine. I did not rely on his generosity and good intentions for my financial well-being and the security of the people in my family who depend on my support. Throughout our marriage I'd taken steps to ensure that I'd always have a roof over my head and the means to support myself no matter what happened to my husband or to our relationship. As a result, I did not

. . . .

Cash is cold comfort under these circumstances. But make no mistake about it: Cold comfort is better than no comfort at all.

. . . .

find myself at age fifty having to start all over again financially, as so many women do in situations like mine.

Cash is cold comfort under these circumstances. But make no mistake about it: It *is* some comfort. And at times like these, we need all the help we can get.

THE THIRD GREAT LIE

"Don't worry, I'll take care of you, honey."

Along with "The check is in the mail" and "I'll still respect you in the morning," this is the biggest falsehood you'll ever hear from a man. That includes your husband, your father, your brother, your boyfriend, your boss—any and all of them.

It's not that the men who utter these platitudes maliciously set out to lie. I'm sure that most of them think they mean what they say at the time they say them. But the fact that they believe that they're telling the truth doesn't make what they're saying any truer.

Statistics, coupled with our own personal experiences, tell us differently. Consider these facts:

- Half of all women married in the past twenty years will eventually divorce, the Census Bureau reports.

- Of those women, only 28 percent will be granted an award of ongoing financial support from their exes. As if that isn't bad enough, more than a third of the women who are entitled to alimony or child support will never see a penny of the money that's due them.

- As a result of these and other financial pressures, the average woman's standard of living drops dramatically in the first year after a divorce—by anywhere from 27 percent to 45 percent, according to various estimates. Meanwhile, the average man's standard of living rises after a split by some 10 percent to 15 percent.

Even if your union lasts, though, you're not out of the financial woods. That's because, unless your husband is a lot younger or healthier than you are, he's unlikely to survive you. As with divorce, the financial ramifications of widowhood can be devastating for women. Just take a look at these facts:

- Women, on average, live seven years longer than men. Indeed, the average widow is only fifty-six years old.

- Almost four times as many widows live in poverty as wives of the same age.

- Of those widows who are now living in poverty, some 80 percent hadn't been poor while their husbands were still alive.

All told, an estimated 80 percent to 90 percent of all women will be solely responsible for their own finances at some point in their lives, according to Long Island University's National Center for Women and Retirement Research.

WAKE UP TO REALITY

It's time for every woman to wake up: *YOU CANNOT RELY ON ANYONE TO TAKE CARE OF YOU BUT YOU. NO ONE.*

Harsh words, I know, but unfortunately true. When you're happily married, you think it can't happen to you. But, of course, it can and it does. I'm living proof. You have to deal from reality. After all, if you lived in a hurricane-prone region, you'd take out hurricane insurance, even though you realize you may get lucky and never be hit by a storm. Well, you can't rely on luck to keep you financially secure, either.

By the way, taking charge of your own financial life doesn't mean that you suddenly have to become your family's main source of income or even that you have to go out and get a paying job, if you're currently a full-time homemaker. There's nothing inherently wrong with the traditional man-as-breadwinner role. If you are dating or married to a man who can afford to pay all the bills and both of you enjoy that arrangement, more power to you. When I was married to Robert, he did indeed take care of all the expenses of our day-to-day lives, even though I ran a multimillion-dollar company and was perfectly capable of paying my bills myself.

No, the only problem with this system is if you view your bread-winner as a sure thing, a forever-after kind of arrangement and there-fore make him your only source of financial security. And it's a partic-ularly dangerous way to live if you have children or other people who depend on you for their financial well-being. During the time that I was married to Robert, for example, I was the sole means of financial support for both my mother and my grandmother, who, as it turned out, passed away just a few months after that fateful phone call. At age fifty, I would have had a hard enough time building my financial life from scratch again, but for them, at ages seventy and ninety-three respectively, it would have been impossible.

I can't—I won't—allow that to happen.

....

Ask yourself: If my relationship shatters tomorrow, will I be able to take care of myself financially and take care of the people who depend on me as well?

....

As a first step toward grounding your financial life in reality, ask your-self a key question: If my relationship shatters tomorrow, will I be able to take care of myself financially and take care of the people who depend on me as well? And keep asking yourself that periodically, throughout the course of your marriage or relationship, even during the most fairy-tale-like, head-over-heels-in-love moments. No, especially during those moments. Because it's almost always when you think everything is going perfectly that trouble strikes. That's when life has the greatest tendency to throw you a curveball.

Now, I know that some women believe that they'll be able to see the warning signs of a disintegration in their relationship or a spouse's terminal illness well in advance of the end result. My response? When it comes to death and divorce, that's simply not the way life usually works. But the more pressing problem is that even if you do see trouble coming, you probably won't be able to act smartly and rationally on your own behalf at that time. You will instead be caught up in the pain of the moment—grief or betrayal or anger or fear or whatever powerful emotions the situation deserves. That's not the best moment to draw up a sound plan for your financial security. In fact, it's the worst.

PROTECT WHAT IS RIGHTFULLY YOURS

If you act on only one piece of advice in this book, let it be this: Do not wait for catastrophe to strike before taking an active role in understanding your financial affairs and managing your money. Do not leave your financial well-being, and that of the people who depend on you, in anyone's hands but your own.

I learned this lesson the hard way after my father was killed. I saw and heard the terror and panic in my mother, who was only twenty-seven years old at the time, as she struggled to figure out how to keep our family together, under one heavily mortgaged roof, with no savings, no job skills, and four children to provide for, all under the age of eight. Had it not been for my grandmother and great-grandmother pitching in to cover our mortgage payments, our family could not have stayed together in those first few months.

If you are married, it is imperative that you become familiar with your household's financial situation, so you are not caught unaware if an emergency arises. Make it your business to be part of the financial decision-making process. And, as a precautionary measure, make sure that your name appears on all of your household accounts and investments, either solely or as a joint owner with your spouse. That way you establish your legal right to at least a portion of those assets if you and your husband become involved in an acrimonious break-up, and ensure that you'll have ready access to financial resources if he becomes ill or otherwise incapacitated.

The single most important asset to secure is the roof over your head, so you'll never be left homeless. During my marriage to Robert, for example, I made sure that my name and my name only appeared on the deed to our apartment in New York City. That way I ensured that my principal residence could never be taken away from me, even if we divorced (as, of course, we eventually did) or he died before me (a particularly pressing concern when you're married, as I was, to a man who's significantly older than you are). I was also listed as a joint owner on our home in Houston, where Robert worked and so consequently we spent much of our time.

I also insisted that the title to the car I regularly drive be in my name only, so that my principal means of transportation couldn't be part of any divorce or probate proceedings, either. Since a car, in many cases, represents your ability to get to work and otherwise run your life, it's a particularly important asset to safeguard. Your name should also appear on the household's checking and savings accounts, so you have access to ready cash in an emergency.

If you don't already have one, you also need to get at least one credit card in your name only to establish your creditworthiness independent of your husband. Although that's sound advice for every woman, it's absolutely essential for homemakers who do not have an independent source of income and therefore would be unable to prove to a credit-card issuer that they'd be able to pay their bills if they suddenly find themselves on their own. If you've been using your husband's cards, the simplest way to do this is to call the companies that issue the cards and ask for an application to become a joint cardholder on the account (as opposed to "an authorized user," who has no financial responsibility for the debt). After six months of being listed on the cards as a joint owner (and making timely payments, which are crucial for building a solid credit history), apply for one or two cards in your name only.

The easiest cards to get, by the way, are those issued by gas stations and department stores. They have drawbacks, though: Gas cards are sometimes useless for building a credit history because many stations don't send information on their customers to the rating agencies. Department-store cards, meanwhile, typically sport the highest interest rates around, sometimes as high as 26 percent. In any event, you may still be turned down for these cards if you don't have an independent source of income. If that happens, consider getting a *secured credit card*, which is a credit card that is backed by a deposit at the bank that you agree to put up as collateral. Since the card issuer can collect its money from your deposit account if you fail to make your payments, it is often willing to accept customers without an established credit history.

> # *Men never give up money and control easily, no matter who they are and how much they have.*

Your home, your car, a checking account, and a credit card—these are the foundation of your financial life that you must keep secure. But don't stop with the bare basics. Mentally walk through your entire life, taking note of your family's major assets. Then make a list of the items that are most meaningful to you, either because they're important to your ability to survive if you end up on your own or because they have extraordinary emotional resonance for you. These are the additional items that you should secure in your name—and they're worth fighting for even if they don't have tremendous monetary value.

The simplest way to make these arrangements is to just matter-of-factly include your name whenever you make a sizable purchase or first set up any savings or investment accounts. You'll find it's a lot harder (but by no means impossible) to change the way ownership is listed after the fact. Men never give up money and control easily, no matter who they are and how much they have. A lot of men will feel understandably threatened if their wives suddenly ask to be listed as joint owners on key family assets or, worse yet from the male point of view, as sole owners. To many men, such a request will appear as if you're gearing up to leave the marriage or don't trust them enough to take care of the family in an emergency. Keeping the assets in the man's name only becomes a macho sort of thing, a testosterone-based point of honor. Then too, most men believe that they're omnipotent, and therefore that they'll never die—or at least not any time soon. And they're not too keen on anyone, including, or perhaps even especially, their wives, suggesting otherwise.

For all of these reasons, I was careful to pick the most propitious times to talk to Robert when I wanted to make a change in the way we listed ownership of some important asset. I'd wait for a vulnerable moment—say, after a friend's husband had just died—so I could use that event as a fresh example of why I was so determined to protect myself. I'd dig down deep and explain what I was feeling and why the change was important to me in a way that I hoped would strike an emotional chord. When I wanted to switch ownership of the New York apartment from both of our names to my name only, for instance, I talked about how unprotected I'd felt as a child after my father died and, as a result, how important it was to my emotional well-being to have the security of a home of my own and to know that no one could ever take it away from me. This was not some coldly calculated ploy on my part; it was the emotional truth, pure and simple.

I don't want to kid you: These conversations weren't easy. Robert and I argued every time. But that didn't stop me from pushing for the financial protection I needed, and it shouldn't stop you, either. In the end, we always worked it out and our relationship was none the worse for it. And when our marriage did eventually unravel, for reasons totally unrelated to issues of financial security, I was enormously relieved that I'd put these safety mechanisms into place.

If no amount of explanation and entreaty convinces your husband that you need and deserve, at the very least, to be listed as a co-owner on the deed to your home and the title to your car, I'd seriously consider turning to a marriage counselor or some other sympathetic third party to help the two of you work through it. If there's anything to be tenacious about, it's securing a place that you can always call home and the financial tools you need to keep your family afloat.

Not convinced? Or perhaps you're simply not willing to risk a serious argument or, worse yet, a rift in your relationship for the sake of getting your name on a few pieces of paper? Let me suggest a simple exercise: Visualize yourself homeless. That's right, think seriously for a few minutes about what life would be like if you had no home to go to, get a picture in your mind of exactly where you would go and what you would do. Of course, you'd have no bed to sleep in, no place to wash your hands and face or go to the bathroom. You'd have no closet to keep your clothes in or store any of your other belongings. No phone to reach out to friends and relatives, no shelter to protect you from the elements, no address to leave for prospective employers. Visualize all of this, and you will understand how vital your home is to your existence, your self-image, the very quality of your life, and you'll see how imperative it is to fight to secure it, no matter how humble that home may be.

DEVELOP AN INDEPENDENT NETWORK

There is more to a financial safety net than a roof over your head and some money to fall back on if you suddenly find yourself on your own. You need the ability to make more money to keep you going when that initial stash runs out, and you need a support network that will help you get back on your feet—financially, emotionally, spiritually, and any other "-ly" you need.

I had neither in 1982, when my emotionally abusive marriage to my second husband, George Barrie, ended. At the time, G.B., as his friends and colleagues called him, was the CEO of Fabergé, the giant cosmetics concern. I'd met G.B. at a party several years earlier and soon after that first meeting went to work for him as a production assistant at the company's feature-film division, Brut Productions. During the years we were together, G.B. and I enjoyed a glittering lifestyle, hobnobbing with Hollywood stars and frequently jetting off to exotic locales. During that period I also moved up the corporate ladder, ultimately becoming a vice president in charge of licensing in Faberge's main cosmetics division.

But I quickly learned that everything I'd relished about my life with G.B. was totally dependent on his good graces. As soon as I made the decision to separate—and no amount of money is worth staying in an abusive relationship for—I had to find another place to live because the apartment we'd shared was in his name only and he wasn't about to let me stay there until I got back on my feet financially. (To be honest, I didn't want to stay there, either, as long as he was still in residence.) Then a week after our divorce became final, G.B. fired me. One minute I had a job and an independent source of income, then poof! it was gone.

I soon discovered I had few real friends I could rely on for help and support, either. When couples split up, I learned, their friends usually stick with the power partner, and that's rarely the female half of the relationship. Indeed, if it hadn't been for some money that I'd managed to save from my salary at Fabergé, I would have been forced by the circumstances to move back in with my mother in Indiana and rebuild my life entirely from scratch.

I swore I'd never again put myself in a position where I was dependent on a man for my livelihood, and I haven't. I seized the opportunities that came my way during my marriage to Robert Mosbacher to forge an independent career as an entrepreneur, ultimately buying and revitalizing a flagging cosmetics company named La Prairie, then selling it for a very handsome profit. I then turned around and used the proceeds of that sale to start a consulting firm, Georgette Mosbacher Enterprises, which I own and operate to this day.

Now, I'm certainly not suggesting that every woman has the wherewithal to buy and sell her own company—or would even want to if she could. But what every woman can and must do is maintain an independent career or at least keep her job skills up to date so that she has an income of her own to fall back on or the ability to generate one if her circumstances demand it.

Of course, these days the majority of women already are working, and their paychecks are vital to their household's economic well-being. But too often we neglect our careers once we have a family or coast on what we've already achieved, as we pour our energy into our husbands, our kids, and the day-to-day routine of our lives. And if we've been able to devote ourselves full-time to being a homemaker, our days quickly become filled with cleaning and cooking and shopping and getting the kids to and from school and soccer practice and Scouts, and we never carve out space to pursue the interests and activities that will ensure our own economic and emotional well-being.

Whether you work outside the home or not, the great excuse is, "I don't have the time." I say if you want to be a survivor, you make the time.

Ask yourself: Are you up to speed on developments in your field? Do you know how to use the latest office technology? Have you kept up with your professional contacts—and tried to make new ones? If you can answer yes to these questions, you ensure your ability to bring home a buck if and when you need to.

You don't necessarily have to follow elaborate or time-consuming professional courses to keep current in your field. But you do have to carve out a small chunk of time for yourself on a regular basis that you devote to pursuing some interest that will help keep your job skills current. Then mark the date and time on your calendar as you would any other appointment. Write, Tuesday, 9:30 p.m. read *XYZ Journal* for half an hour, or Friday, 1:30 to 2:30 p.m., take computer class. And take advantage of opportunities to build your Rolodex with future contacts wherever you find them. For instance, the next time you attend a business function with your husband, father, or boyfriend, strike up a friendly but professional conversation with someone you don't know instead of mingling idly, and make sure to exchange business cards or phone numbers with that person before you leave the event. You never know when that contact might come in handy, for a new business idea, a referral, or even a new job down the road.

Whether you work outside the home or not, you must also develop some interests that do not require your husband's participation—or your children's, for that matter. Pursuing independent activities will make you a more interesting person in the long run and enable you to find fulfillment even if your marriage doesn't last or your children are no longer at home.

And it's just as vital to have friends and professional acquaintances that are independent of the circles that your husband or boyfriend moves in. Keep up your membership in your professional association, whether you currently have a job in the field or not. Attend an occasional get-together of your college alumnae organization. Join a book club. Go to lunch or brunch or dinner with friends on your own from time to time—friends that you had before you met and married your spouse or people you've gotten to know independently. That way, if your relationship falls apart or the marriage ends, you'll have a support network to help you find the strength to turn the corner. If you haven't built this system in advance, you're likely to find yourself broke in every respect when trouble hits—financially as well as emotionally and spiritually.

A good friend of mine, whose husband of twenty-odd years recently left her for a much younger woman, sometimes calls me in despair, and all she can say over and over again is "I just want my life back." I understand how she feels, and even confess to similar thoughts in the aftermath of my break-up with Robert. But most of the time I just want to shake her and say, "Wake up! If you hadn't handed your life over to someone else, it wouldn't be lost now, and you wouldn't need to ask for it back."

Share your life with the man you love, but don't give it over to him. There's a difference. And understanding and acting on that difference is the key to your long-term financial security.

....

The bottom line: Don't ever hand your life over to someone else.

....

ACTION PLAN
To stop living in denial and take the first giant step on the road to life-long financial security, make a commitment to yourself to do the following:

1. **Visualize how you would cope financially if your husband suddenly disappeared from the picture.** Could you handle your mortgage and car payments? Afford to buy food and clothes for yourself and your kids? Take a vacation? Have any fun?

2. **Make a list of your household's most valuable assets, including your home, your car, and other prized possessions.** Then check the ownership agreements on each one to make sure you are listed as either the sole or joint owner. If you aren't, make an appointment with your husband to discuss the matter and lobby insistently to get your name on all of the household's deeds, titles, and savings and investment accounts.

3. **If you don't have a credit card in your name only, apply for one immediately.** If you don't have an independent source of income, ask to be listed as a joint cardholder on your husband's accounts instead of just an authorized user. After a few months of making timely payments, you will have established an independent cred-

it history and can apply for a card in your name alone. The easiest to get: secured cards or ones issued by gas stations and department stores.

4. **Maintain an independent network of friends and professional acquaintances.** Schedule time for a phone call once a week to a new professional contact, a former colleague with whom you've lost touch, or a friend you palled around with before you met your husband or current boyfriend.

5. **Pursue your own interests.** Sign up for a book-reading club, a women's support group, a dance class, or some other regular activity that you can attend without your significant other.

6. **Commit to at least one activity a month that will enhance your job skills or earning potential.** Make it a point to take a computer class, read a professional journal or attend an industry function. Treat the activity seriously by scheduling it on your calendar as you would any other important appointment.

Step 2:
Dream Big, Aim High

I've often said that I wasn't born a redhead, but I was born to be a redhead. Well, the same sentiment is true when it comes to me and my money: I wasn't born rich, but I was certain from a very young age that I was born to *be* rich. And if that's what you want, it's altogether possible that you can be rich, too.

In fact, I'm convinced that you can achieve just about any goal you put your mind to, no matter how far-fetched or unattainable it may seem now—whether that goal is to run your own company, travel around the world, retire early, or simply achieve a degree of financial independence that allows you to do whatever you want, whenever you want to do it.

The first step is crucial, though: You must drum up the courage to dream big and reach for the stars.

Like so many people who come from humble beginnings, my own dreams were born at the movies. As a child I used to go to the cinema faithfully every Saturday (no matter how strapped we were for cash, I somehow managed to scrounge up the money), using the larger-than-life images on the big screen as a temporary escape from the heavy family responsibilities I'd taken on since my father's death. I was particularly enamored of Maureen O'Hara and Katharine Hepburn. I loved the fact that they were both glamorous and gutsy.

Though they were decked out in silks and satins, with upper-crust accents and patrician lifestyles, I knew I could count on Maureen and Kate to get down and dirty if they needed to and to always have a glorious adventure.

Watching them, I knew instinctively that plenty of food on the table, a roof over my head, and other traditional hallmarks of financial security would never by themselves be enough for me. Lord knows, I understood from firsthand experience that financial survival must be every woman's first and most important priority. If you constantly have to worry about whether you can afford to pay your rent, feed your kids, and keep up with your bills, the battle to stay afloat financially consumes all your physical and emotional energy. You have nothing left for dreams. I promised myself as a child that I'd find a way to free myself and my family from the daily struggle for food, clothes, and shelter. But once I'd guaranteed myself those basics, I wanted more. Much more. Like my movie heroines, I wanted a life that sparkled with limitless possibilities and, yes, luxury.

Of course, as a seven-year-old I didn't phrase it quite like that. Instead I had a litany of wants: I wanted adventure, I wanted to travel, I wanted to wear pretty clothes (I loved pretty clothes!), I wanted a beautiful home filled with beautiful things and, because I so often had to sleep on the floor, I wanted an oversized bed with feather pillows, plush comforters, and exquisite linens. And having those things all by myself wasn't enough. With my constant awareness of the sacrifices that my mother and grandmother made daily for our family, I wanted them to be surrounded by beautiful things as well.

It wasn't a great leap from wanting to live the life I saw in the movies and on television to visualizing myself doing exactly that. I closed my eyes and saw myself as Loretta Young, descending a long spiral staircase in a breathtaking designer dress, then flinging open French doors to let guests into a sumptuously furnished living room, just as the real Loretta did each week on her TV show. The more I visualized the scene, the sharper the picture came into focus and the more determined I became to devise a strategy that would make the vision come true.

In short, I dreamed rich and ultimately became rich, in life experiences as well as in money. I am living proof that dreams really can come true.

DARE TO DREAM

Don't take my word for it. Look around you. Inspirational stories are everywhere. Small dreams, big dreams, career dreams, romantic dreams, against-all-odds dreams—you name the brand of aspiration, there's a woman out there to show the rest of us it can done.

Consider Guadalupe Quintanilla, a Mexican immigrant who moved to Brownsville, Texas, with her parents at age thirteen. Administered school IQ tests in English, the Spanish-speaking Lupe was erroneously labeled mentally retarded and placed in the first grade, despite the fact that she was perfectly proficient in her own language. Frustrated and humiliated, she soon dropped out of school, and spent the next fifteen years or so just scraping by, eventually marrying and having three children. Still unable to read, write or speak English at age thirty, Lupe feared that history would repeat itself when her children, then five, six, and seven years old, were evaluated at school and also labeled "slow." That's when she began to dream, and the dream was simple: to become a role model for her children so that by example she could motivate them to do and become their very best.

Lupe decided that the best way to accomplish that goal was to return to school herself. No one made it easy. Her neighborhood high school refused to accept her, as did the local community college, until in desperation she staked out the registrar's car and begged him tearfully to give her one shot. Working furiously at her studies, she made the dean's list in her first semester and went on, after earning her high school equivalency and undergraduate degree, to earn a doctorate in multicultural education. To pay for her tuition and help support her family, Lupe regularly worked two jobs during this period (various jobs at the university during the day and teaching Spanish at the local YMCA at night), then studied until two in the morning to keep up her grades. She says, "My motivation was my children's future."

Now sixty, Lupe these days earns a six-figure income from two jobs, one as CEO of her own cross-cultural training company and the other as an associate professor at the University of Houston. She's also served in a number of appointed positions in the Carter, Reagan, Bush, and Clinton administrations, most recently as vice-chair of the President's Advisory Committee on Educational Excellence for Hispanic Americans. Her "slow" children haven't turned out too badly, either. Two are successful attorneys, while the other is a doctor.

Then there's Marlene Seiford, a former real estate broker who, unlike Lupe, was professionally successful from the outset selling high-end homes in scenic Bainbridge Island, Washington. But despite earning a comfortable $70,000 a year, Marlene was miserable. A physical fitness buff who preferred walking and biking to driving prospective home buyers around the island, Marlene secretly yearned to become a personal trainer. The hitch: She was nearing fifty by the time she acknowledged her dream, and she was convinced that no sane person would hire a woman her age to help get them in shape.

But the dream wouldn't go away. After two years of depressed dithering, Marlene determined that if she cut spending to the bare bone (no vacations, no new clothes, no dinners out) and withdrew some of her savings from the bank, she'd have enough money to survive temporarily without a salary and finance her training as fitness instructor. She quit the real estate business in 1996 and spent ten months learning her new trade—taking fitness classes, learning techniques from other trainers, and studying for her certification from the American Council on Exercise. Shortly after celebrating her fiftieth birthday, Marlene was ready to hang out her shingle as a personal trainer.

To her amazement and delight, the answer to her question about who would hire a woman her age turned out to be just about anybody over age thirty-five; in less than a year, Marlene had signed up more than sixty baby boomers and seniors as clients. These older exercisers, it turned out, were universally unenthusiastic about entrusting their physical fitness to the usual lithe young hard-bodies in the personal-trainer business, convinced that the younger trainers would be unable to relate to their problems and concerns. "My age not only hasn't been an impediment to my success, I'm convinced it's *the* reason I've done so well," says Marlene. In fact, she's now expanding her business into weight-management and fitness retreats. Looking ahead, she envisions herself still at it in her sixties, leading fitness classes on senior cruise lines.

Of course, some women refuse to let any time pass pursuing their dreams. Take Lisa Renshaw. At twenty-one, with only a high school education behind her, Lisa fantasized about owning her own business. So she convinced the owner of a failing parking garage in her native Baltimore to let her work there for three months without pay; her reward, she hoped, was that if she helped turn the business around, he would make her a partner. The owner promptly convinced her to borrow $3,000 and turn it over to him so he could meet his next rent payment on the facility. Instead, as Lisa told *Cosmopolitan* magazine in May 1996, her boss disappeared with the cash.

At that point most of us would have given up in despair. But not Lisa. Instead she seized the opportunity to run the business herself. She immediately moved to lower the garage's overhead, negotiating a lower rent and retaining only one employee. The rest of the time she parked the cars herself and washed them, too, in order to offer customers a unique service. Business soared. Within four years, Lisa was successful enough to buy a second garage, and then a third. By the time she hit her early thirties, Lisa Renshaw was a millionaire, running a mini-empire of more than fifty parking garages in Maryland, Washington, D.C., and Virginia, with collective revenues of over $25 million annually.

UNDERSTAND THE PRINCIPLES OF SUCCESS

What all of these very different women have in common with me and with so many of the other women you'll meet in this book is their willingness to acknowledge and follow their dreams, no matter how frightening the first steps felt or how slim their chances of success seemed at the outset. As different as their individual background and career paths were, they followed the same three simple principles to make their dreams reality:

- They clearly identified what they wanted.

- They devised a pragmatic game plan for achieving their goal.

- They took concrete action, despite the odds against them.

Then, with each victory that Lupe, Marlene, and Lisa scored, they set the bar a little higher and moved on to conquer the next goal. After graduating from college, for instance, Lupe went on to earn graduate degrees, get an associate professorship, and eventually opened her own business. Once Marlene successfully established herself as a personal trainer, she began branching out into weight-management and fitness retreats. As soon as Lisa's parking garage became prosperous, she opened another and another and another.

With each subsequent goal that these women set for themselves, they followed the same three principles to success. The formula can be boiled down to three simple words: IDENTIFY, PLAN, ACT.

Repeat them to yourself until you're tired of hearing yourself speak, until you've well and truly adopted them as your very own. IDENTIFY, PLAN, ACT.

Got it? Good.

AVOID MENTAL TRAPS

The one last trait that Lupe, Marlene, Lisa, and I share was perhaps the most critical element of all in our success. We understand at our very core the most basic truth about dreaming, and it is this: THE ONLY REAL BARRIERS TO ACHIEVING WHAT WE WANT IN LIFE ARE THE ONES WE ERECT IN OUR HEADS.

That's where we imprison ourselves.

Unfortunately, too many women remained locked in these mental jails. We get so caught up in trying to achieve a measure of security in our lives that we fail to dream big. Ever the pragmatists, we focus on making sure that we'll always have food on the table, clothing on our backs, and a roof over our heads. But while satisfying our needs must indeed be our paramount concern, we've got to make room for our wants, too.

....

The only real barriers to achieving what we want in life are the ones we erect in our heads.

....

We're also stymied in our dreams by our traditional role as nurturers. We're so used to taking care of others that we feel guilty about taking anything for ourselves—time, money, even dreams. It's okay to want for our children, our parents, our husbands, our friends. But somehow we're not good people if we want something for ourselves.

Simply put, we set our sights too low.

I say it's time to raise the bar, just as Lupe, Marlene, and Lisa did. Understand that if you focus too much on achieving security and security alone, you'll never achieve anything more than that. Security is an absolute must for us, but it should not be enough.

In fact, the very idea of financial safety can be contrary, even downright dangerous, to your dreams because being safe implies taking no chances. To think big and achieve big, you have to take risks. There's no way to be safe and reach high at the same time.

If you don't take chances, it's a done deal that you won't ever get what you're yearning for. I say, at least leave yourself the possibilities.

TAKE MENTAL EXERCISE NUMBER ONE

So go ahead and look into the future and picture what you'd really like to see there. Literally close your eyes and conjure up a mental image of yourself as you would like to be in a few years' time.

Then take the all-important next step: Tell yourself that you really can achieve whatever it is you truly want. It's a matter of learning to exercise your inner voice the same way that you exercise your body. Say to yourself: *I DO NOT HAVE TO BE WHERE I AM IF THIS IS NOT WHERE I WANT TO BE.*

In my case, I said to myself, hey, I may have come from humble beginnings, but I'm going to be somebody. To make something happen you have to visualize it happening. In my case, I visualized myself rich, and eventually I became rich.

....

To think big and achieve big, you have to take risks. There's no way to be safe and reach high at the same time.

....

These mental exercises are as critical as your push-ups or your abdominal crunches or your turn on the Stairmaster. As you develop a plan for reaching your goals and begin taking the necessary steps toward achieving them, here's what you have to do:

- Develop a mantra that summarizes your dream and your ability to achieve it. The saying doesn't have to be particularly clever— just a few words or a short sentence that encapsulates what you're trying to accomplish and when you hope to reach that goal. For instance, you might say, "I will get that red sports car by my thirtieth birthday." Or, "I will write a novel by the year 2001." Or even, "Within five years I will be living on Park Avenue, and I won't let anyone stop me."

- As I did (and still do every day), repeat your mantra to yourself on a regular basis, just as you incorporate physical exercise into your daily routine. First thing in the morning and last thing at night are key moments.

- For added incentive, place a Post-It with your goal printed in blunt letters on your makeup mirror and your refrigerator door and any other place you can think of where you'll see it often, reminding yourself of what you intend to accomplish.

GET PRACTICAL

Of course, motivational talk alone won't get you where you want to go. You've got to translate your dreams into a concrete set of goals over the near, medium, and longer term.

In my case, I knew that getting a college degree was fundamental to the ability to better myself in life, so figuring out a way to pay for college became my most immediate goal. The next goal was getting the degree itself. I knew that I'd never find the kind of opportunities and lifestyle I was looking for in Indiana, so my post-college goal was to move to a big city (preferably Los Angeles, since I was still in my starstruck phase as a teenager), where I aimed to land a glamorous job—or, at least, one a lot more glamorous than I was likely to find in Highland. Once I was working, I knew the next step would be to build a firm financial foundation so that my family would never again have to worry about the basic necessities of life. Specifically that meant paying off the mortgage on my grandmother's house and, eventually, buying my mother a home of her own.

I knew that only after all those needs had been met could I concentrate on the wants—the "rich" part of my dream. As you pursue your dreams, bear these general rules in mind.

- **The more specific you are about your goal, the clearer the path you must take and the better your chances of achieving it.** Better to say, for example, I want to buy a new car in two years when I turn twenty-five, than it is to say, I want to save more money. It's hard to get yourself fired up about saving money for the sake of saving. But if you're saving for something tangible—whether it's buying a fancy dress, taking a trip to the Caribbean, or building a nest egg for your retirement—much of the natural distaste for financial discipline melts away. And make no mistake. Financial discipline is exactly what it takes to make your dreams come true.

- **Be frank with yourself about what you really want.** If you're currently living in a studio apartment and dream of moving to a bigger place, don't convince yourself that you'd be happy with a one-bedroom apartment if what you really want, in your heart of hearts, is two bedrooms or more. It's that dreaded curse of women, again; we constantly aim too low and consequently end up with less than we want and deserve. In your quest for roomier quarters, you may indeed have to settle for a one-bedroom place as an interim step, until you save enough for the apartment of your dreams. But if you say to yourself at the outset, I can manage with a one-bedroom apartment, you can be sure that a one-bedroom apartment is all that you'll ever get.

- **Commit your goals to paper.** The very act of writing them down makes them real, a public acknowledgment to yourself that you want more out of life than you currently have and you plan to take action to achieve it. Then give yourself some deadlines by which you aim to achieve these goals.

Try the following exercise: Buy yourself a blank writing pad that you designate as your dream notebook. On the first page, write down everything you hope to accomplish over the next year; on the second page, jot down your aspirations for the next two to five years; then use page three to list your goals for five years and beyond. Don't be shy, at least at the outset, about covering the sheet with your dreams, large and small, noble and frivolous. On the first-year page, for instance, you might say: I'd like to buy a new cashmere winter coat, visit a spa, learn how to invest, see a Broadway show, and land a better-paying new job. For your medium-term goals, maybe you'd like to renovate your kitchen, take tango lessons, vacation in Paris, and go back to school to earn your M.B.A. Longer term perhaps you're hoping to launch your own business, write a best-selling novel, appear on the

Oprah Winfrey show, amass enough money to retire early, and then divide your time between charitable works and traveling around the world. Whatever comes to mind, just jot it down and close the book. (Note: If you're adept at working on a computer, you can just as easily create a Dream File, and record your goals there instead.)

- **Prioritize your goals.** A short time after you commit your dreams to paper—a day or two or even a week, but no longer—make an appointment with yourself to go back over each of your lists and prioritize those goals. You might even assign numbers to each of your dreams to see which ones matter most to you, then cross off those at the bottom of your list (at least temporarily). Over the next year, for example, you might decide that you really want to throw your energy into looking for a new job because so many of your subsequent goals are tied to your ability to earn more money. The new job becomes your major goal for the next year and, because your old winter coat is really threadbare, you make up your mind to set aside $15 a week for a new coat as your secondary goal. You figure the spa and the Broadway show will just have to wait.

WATCH OUT FOR EMOTIONAL ROADBLOCKS

What if you don't have any particularly compelling dreams or unfulfilled desires that leap to mind? Hogwash, I say. We all have dreams. If you think you don't, you may simply be too caught up in survival mode to tune in to yours. It's hard to fantasize about the future when you're worried about how you'll put milk on the table tomorrow and you'll be able to pay the rent next week. If that describes you, your first order of business must be to build a financial foundation strong enough that mere survival will no longer be an issue. And right there you have your first dream: To achieve a degree of financial security so that paying for the necessities of life no longer consumes all your physical and emotional energy (and you will learn exactly how to do that in the next few chapters). Once you are on your way to achieving that goal, once you eliminate the bare-bones struggle to survive, you will dream bigger dreams again. I guarantee it.

....

Your first order of business
must be to build a financial
foundation strong enough
that mere survival will
no longer be an issue.

....

Or perhaps you're simply frightened to dream without even realizing that you're afraid. When we have no faith that our dreams can become reality and no confidence that we have the inner resources to make them happen, it sometimes becomes easier not to dream at all. Fear of failing and fear of disappointment block dreams as surely as storm clouds obliterate the sun. For some of us, then, dreams become a painful reminder of what our lives could have been but never will be. Trust me, though, the greater pain lies in not dreaming at all, because then we are truly doomed to the life we're currently leading. At least leave yourself the possibility for change.

One more consideration: Don't worry about whether your dreams are truly worthy of fulfillment. They're your dreams, after all, and the only thing that really counts is if they're important to you. I know, for example, that some people think it was somehow unbecoming, even vulgar, for me to dream of being rich. But, hey, it was my dream, not anyone else's. As long as I don't hurt anyone in pursuit of my goals, I don't have to apologize for my dreams to anyone. And you shouldn't, either.

I daresay if I were a man, the notion of aspiring to be rich would seem a lot less vulgar. As a society, we're not used to associating riches with women; we've come to think of wealth as a male sort of thing. A woman can be comfortable, she can be able to take care of herself and her loved ones financially, but rich? Only if her husband was rich first. Well, that's just wrong-headed thinking. When we women start to visualize ourselves as rich, when we stop feeling that we have to apologize for wanting money, when we stop being frightened of the concept, only then can we mobilize our thoughts and actions in ways that will attract the opportunities that will in turn really make us rich.

When it comes to dreams, I say: *If it's not illegal, immoral, or fatal, go for it.*

....

If it's not illegal, immoral, or fatal, go for it.

....

ACTION PLAN
To help identify your financial dreams and translate them into concrete, achievable goals, follow these steps:

1. **Close your eyes and visualize yourself as you'd like to be in a few years' time.** Remember, the more specific you are about what you want to achieve, the clearer the path that you must take to get there becomes, and the better your chances of actually reaching your goal.

2. **Commit your dreams and goals to paper.** Take a blank notebook and use the first page to jot down everything you hope to achieve over the next year. On the second page, note everything you want to do over the next two to five years. Then on the third page, write down all your ambitions for five years and beyond.

3. **Prioritize your goals.** Go back over each of your lists and select one major accomplishment and one minor one to concentrate on for each time period.

4. **Develop a mantra that summarizes your dream and your ability to achieve it.** Repeat this motivational phrase to yourself at least

once a day. Say: I do not have to be where I am if this is not where I want to be. I can achieve _____ (fill in your goal) if I really set my mind to it.

5. **Print your goal in blunt letters on several Post-It notes and place them strategically around your home.** Put them on your make-up mirror, refrigerator door, and any other location where you can't miss seeing them to remind yourself of what you hope to accomplish.

6. **Remember: If it's not illegal, immoral, or fatal, go for it!**

Step 3:
Put a Price Tag on Your Dreams

Once you've decided on your goals, you have to figure out exactly how much it will cost you to accomplish them. All dreams have a financial component. Some price tags are simply more obvious than others.

Tangible goods and services are the easiest to calculate. If you're hoping to buy a new computer, for instance, all you have to do is look at some ads in the newspaper, skim a few articles in a computer magazine to get a good sense of what's out there, and visit a few stores to compare prices. Or if you've always wanted to get away to Florida in the middle of winter, just a call a reputable travel agent or two to get rates on airfare and lodging, and you've pretty much got your answer.

Figuring out the cost of a dream that you can't reach out and touch takes a little more ingenuity. In the case of Lupe Quintanilla, the high school dropout turned university professor and successful entrepreneur whom you met in Chapter Two, the price of becoming a better role model for her children turned out to be the cost of going back to school to earn her undergraduate and graduate degrees. For a working woman who yearns to stay home full-time with her children, the cost might be her salary, minus all the expenses she incurs by working, such as child care, commuting, and maintaining a professional wardrobe.

One thing's for sure, though. If you don't have a realistic idea of how much money you'll need to reach your goals, you'll never be able to devise a practical plan for achieving them.

DO YOUR HOMEWORK

Before you start the tally, gather all the hard information you can about the expenses you're likely to incur, direct and indirect, in pursuit of your dream. When I made up my mind to go to college, for example, I called Indiana University and found out exactly what I'd have to pay per semester for room, board, and tuition and got an estimate for books and other incidentals as well. Then I figured in the cost of my transportation to and from home on school breaks and holidays, and gave myself a modest clothing allowance. I listed every cost I could think of in a big ledger and added them up. I literally knew almost down to the dollar what that B.A. would run me.

So whip out your dream notebook and make yourself a crude ledger on which you can add up just how much money you'll need. And don't forget to take into account all the ancillary expenses that can really jack up the price tag—the clothes you'll need, any commuting expenses you may incur, tools or equipment you'll have to buy, classes you'll need to take, child care for your children. If it costs money, write it down.

RUN THE NUMBERS

Let's consider a test case. Say you're currently renting an apartment and your dream is to buy a home of your own. Your first step in calculating your costs is pretty obvious: You get a rough idea of the prices of apartments or houses in the area where you want to live by scouring the classifieds and talking to real estate agents. Those same agents can also give you an estimate of the property taxes on houses in your price range. Once you know the going rates, you can figure out how much you'll need for a down payment (20 percent of the purchase price is standard, but many lenders accept as little as five percent to ten percent, as long as your credit rating is solid and your income is ample enough to cover the higher loan payments) and how much your mort-gage payments will be at current interest rates. Any bank or mortgage lender will be happy to help you with those calculations, at no cost.

Now, many people would stop there, but that's actually just the beginning. You also have to figure out how much it will cost to get the mortgage and to close on the house (that's the real estate term for legally settling the purchase transaction). You'll probably, for example, have to pay an origination fee and points to the bank; these charges for processing and finalizing the loan will run you anywhere from one per-cent to three percent of the amount you're borrowing. You'll also have to cough up money for a home inspection, a title search (legal research to make sure no one else has a claim on the house), an appraisal of the property, lawyer's fees, a credit report, and title insurance to protect you against future claims on the property. A mortgage lender should be able to estimate these costs for you. And, of course, you'll need homeowner's insurance as well (even if you were willing to take the financial risk of something happening to your property, no lender will take such a gamble). These myriad incidentals will add up to anywhere from a few hundred dollars to several thousand by the time you're done.

But your calculations aren't over yet. The final step is to estimate the cost of getting the place in living condition. Are you likely to be buy-ing a fixer-upper that will need extensive repairs before you move in? Have you budgeted at least for a fresh coat of paint on the interior walls? If you'll be buying a larger place than you live in now, do you have enough furniture to fill the space? Are your draperies likely to fit the windows? If you're unlikely to be able to afford to get the place in the shape you'd like right away, you need to calculate the emotional cost of that as well. Are you the type who can shrug off chaos around you, or will you be suffering through two years of hell until you have enough cash to fix up the place right?

Next you need to figure out what resources you have to work with. Do you have any savings you can tap, if need be? For example, you might be able to borrow against your retirement-savings plan at work, if you have one, for a portion of the down payment. Do you have any assets you're willing to sell—from stocks to old furniture, clothes, or jewelry? Are you able to generate additional income by offering some service on a freelance basis (for instance, typing term papers or baking for holiday parties) or taking on a second job? Any amount you can come up with, however small, brings you that much closer, that much faster, to achieving your goal. And many small sums add up to a big chunk of change over time.

The last factor in the equation is to give yourself a reasonable length of time in which to accomplish your goal—not so short that you doom the project from the outset, but not so long that you allow yourself to get lazy about it, either. I truly believe that work expands into the amount of time you allot to do it. In other words, if you give yourself five years to come up with enough money to buy the house, it will take you five years; if you give yourself two years, you'll do it in two. Sooner is always better than later.

DEVISE YOUR GAME PLAN

Okay, now you have a realistic idea of how much money you'll need to achieve your goal, the resources at your disposal, and a reasonable deadline by which you aim do it. The next step is to move on to the grunt work of dreaming: You have to come up with a step-by-step strategy to make it happen.

As I've learned from long years of experience, you have to be utterly practical in getting from Point A to Point B. I was only seven when I developed my first goal-oriented game plan, although I had no idea at the time, of course, that was what I was doing. I remember the occasion vividly because it came on the day that my father died. Our house was filled with people that day, well-meaning friends and neighbors who were moved by our tragedy. But they were so caught up in the moment that they seemed to forget about the four children milling around who'd just lost their father and, with him, any claim to a normal, worry-free upbringing. I heard sentiments expressed that day that made my blood chill: *I hope they're not going to have to split up the kids.* Nothing could have been scarier to me since now all we had was each

other. I made up my mind there and then that it was my responsibility
to keep us all together.

So I developed an escape route. If anyone knocked on the front door
looking for us kids, I planned to sneak all four of us out the back way.
Then we'd walk to Grandma's house, with me carrying my two-year-
old sister Lyn in my arms and six-year-old Melody and four-year-old
George trailing behind. Now, Grandma's house was a long way away,
and I'd never walked there alone before. But I knew the route and was
sure I could get us there if I had to. Once we arrived, I figured we'd
hide in the apartment Grandma had in her basement. At seven, it didn't
occur to me that was one of the first places people were likely to look
for us.

Thank goodness I never had to activate my plan. But believe me, I
was ready if the need arose. Like the Girl Scouts, BE PREPARED has been
my motto ever since.

Indeed, by the time I was seventeen and ready to launch my pursuit
of college financing, I'd become almost ruthless in my pragmatism.
Remember, I'd computed down to the dollar how much money I'd
need to get my degree and now I broke that amount down to figure
just what I needed to earn the summer before school started to meet
my first tuition bill in September. The number wasn't pretty. We certainly had no savings I could use for college. The only resource I had to
work with was me.

So right after graduation, I hopped on a train and headed to Chicago,
where I figured decent jobs for newly minted high school graduates
would be more plentiful than in Highland. (Sometimes one of the sacrifices needed to achieve your goal is to move to an area with more
opportunities.) I bought newspapers, scoured the want ads, and went
from interview to interview. I was fearless in asking for jobs, so singu-
lar was I in my purpose. I was willing to do just about anything—wait
on tables, wash windows, anything. By the end of the first day, I'd
landed a job as a switchboard operator, but only by fibbing about my
college plans, telling my employers that I was looking for a permanent
position.

That wasn't enough. When I got home and rechecked the figures in my ledger, I realized that I'd have to get a second job or else fall short when the tuition bill came. Because the switchboard was a nine-to-five position, a nighttime job was the only possibility. So I hit all the retail stores that stayed open late in Highland, and was quickly hired as a salesperson in a local department store that stayed open until nine o'clock every night. Then I went back to my ledger and ran the numbers again, adding the salaries from both my jobs, then subtracting the train fare to and from Chicago and my bus fare to and from the department store in Highland. This time the math looked right, and when September rolled around, I made that first tuition payment on time, with change to spare.

APPLY THESE PRINCIPLES OF SUCCESS

From these experiences and scores of other game plans I've devised over the years, here's what I believe are the three secrets to success:

- **Break down your goal into do-able chunks.** Think of it as working your way up the dream ladder. For example, I had many sub-goals—getting a B.A., paying off the mortgage on my grandmother's home, buying a place for my mother—each of which seemed eminently more achievable than my ultimate goal of becoming wealthy, or even modestly well off.

- **Make an absolute 100 percent commitment to your goal.** If you feel passionately that what you're trying to accomplish is right for you, you'll be much better equipped emotionally to endure whatever hardships are involved and to push past the unexpected obstacles that are bound to crop up in your path.

- **Be utterly without false pride in what you are willing to do to achieve your dreams.** As long as you don't hurt yourself or anyone else in the process, do whatever it takes.

PUSH PAST THE EMOTIONAL ROADBLOCKS

Are you ready now for the really hard part? Once you've decided on your goals and developed a plan of action, you've got to follow Nike's advice: Just Do It. And do it quickly. The longer you put off taking the first step toward your goal, the more reasons you'll find not to do it.

Time works against courage.

....

> *The longer you put off taking the first step toward your goal, the more reasons you'll find not to do it. Time works against courage.*

....

Ask yourself, as I always do when I have to drum up the courage to take some step that I'm unsure about, what's the worst thing that can happen to me? Maybe you'll be embarrassed by some people's reactions to what you're about to do, but remember that no one ever dies from embarrassment. Maybe you'll lose some money, but then you'll just have to work a little harder to make it up. Maybe—and this is the one I suspect is the real sticking point for many women—you'll fail, and possibly end up more disappointed with your life than you were before. Well, sure, that's possible. But it's a lot more likely that you'll discover the risk was well worth taking, even if you do have to temporarily scale back your dreams or rework your goals.

In fact, there is no real way to fail if you truly put your heart and mind into pursuing your goal. An initial lack of success is like an early warning signal. It simply tells you that you need to review your game plan to make sure it's the best possible way to get what you want.

Maybe you need a different strategy. Maybe you need to revise your time line. Even if it turns out you should have done things a different way, though, you'll bounce back. Mistakes can be the most powerful teacher of all; learn from them and move on.

So no more excuses. Force yourself to get up off your rear and do something.

TAKE BABY STEPS FIRST

But how, you say? Well, let's consider another test case. Say you're miserable in a dead-end job and are anxious to find a better position. You know you should update your résumé or, at least, call a few employment agencies or recruiting firms to get a good feel for the current job market. You've thought about networking with friends and former colleagues who might be in a position to help and toyed with the idea of taking a professional course to boost your career skills. But somehow you just can't bring yourself to do any of it. Maybe you're secretly afraid that no one else will want to hire you or that you're not really qualified to land something better. Maybe you're concerned that a new job won't pay as much as your current position. Or maybe you're simply too busy.

Whatever the reason (and if by reason you think that I mean excuse, so be it), get past it by making one very concrete move toward your goal, even if it's a baby step. In this case, say, decide that you're finally going to revamp that résumé. Make an appointment with yourself and write it down in your calendar just as you would any other appointment—Saturday, 9 a.m. to 10 a.m., get haircut; 10:30 to noon, dentist appointment; 1 p.m. to 2 p.m., update résumé. Then enlist the help of a supportive friend to keep you on track. Ask the friend to read your résumé when you've finished with it and to give you some feedback, and schedule a time to do that, too.

Trust me. The very act of doing something, particularly something you were apprehensive about, will boost your self-confidence immeasurably and motivate you to take the next step and the step beyond that. As renowned career counselor Barbara Sher says in her book, *I*

Could Do Anything If Only I Knew What It Was, "Even if someone slams the door in your face, refuses to answer your letter, or yells at you—the worst outcome you can imagine—it doesn't matter. You're a success every time you face down fear."

STICK WITH THE PROGRAM

I can't think of anyone who better epitomizes the process than Ella Williams, who is founder, president and CEO of Aegir Systems, a multimillion-dollar engineering support and computer-services firm in Oxnard, California, that specializes in defense contracts. A divorcee with two daughters, Ella was working as a secretary for an oil refinery and collecting aluminum cans in her off-hours to supplement her income when she dreamed up the idea for her company seventeen years ago. She didn't have an engineering degree or even an M.B.A. But Ella was convinced she'd acquired enough technical and marketing expertise during a previous twelve-year stint with Hughes Aircraft to be a success. And while she'd quit Hughes's payroll department a few years earlier to earn her college degree, she had kept in close touch with many of her former colleagues and felt confident that they'd lend a hand with her new venture. So she gave herself what she considered a reasonable deadline by which to make it work—two years or bust— and set out to make her dream come true.

Her first challenge was how to meet the price tag on her dream: the $60,000-plus she estimated she'd need to support herself and her family while she scoped out projects, developed detailed proposals, and visited prospective clients. Her solution was to take out a $65,000 second mortgage on her home (at the time the interest rate on such loans was 21 percent!), which, in addition to sporadic child support, was the only asset she'd acquired in her divorce several years earlier. But since she also needed capital for the business itself—hiring consultants occasionally to help her put together proposals, getting materials for her presentations, and traveling to and from prospective clients—the loan, as it turned out, wasn't enough. So she took a job with a temporary agency, doing secretarial work three days a week, earning $200. She was then free to spend the rest of her time making presentations to potential clients at military bases, often accompanied by her engineer friends or by a retired Hughes marketing executive who acted as her chief consultant.

Not a single client bit. Ella recalls that she often cried herself to sleep during this period, feeling guilty that her kids had to live so frugally while she pursued her dream. She'd feed the girls at night, encouraging them to clean their plates, although the only food she had to eat herself were their leftovers. But Ella didn't waver, so convinced was she of the rightness of what she calls "my mission." Notes Ella, "I knew in my heart it was just a matter of finding someone who would give me my first chance."

Dejected as her two-year deadline stretched into three and sinking rapidly into more debt to continue financing her efforts, Ella knew she needed to try something new. A terrific baker, she began taking homemade breads, cheesecake, and muffins with her to her presentations. And, as she puts it, "something magical happened through that food." Soon she started getting her first callbacks, and within a year she won her first contract: an $8 million job to test and evaluate missile systems for the Navy. After that the projects started to roll in and the business really took off, generating over $5 million in annual revenues by the early 1990s.

Now Ella even has a sideline venture: Ella's Worldclass Cheesecakes, Breads and Muffins, which employs inner-city youths to make products for Los Angeles bakeries. It's her way of giving a little something back to the community for all the financial success that she has achieved.

When it comes to pursuing your dreams, take a page from Ella's book: Just believe in what you are doing and keep at it, no matter what. Look for creative ways around the inevitable roadblocks you'll come across. Don't be afraid to reach out to friends and colleagues for help. And never, ever give up.

Tenacity will win in the end, every time. I promise.

ACTION PLAN
To finance the pursuit of your dreams and develop a workable game plan to achieve them, follow these steps:

1. Gather as much hard information as possible about how much it will cost for you to actively pursue your dream. Remember to calculate indirect costs—such as the price of any clothes or equipment you might need—as well as your direct expenses.

2. **Assess where you stand financially.** Create a ledger in your notebook or computer file in which you list all of the expenses associated with your goal as well as the financial resources you have at your disposal. Then calculate how much more money you'll need to accomplish your goal within the time frame you've set for yourself.

3. **Devise a practical step-by-step strategy for pursuing your goal.** For big dreams, consider creating a series of sub-goals, with game plans for each, to make the process more manageable. Record the game plan in your notebook or computer file, and review it periodically to help you keep track of your progress.

4. **Force yourself to take one very concrete step toward your goal, at least once a week.** Schedule an appointment with yourself to do it, put it on your calendar, and always keep the date.

5. **Enlist the help of a supportive friend.** Talk about your goals periodically and about the actions you're taking to achieve them. Your friend's inevitable questions about your progress will help keep you on track.

6. **Keep at it, no matter what.**

Step 4:
Arm Yourself with the Right Tools

You can't build a house without first laying a foundation. And you can't lay a foundation unless you have the right materials and equipment. Now, I'm no architect and I'm certainly not a builder, either, but even I know that to make that foundation, at the very least, you need a tractor and dump truck to clear the ground and a concrete mixer and molds in which to pour the cement. If you don't have those basics, you'll never get the job done.

Well, the exact same principles hold true in fulfilling your financial dreams. You can't achieve your goals without first laying a financial foundation that ensures that you and your loved ones will never go hungry or homeless, and that you'll always be able to provide for the necessities in life. And you can't build that foundation without the skills you need to earn a decent living and attract the right opportunities, which in turn requires that you have a certain amount of education and training and the personal style to put them to good use.

Simply put, a college education, professional skills, and a winning attitude are the bricks and mortar of financial freedom. It's up to you to do what you have to do to get all three.

START WITH YOUR HEAD

To acheive what you want in life, the most important first step is to get a good education. I'm convinced of that. Money, self-esteem, the career, man or lifestyle of your dreams—whatever you most desire—the right schooling is crucial to achieving it.

At the most basic level, this means going all-out to get a college degree, if you don't already have one. Whether you're eighteen or eighty, that academic credential is essential to your ability to land a well-paying job and to advance in your chosen field or to help you discover the field that's best for you if you're not sure about what you want to do. In today's tough job market, smart employers simply demand a degree, whether you're a secretary or a CEO.

In fact, a college education does a lot more than simply improve your job prospects. It broadens your horizons, enhances your ability to speak intelligently on a variety of topics, teaches you critical thinking, instills discipline in meeting deadlines, and introduces you to many, many more opportunities than you would otherwise have. No matter what you major in, no matter how well you do academically, you'll graduate from college a more interesting person than you were going in, and that in turn will attract more interesting people and opportunities to you for the rest of your life.

My experiences certainly bear this out. If I hadn't gone to Indiana University and gotten my bachelor's degree, I never would have had the credentials to land a job in advertising, which was my ticket out of Highland right after graduation. And then I wouldn't have gained the experience and self-confidence to believe I could be just as successful at my career in Los Angeles, where I'd dreamed of moving since I was a child. My college education gave me the grounding I needed later in my life to hold my own admirably in conversations with business leaders and politicians and foreign dignitaries. And it helped pave the way for me to buy and run my own cosmetics company, La Prairie, which in many ways turned out to be the pivotal experience of my career.

But you don't need me to convince you of the benefits of formal higher education. Just look at the dollars-and-cents evidence:

- The average female college graduate makes almost 50 percent more than a woman with just a high school diploma—$33,525 a year for the college grad in 1996 (the most recent statistics available at this writing), versus $21,175 for her less educated sister, the Census Bureau reports.

- Women who go on to earn a professional degree in turn earn $57,624 a year on average, or over 70 percent more than women who stop at a B.A. and more than one and a half times (172 percent, to be exact) as much as those who quit after high school.

- The gap between those with a college degree and those without has been widening in recent years. In fact, women with just a high school diploma have actually been losing ground in recent years once you take inflation into account. Their so-called real wages (that is, adjusted for inflation) dropped nearly four percent during the fifteen-year period that ended in 1995, according to an analysis of Census Bureau data by the Economic Policy Institute in Washington, D.C. Meanwhile, women with undergraduate and advanced degrees saw their salaries rise roughly 20 percent over the same period.

The lesson is clear: If you don't already have a college degree, make up your mind now to get one. And if you already have that B.A., seriously consider going back to school to buff up your credentials with postgraduate courses or an advanced degree.

DO WHAT IT TAKES

I don't mean to be flip here. I'm certainly well aware that unless you're lucky enough to have parents who paid your tuition straight out of high school or talented enough to win a sizable scholarship, pursuing a degree on your own is a lot easier said than done. And not just because college these days can cost a small fortune. As adults, we have families and jobs and a whole host of other responsibilities that demand our time and our energy; it may seem close to impossible to figure out how to fit school into our schedules as well. And let's face it, it's emotionally difficult to get yourself up for studying and homework and tests again, particularly if you'll be attending a program where you'll be surrounded by eighteen-year-olds.

But I'm not trying to convince you that it's easy. Life *isn't* easy. What I am saying, though, is that going for your degree is almost guaranteed to be worth the sacrifices you'll have to make to pull it off.

That's certainly been the case for Helen Barrios. Helen grew up in the tenements of East Los Angeles to Mexican-born parents who couldn't afford to send any of their four children to college. Nevertheless her mom and dad actively encouraged her three brothers to attend college any way they could manage. They pushed Helen instead to take secretarial courses, which they said would give her a marketable skill, and her high school teachers did the same. Helen followed their advice and even took a job as a secretary, but only to finance her studies at Cal State, where she enrolled straight out of high school.

Her salary as a secretary wasn't enough to allow her to attend school full-time. To earn more money for her studies, Helen later became a flight attendant, working nights and weekends. Monday through Thursday, she'd hop on a one a.m. red-eye flight to Minneapolis, reboard after a two-hour layover for the trip back home, land in Los Angeles at 10 a.m., and head straight for school. Then on Saturday and Sunday, she'd fly three round-trip flights between L.A. and Las Vegas. It took ten years of working and studying in this way, but eventually Helen did get her degree. She notes, "I always say my diploma should be written in blood."

Helen has never had cause to regret her sacrifice. Straight out of college, she got a job as a sales trainee at IBM. "At that time they required a college degree to be hired, but didn't care what the degree was in," says the political science major. She moved quickly into and up the managerial ranks, specializing in sales of computer equipment to the construction industry. Four years ago, after Helen had been with the company for fifteen years, IBM began offering buyouts to qualified employees. Helen grabbed the opportunity and the cash, and set out to build her own construction company, Aztech Contracting, in Marietta, Georgia. The firm generated $8 million in revenues last year, and Helen, as founder and president, now earns a comfortable six-figure salary. "I still believe the smartest thing I ever did was to go to college," she says. "That's made everything I've achieved in life so much easier."

JOIN THE CROWD

Don't worry if you're long past traditional co-ed age. You'll have plenty of company.

Just consider:

- More than a third of all college students today are older women.

- Their numbers are growing rapidly. Over the past decade the number of college women over the age of twenty-five has grown by 75 percent, compared with a mere 15 percent increase in enrollment among students in the traditional eighteen- to twenty-two-year-old range.

- The fastest-growing age group on campus is the one labeled "women over sixty-five," the American Association of Retired Persons reports.

- By the year 2000, adult women are expected to constitute the majority of students, no matter what kind of educational setting you're talking about. Vocational school, college, corporate training programs, you name it, women will be the force to be reckoned with.

In fact, older women on campus have become so commonplace that a virtual cottage industry has sprung up to help facilitate their academic careers. (Older, in this context, typically means anyone who's at least twenty-five years of age.) In other words, there are many groups out there and many different programs specifically designed to make the process of going back to school a whole lot easier for you.

To see if there's help out there for you, here's what I suggest:

- **Contact federal or state educational agencies.** These offices, which are usually listed in the blue pages of your local phone book, often have financial-aid programs specifically aimed at older women.

- **Look into scholarship and special assistance programs sponsored by professional organizations.** Two particularly good groups to check out are the **American Association of University Women** (800–326–2289; www.aauw.org) and the **Business and Professional Women's Foundation** (202–293–1100, ext. 169; www.bpwusa.org).

- **Visit your local bookstore or library to browse through guides that list financial-assistance programs.** One of the best among the hundreds out there: *Directory of Financial Aids for Women*, which is published every other year by Reference Service Press (415–594–0743) in San Carlos, California.

- **Search the Internet for additional sources of aid.** One of the best web sites that I've come across for this purpose is sponsored by the **National Association of Student Financial Aid Administrators**. The address: www.finaid.org. Just go to the "Special Interests" category, click on "Female Students," and you'll find information about scholarships and fellowships specifically designed for women as well as a link to an outstanding bibliography of books about financial aid for women.

- **Check out some schools directly.** Many community colleges across the country offer tuition breaks and loans for women returning to school. So do many other women- and older adult-oriented academic institutions, from Smith and Mt. Holyoke to the New School in New York.

The potential payoff for doing this sort of research is huge. Savings off the cost of a degree through these various programs range from a few hundred dollars to $10,000 a year or more.

CHECK OUT ALTERNATIVE PROGRAMS

Of course, not only money prevents many women from going back to school to get the training they need. It's life, and all the responsibilities that go along with it. Maybe you have young children who need you at home, or perhaps your household is dependent on the income you earn from a job—you can't just drop everything and head off to campus full-time.

Well, these days you don't have to. Hundreds of institutions of higher learning offer nighttime, weekend, and part-time solutions for adult students. Community colleges in particular are notoriously accommodating. Then too, more than two thousand colleges and universities (practically every accredited school in the nation) grant at least some credit for life experiences and other college-level learning outside the classroom. Pursuing credits that reflect what you've learned on the job, as a homemaker, through hobbies or volunteer work or independent study can reduce the time needed to get your degree by as much as a year or more. The resulting cost savings can be enormous—as much as 25 percent or more off your college bill, or the equivalent of a tuition scholarship of $8,000 or more, according to a recent report by the American Association of Retired Persons.

Of course, you'll have to prove to the college of your choice that the informal learning experiences that you've had are really worth college credit. To do that you can either take a standardized test to demonstrate your knowledge of a particular subject (costs generally range from $50 to $150 per exam), or you can put together a portfolio that documents your experience (for instance, you might include your résumé, any commendations or awards that you've received, examples of the work that you've done, and so on). You can get some guidance in putting together a request for life-experience credit from the **Council for Adult and Experiential Learning** (243 South Mahash,

Suite 800, Chicago, IL 60604; 312–922–5090; www.cael.org).

These days you can even attend college right in the privacy of your own home through any one of hundreds of off-campus study programs, conducted by mail, videotape, or even a home computer. Although the quality and costs of these programs vary dramatically, some are top-notch and the cost is typically a fraction of what you'd pay to earn your degree on campus: $60 a credit, on average, compared with $300 a credit at a traditional school. Not all of these so-called distance-learning programs are accredited, however, and many traditional colleges do not accept credits earned in this way. So you'll need to check out the program thoroughly before you begin. To inquire about an off-campus school's accreditation, contact the **Distance Education and Training Council** (1601 18th St., NW, Washington, DC 20009; 202–234–5100; www.detc.org). For more general information on these programs, get in touch with the **United States Distance Learning Association** (P.O. Box 5129, San Ramon, CA 94583; 510–820–5845; www.usdla.org).

The bottom line is that it's a whole lot easier for women today to pursue college and advanced degrees than for women like me and Helen Barrios twenty-five years ago. So go ahead and take advantage of what's out there.

GET THE TRAINING YOU NEED

Of course, you don't have to enroll in a formal degree program to boost your career skills and earning power. You can also up your professional ante by taking job-related courses offered by professional associations, colleges, and business-training centers. Over the years, for example, I've taken debate lessons, computer courses, public-speaking classes, voice-modulation lessons, and instruction on makeup and on-camera body language in preparation for my TV appearances. These courses have helped me enormously in my career, not just because of the specific skills I learned but also because they boosted my self-confidence, which in turn helped me to do a better job, whatever the task at hand happened to be.

Your best bet is to build your so-called portable skills—that is, to get training that will serve you well in any position at any company, rather than knowledge that is specific to your current job. The days of working for one company for life are long gone—the average woman nowadays switches jobs every four to five years. The skills most in demand now, career counselors tell me: public speaking, technical writing, foreign languages (especially those spoken in Eastern Europe, as well as Japanese and German), management techniques (such as team building and negotiating), and computer expertise of any kind.

If you do nothing else, concentrate on becoming computer literate, if you aren't already. At the very least, you should be able to operate a word-processing program and get yourself onto the Internet; knowing how to work with spread sheets is a major plus, too. Nothing will stop a prospective employer from hiring you faster than finding out that you don't know your way around a computer, even if the job you're after doesn't specifically require working the keyboard. Computers are used everywhere in business these days, from the factory floor to the executive suite. From the boss's standpoint, then, not knowing how to use one suggests that your skills are outdated and that you're resistant to change—two deadly qualities in an employee, no matter what the job is.

And knowing how to use a computer not only helps you land a job, it also helps boost your salary once you're employed. Indeed, a Princeton University study has found that workers who use computers earn 15 percent more on average than those who do not.

So make up your mind to sign up for a class right away. Even if you're techno-phobic, I promise you, it's easy—*really easy*—to learn the basics. I made up my mind to conquer the computer a few years ago while I was putting in some weekend hours at my office. I needed information on some clients that my secretary kept on a computer file, but since she didn't work on Saturdays and I didn't know how to operate the computer, I couldn't retrieve the file. I promised myself that when it came to my business I would never again be at someone else's mercy, let alone the mercy of a piece of machinery. So I looked in the yellow pages for computer training courses and signed myself up for one right away. I've since learned word processing, spread sheets, money-management programs, and research techniques for the Internet, and continue to take specialized instruction every time I acquire an important new software program.

You can pick up a computer class at almost any community college, adult training center, or computer store or lab, often for a fairly nominal fee. Many employers—even temporary agencies—also offer some sort of computer training. And if you don't have a computer to practice on at home, check out your local library, which probably provides computers with Internet access for its patrons. Or ask a friend if you can occasionally use her computer for practice.

Don't become familiar with your PC just for the sake of a job, either. Knowing how to use the computer (even at the most elementary level) can help you better manage your money, access great on-line travel and shopping bargains, and retrieve up-to-the-minute news and medical information at the click of a mouse. It's educational and it's fun. Honest.

GET A HELPING HAND

If you already hold a job, you may be able to get your employer to pick up the tab for at least some of your training, no matter what kind of courses you're considering. Nine out of ten large companies now have programs in place that pay all or part of tuition or training costs for their employees, as do more than 80 percent of medium-sized firms, according to the National Institute for Work and Learning.

Even if your employer doesn't have a formal program, ask your supervisor if the company can partially reimburse you anyway. The worst thing that can happen is that the boss will say no. In the process, though, you'll come across as a go-getter eager to improve your performance, so you'll still come out ahead. And at best you'll get the money for your class *and* the additional training *and* the enhanced reputation—a pretty terrific deal all around.

What if you're a homemaker who's never held down a job outside the home (or at least not in more years than you care to remember) and you're suddenly pushed back into the work force by economic necessity? Maybe your husband lost his job unexpectedly and is having a hard time finding another one, or maybe you've recently been widowed or divorced and were left without adequate insurance or financial support. You need a job badly, but your skills are too rusty or nonexistent for you to qualify for any position that pays a decent wage.

Well, there's plenty of help available for you, too. Virtually every state and most sizable cities have programs for so-called displaced homemakers—in other words, women just like you—which offer training as well as loans and tuition breaks for furthering your education. Again, your state or local education or labor department can probably tell you about programs in your area. For a list of schools with centers specifically set aside for displaced homemakers, you can also get in touch with **Women Work! The National Network for Women's Employment** (1625 K Street, NW, Washington, DC 20006; 202–467–6346; www.womenwork.org).

SEEK OUT ON-THE-JOB TRAINING

You don't need to get all your training in the classroom, either. Hands-on experience is often as good or better than the theoretical knowledge you pick up at school. Ask your boss to put you on the team whenever projects come up at work that can expand your job skills. You can also try doing volunteer work to pick up some expertise in a particular area—a particularly useful strategy for anyone considering a career change.

That's exactly what Shirley Jowell did when, at age fifty-nine, she decided to quit her job as publications manager for a computer-science book company and pursue a totally new line of work: alcohol-abuse counseling for seniors. While taking courses to get the proper accreditation, Shirley also volunteered at a local counseling center in the San Francisco area, where she lives. "I knew I needed to gain experience and make contacts to break into a new field at almost sixty years old," she told *Good Housekeeping* magazine a couple of years ago. "I was prepared to call everyone I knew for help when I was ready to look for a job, and I wouldn't have really had any contacts if I hadn't done some volunteer work first." The strategy worked. She got a job in the field shortly after finishing her course work through a lead she picked up from one of her colleagues at the counseling center.

Don't get all high and mighty about the kind of work you'll take to get the experience you need. When Charlotte Ferguson decided she wanted a career in the nonprofit world, specifically working with women in transition, the only job she could find was as a $6.50-an-hour file clerk reporting to the secretary of a small women's services agency in San Francisco. In her previous job Charlotte had been a high-level insurance executive managing a large underwriting department for a major financial-services company, so a position as a file clerk was a quite a comedown. But Charlotte, who was fifty at the time, didn't care. "All I wanted was a foot in the door so I could gain the experience I needed," she says. "I knew I wouldn't be a file clerk for long."

She wasn't. Charlotte set out to be the best, most reliable employee that agency could have hoped for. A few months after her arrival, she struck up a conversation with the director, explaining her background and offering to help in any way that was needed. "She looked as if she had won the lottery," recalls Charlotte, who began working directly for the manager of the agency a short time later. She continued to climb through the ranks of the agency's staff until finally she was running the place. "You've got to be prepared to do things that aren't in your job description to learn," Charlotte notes. "And you've got to be convinced of the truth of what you're doing. If you're wishy-washy or half-assed about it, it's not going to work."

Now seventy-two, Charlotte these days heads a scholarship fund for women sponsored by a local nonprofit women's organization. And she's still growing professionally—and personally. As she notes, "Every encounter you have in this life is a learning experience."

VIEW EDUCATION AS A LIFELONG PROCESS

That approach, more than any specific knowledge or training you'll pick up in the course of your career, will enable you to fulfill your dreams, whatever they are.

Either you're growing or you're dying. Staying where you are shouldn't be an option. That's not surviving; it's withering.

So don't consider your education over just because the ink is dry on your diploma. Understand that education is an ongoing process. It shouldn't end until you do.

Recruiting consultant Marion Manigo-Truell, fifty-three, has built her career around that concept. Marion started out in the 1960s as a long-distance operator for Southern Bell Telephone in Savannah, Georgia (at the time she was only the second African American person ever to work there). In the thirty-two years since, she's held positions in banking, computers, market research, financial services, meeting planning, and, most recently, recruiting. "I've never made the mistake of thinking one field is my career," she says. "Industries die, companies downsize, the world changes—and we've all got to change along with it."

Education is an ongoing process. It shouldn't end until you do.

With each career change Marion went back to class to brush up on her job skills or add new ones. Along the way she acquired two under-graduate degrees (in social studies and business administration), a license to sell securities, and her accreditation as a direct-mail mar-keter, life and health insurance agent, travel agent, and meeting plan-ner. She also asked every employer she ever worked for to send her to computer classes to learn different programs. She says, "To me, school was like the sun—everything radiated from there." But she doesn't confine her learning to the classroom. She also reads *The Wall Street Journal* and *The New York Times* every day, subscribes to several com-puter magazines, and regularly attends seminars and events sponsored by the various professional associations to which she belongs to keep abreast with changes in her field. She says simply, "I keep up."

As Marion has figured out, education doesn't always come in the form of a degree or training program. Pursue anything that you're interested in, and you'll become a more interesting person in turn. Take a wine class, make up your mind to read a book a week, read the newspaper every day, sign up for karate classes—anything that strikes your fancy.

Understand that if you never pick up the newspaper, read a book, and otherwise expand your interests, you'll dry up, even if you have a college education. Curiosity is one of the most important traits that you can cultivate. A curious person is a person that successful people want to be around because successful people are doers, too. People surround themselves with like people. And everyone is attracted to people who strive to excel.

ACTION PLAN
To make sure you have the education, skills, and training you need to achieve your life goals, follow these steps:

1. Seriously consider going back to school for your B.A. or an advanced degree, if you do not already have one. A college or postgraduate degree will greatly improve your job and salary prospects, broaden your horizons and introduce you to many more opportunities in life than you would otherwise have.

2. **Investigate alternative degree options.** Part-time, night, weekend, or off-campus programs can make it a lot easier for you to carry on with your other responsibilities in life while you attend school.

3. **Vigorously pursue financial aid.** Assistance programs, particularly those specifically aimed at women aged twenty-five and older, can sharply reduce the cost of getting your degree or additional training. Federal and state agencies, nonprofit groups, professional associations, the schools themselves, and even your own employer are all possible sources of serious money.

4. **Build your so-called portable skills.** Concentrate on training that will come in handy no matter what job you're in. Your best bets include public speaking, technical writing, foreign languages, and managerial training.

5. **Learn how to use a computer *now*!** At a minimum, you should be able to operate a word-processing program and navigate the Internet. Being able to work with spread sheets is a major plus in the skills department, too.

6. **Seek out on-the-job training, whenever and wherever available.** Volunteer for projects that will stretch your current skills or teach you new ones.

7. **Understand that education is a lifelong process.** Higher learning doesn't have to take place in a formal classroom when you're eighteen to twenty-two years old. Make up your mind to pursue at least one activity a week—say, reading a book, learning about fine wine, or taking piano lessons—that will exercise your brain and keep you growing.

Present Your Personal Best

*A*ppearances don't matter." "You look fine." "It's only what's inside that counts."

How many times have you heard a friend or relative utter those phrases, or words to that effect, in a well-meant effort to reassure you about your looks or what you're wearing or some other physical attribute? If you're like me, probably too many to count.

But there's a serious problem with such sentiments, and it's this: They're simply not true. In fact, they're drivel. What you wear and how you look speak volumes about who you are and what you can accomplish to anyone who's looking. Don't let anyone convince you otherwise.

To see exactly what I mean, I invite you to do the following simple exercise: Go for a walk through a busy neighborhood in your city or town, and take a few minutes to really observe the people who happen by. Pick several candidates at random and note your immediate impressions about them. What's the first thing that you think of when you see a woman dressed in a simple suit that's clean and pressed, with neat hair and well-shined shoes? What pops into your mind when you see someone in leggings and an oversized shirt, with long, dangly earrings, platform shoes, and hair streaming down her back? What's your gut reaction to a woman in a tube top and miniskirt, with what appears to be a navel ring decorating her midriff?

Now imagine that you are a prospective employer looking to hire someone for a key position in your home or company and the passersby were all applying for the job. Which one of those candidates would you hire?

To be sure, these examples are extremes. Most of us know better than to wear Spandex to a job interview. But we do sometimes, in the hustle and bustle of everyday life, neglect to put our best foot forward—particularly if we're feeling down about ourselves or some other aspect of our lives.

Those, of course, are the very moments when you need to pull yourself together the most. If you look like you're together, other people's perception is that you *are* together—even when on the inside nothing could be further from the truth. If you're genuinely interested in reaching your financial goals, you'll do everything in your power to put that message across. And there's a bonus to this little exercise: When you dress smartly and carry yourself with confidence, after a while you fool yourself as well.

COVER THE BASICS FIRST

Good grooming is vital to achieving the look of success you need. Start with what I refer to as the ultimate basics: clean hair, clean body, clean nails, and clean clothes, all brushed, buffed, polished, ironed, and in generally good repair.

Now, this may sound so simple that you wonder why I even bother to mention it. Well, when you're so strapped for cash that you're struggling to pay the rent and put food on the table, soap and detergent and all the other tools of cleanliness may sometimes seem like luxuries, rather than the necessities they ought to be. Under those circumstances, something as simple as keeping clean isn't simple at all.

More commonly, though, we have the money to keep ourselves physically together, but we've run out of the emotional capital to do it properly. When you're feeling overwhelmed or otherwise beaten down by life, it's easy—too easy—to let your personal appearance slide. Maybe you forget to run a brush through your hair before going out. Or you're in too much of a hurry to sew a button back on your coat or change a blouse after you spot a stain on the sleeve. No one else will notice, you figure, so you just let it go.

Trust me on this: Someone *always* notices. And when they do, the subconscious conclusion they draw is that you don't have your act together. That's not the kind of person who attracts opportunity, either of the personal or professional kind.

The good news is that it doesn't take a lot—of money, time, or emotional energy—to look good. Soap, water, comb, brush, iron, needle and thread, and a nice dress or suit are all you really need. Even just one nice dress or suit will do. As long as that outfit is clean, pressed, and in good repair, you're going to be able to circulate with anybody, anytime, anywhere you want.

For Maureen Peabody of Dallas, one nice outfit turned out to be the catalyst for a whole new life. Maureen had been married for eight years to a drug-addicted schizophrenic with whom she had three sons. Although her husband had been abusing her physically and emotionally for years, it was not until he turned his wrath on their baby son, attempting to burn him, that Maureen finally got up the courage to leave him for good. With her self-esteem and finances at an all-time low, she worked hard to provide for herself and the kids. She did clerical jobs at some local warehouses, where she didn't have to worry about the ratty clothes that were all she had, and at budget motels, which provided her with a uniform.

Determined to do better for herself and her children, Maureen enrolled at a local college, taking regular academic courses as well as a workshop for displaced homemakers that taught job-hunting and interview skills along with grooming, makeup, and dress-for-success lessons. Inspired by the class, Maureen scheduled an appointment at Attitudes & Attire, a local nonprofit group that helps low-income women get back on their feet by providing them with an interview outfit and accessories. They gave her makeup tips, convinced her to let her brassy bottle-blonde hair grow out to its natural ash color, and brought out a beautiful turquoise suit for her, Maureen recalls. She protested, asking for a black one instead. "The turquoise suit is something that a successful, important woman would wear, not me," she told them. But, at their insistence, she tried it. "I put on that suit, and immediately I felt like Cinderella," Maureen remembers. "To this day, when I want to feel really special, I put on that suit."

Maureen quickly landed a job as a receptionist for a local meeting-planning business, and moved up to the position of systems administrator within a year, at a $30,000 annual salary—double what she'd been earning before she put on the suit. She's also continuing her college studies, hoping to earn a degree in computer sciences. "The suit was a tremendous boost to my self-esteem because it gave me a glimpse of what I could be," says Maureen. "I'd become so mired in my problems, I couldn't see the possibilities anymore."

WARNING: PRETTY COUNTS

No one's going to like this, but pretty does count. People are naturally attracted to people who look good—whether those people are prospective employers, clients, friends, boyfriends, or spouses. Maybe they shouldn't be, but they are. It's just a fact of life.

Studies prove it. One recent study into how physical attractiveness and appropriate attire influence hiring decisions found that unattractive subjects gained an 8 percent advantage by being appropriately dressed, while attractive ones gained 18 percent. The reactions of both male and female interviewers were compared, and the only significant difference was that the women judged their fellow women much more harshly than men did.

We can spend a lot of energy arguing about how that isn't fair but, hey, *life isn't fair*. So let's just get past the resentment, acknowledge what we're up against, and figure out what we have to do to win.

In this case the solution is to do everything you can to make yourself look as attractive as you can possibly be.

Fortunately, there are a million ways to enhance your appearance these days. If you think you have mousy brown hair, put in red or blonde highlights or change the color altogether. If you worry that your nose is too big, learn makeup techniques that will downplay its size or save up some money to get yourself a nose reduction. If you have a few bulges in the wrong places, buy clothes that camouflage the weak spots (of course, it wouldn't hurt to jump on the treadmill or take an aerobics class, either). Good teeth are particularly important. If yours are crooked or badly stained, get braces or a retainer to fix them, a professional whitening job (there's also a do-it-yourself version that you can buy over the counter), or a bonding job that can inexpensively re-create the look of your teeth in hours. If you can't afford those solutions, find a dentist who'll work out an extended payment plan with you. It's that important.

The truly best ways to enhance your looks, however, don't cost a dime. Take good posture. If you walk into a room with quiet confidence, standing tall and sure, your stance projects attractiveness and commands attention before you even utter a word. When you do speak, be sure to use your most professional voice—and if you don't have that tone of voice mastered, work on it. With practice you should be able to clean up your grammar and eliminate such bad speaking habits as raising your voice at the end of sentences so that they sound like questions, apologizing frequently, and constantly dropping the word "like" or the phrase "you know" into conversations. Like, uh, you know what I mean, right?

Of all the qualities you can cultivate, however, none is more important than a good smile. Use yours often. When you smile, you project self-confidence and a zest for life that naturally attracts outstanding people and opportunities to your side.

CONSIDER A MAKEOVER

Simply put, there's no such thing anymore as a person who cannot look good.

Easy for you to say, Georgette, you may be thinking, and I can understand why. After all, I've certainly got the financial resources to make the most of my appearance, whether that means going to the top salons, hiring personal trainers, or buying couture outfits from top designers.

But I don't do any of those things and, Lord knows, I didn't always look as glamorous as I do today. In fact, I was downright dowdy as a girl, with nondescript brown hair, frumpy clothes, and an extra ten to twenty pounds, at all times, in all the wrong places. Even as a teenager, though, I knew that I'd never get to where I wanted to go looking the way that I did. So I set about reinventing myself. I certainly didn't call it that at the time or perhaps even realize consciously what I was doing. But in retrospect, that's what it was.

I began my transformation modestly enough by copying the hairstyles I saw in the glamour magazines I loved to read. Soon I became so good at styling that to earn extra money, I began doing my neighbors' hair as well. The next step was experimenting with makeup to enhance my best features and downplay my worst (no expensive cosmetics for me, just the cheapest brands I could find in our local five-and-dime). Looking better from the neck up soon motivated me to work my way down, and I began exercising regularly (but not obsessively) to shed my extra weight.

To this day, by the way, I still do my own hair and nails and, like nearly all the women in my family, wage an ongoing battle with the bulge. But while I admit to occasionally drowning my sorrows in a box of Dunkin' Donuts—don't ask me how many Boston creams I devoured in the months after Robert requested the divorce—I do not let it get too out of hand. I forgive myself my weakness, get back on track (in this case, the NordicTrack), and move on.

DEVELOP A PROFESSIONAL LOOK

If your financial dreams include a work-related goal—maybe you've set your cap at a particular position or are yearning to launch your own business or simply need a better-paying job to make the rest of your dreams come true—you also have to acquire a professional style that will serve you well in any business situation.

Remember, your appearance contributes mightily to the first impression you make, in business as well as in your personal life. Once that impression is made, it is very, very difficult to change. So get it right from the start.

Happily, there's a simple dress code that works in nearly all workplace situations. Whether you're preparing for a job interview, applying for a business loan, or making a presentation to a prospective client, follow this formula and you should do fine:

• **Choose a conservative outfit.** Your best bet is a nicely tailored business suit with a mid-length skirt in a subdued color (navy or black, preferably) and matching low-heeled pumps. Dress that way even if it's completely antithetical to your personal style. A business meeting is not the place to express the real you, especially if your tastes run to peasant skirts and ruffled blouses or, worse yet, Spandex. While you can show a small touch of flair if you're trying out for a creative field, such as advertising or publishing, in most cases you should dress as if you were interviewing for a position as president of the company you're going to see. Then dress that way no matter what position you're really going after or what purpose you're actually there for.

• **Keep the makeup subtle.** Nothing frosted or iridescent and no bright colors. Hot pink or red lipstick, for instance, suggests you're a party girl, not a capable businesswoman. And if you typically favor the big-hair look, tone it down for the interview—or better yet, pull it up and away from your face.

• **As always, good grooming is critical.** If you spend time in an interview constantly brushing wisps of hair off your face and hiding the missing button on your blouse, you can be sure your prospective employer will be thinking, If she can't get her act together enough to comb her hair and mend her clothes, how can she possibly get it together to do the job the way the job should be done?

Make sure, too, that the tools of the trade that you bring with you—your résumé, work samples, reports, presentations—look just as professional as you do. Fortunately, there are a thousand places you can turn to these days for help with sprucing up business documents, including books, office-services companies, software packages, and the Internet. They are well worth the investment of your time and money. Or if you'd rather have someone do it for you, just walk into your local Kinko's or Pip's for assistance.

Last but not least, no matter what kind of business situation you're in, be on your best behavior. Be on time, act attentive, show enthusiasm, and practice unfailing courtesy. Sure, we all know of highly successful people with bad, maybe even rotten manners. But believe me, it's a lot harder to achieve success that way than the other way around. At the end of the day, most people want to be with people who make them feel good about themselves and where they are. They don't want to be around people who make them feel uncomfortable, or who are crude and rude. Never use four-letter words. And always treat other people with dignity and respect, no matter who they are—even if they are "just" the secretary or receptionist or mailroom clerk. That's the most basic of advice, but it will serve you well.

CULTIVATE THE RIGHT ATTITUDE

It's a law of nature, like gravity and perpetual motion: You attract what you project. How you see yourself is how the world sees you. If you think of yourself as successful and dynamic and financially secure, if you act dynamically and as if you're on your way to financial success, then you will naturally attract opportunities for that success, including meeting people who are dynamic and financially secure themselves.

How do you get there from here? Once again, you have to start by exercising that inner voice. In essence, you have to sell yourself first on the notion that you can do whatever you're setting out to do and, what's more, that you deserve to win whatever prize you're after—a new dress, a sportier car, a promotion at work, a terrific man. Then you put on the uniform of success so that you really feel the part. You dress the way the situation calls for, you stand straight and tall to project self-confidence, you speak forthrightly and with conviction about whatever you're setting out to do. Rehearse daily in front of the mirror if you need to. Then get out there in the world and practice.

You'll be amazed at how far attitude alone can get you.

Remember Marion Manigo-Truell, the recruiting consultant you met in chapter 4? Well, the right attitude got Marion the apartment of her dreams, even though at the time she signed the lease, she was out of work and didn't have a penny to pay for it.

It was right after her divorce and, instead of child support for her young daughter, Marion had agreed to a lump-sum settlement from her ex-husband, largely her half of the proceeds from a house they'd owned together and were in the process of selling. She wasn't due to get the money for at least six months, though, and in the meantime she needed someplace to live. But she had no other source of income since she'd quit her job to work through the depression that hit her after her divorce, and she didn't have any savings to fall back on, either. To support herself and her daughter, she was selling off her jewelry, piece by piece.

Marion could have settled for cheap digs until she could afford better, and perhaps that would have been the smarter way to go. But instead she found a fabulously roomy apartment on the eighteenth hole of a golf course, with a view from the terrace of beautifully manicured lawns and greenery for as far as the eye could see. After the trauma of her divorce, she wanted that beauty and comfort in her life and she wanted it *now*. She went directly to the management office, explained that she'd be unable to pay the rent for six months, but would then write a check for the entire amount owed, and she backed up her statement with a letter from her attorney outlining her divorce settlement. To Marion's amazement, she got the apartment without any hassle, moved in immediately, and lived there without paying a dime for six months. Then, just as she had promised, she paid the back rent in a lump sum when her divorce check came through. "You have to have the guts to stand there and ask for what you really want and act like you expect to get it," says Marion. "Even if inside you're saying to yourself, 'What in heaven's name am I doing?', you can't be mealy-mouthed. You've got to be strong."

Marion's advice? "If you know what it is you need, you must not be willing to go gently into that good night without getting it. You have to know deep inside yourself that it's going to work—that it *will* happen—and then refuse to accept anything less."

LEND YOUR ATTITUDE A HELPING HAND

Of course, once you have the right attitude in place, there's nothing wrong with helping nature along a little bit by placing yourself in situations where you're likely to meet the kind of people and opportunities you're looking for.

If, say, the man of your dreams would live in a certain kind of neighborhood or take certain kinds of vacations or be involved in certain kinds of activities, then I'd try to put myself in those same kinds of situations. Ask yourself, are you more likely to meet a man like that at the corner bar or at a political rally, on a public beach or at a civic event? Then go there. My personal favorite technique: Walk your dog in the neighborhood you want to live in rather than the neighborhood where you're currently living. If you're going to meet someone at the park where your dog's playing, why not meet someone who's already arrived at the place you want to go?

Once you're in the situation, don't just sit on the sidelines. If, for instance, you see a man who interests you at that civic event or in the park, figure out a way to meet him. Right there and then, if possible. Don't wait or pretend you're not available when he calls or play any of those other silly games that women are sometimes advised to do. Those kinds of rules may make entertaining reading when they're spelled out in books on how to snare a man, but they don't work in real life—at least, not on the kind of men a smart woman is likely to want.

This kind of forthright attitude and willingness to seek out opportunities, rather than wait for them to come to me, is how I met my first husband. Just a few weeks after I'd moved to Los Angeles from the Midwest, I was sharing an apartment with my brother George to save money. One Sunday afternoon I convinced him to attend an auction of movie memorabilia that Sotheby's was running for Twentieth-Century Fox. We couldn't afford to buy anything, but I was sure it would be an interesting experience attended by lots of interesting people.

And how. Midway through the proceedings, my attention was captured by a confident but gentle-looking man who'd purchased several fifteen-by-twenty-foot replicas of World War II ships used in the filming of the movie *Tora! Tora! Tora!* I couldn't imagine how anyone could afford such an extravagance or what he'd do with them once he took ownership. Even after we left the auction and were on our way home, I couldn't get that man out of my mind. On a whim, I asked George to drive back and wheedled the buyer's name out of the woman in charge by pretending to be a reporter from *Time* magazine doing a feature on Sotheby's. (Hey, it was the first story that popped into my head.) Then I used the same line to arrange a face-to-face interview with the buyer himself. By then I'd learned that he was a successful real estate developer named Robert Muir who just happened to be single.

Now, don't worry. I confessed to my tall tale almost as soon as our "interview" began. Far from being angry, Robert, bless his heart, was amused and flattered. We began dating and were married a year later. Just a year after I first moved to Los Angeles, I found myself living the life of my childhood dreams, married to a man I loved, living in a lovely home in Beverly Hills, and wearing the beautiful clothes I'd always coveted.

··

You should always be taking steps in the direction of the life you want, even if they're baby steps

··

As it turned out, the marriage didn't last and I had to rebuild my life again. Sometimes, when you think you've reached your goal, you blow it. In this case I was simply too young and too immature to appreciate my good fortune. But I learned an important lesson from the experience: You should always be taking steps in the direction of the life you want, even if they're baby steps or you're forced to retrace some of those steps later on. Just because it didn't work out doesn't mean the goal wasn't worthy; you just have to figure out another route to get where you want to go.

ACCENTUATE THE POSITIVE

Now, let's get real here. I don't expect you to be able to put on your best face and maintain an upbeat attitude about everything, all the time. I can't do it, you can't do it, no one can—or should. We're all besieged by self-doubt, even depression, from time to time. The trick is not to let yourself be consumed by it. Recognize it, work through it, and then get on with the business at hand.

Here, when it comes to attitude, are the big don'ts:

- **Don't dwell on what you can't afford or other ways in which life is shortchanging you.** First of all, it's an incredibly unattractive trait, in a man or a woman, and one of the quickest ways I know to lose friends and alienate colleagues and loved ones. Second, it's unproductive. Complaining will not help change the circumstances that you resent one bit. In fact, it's downright counterproductive because when you put negative energy out there, negative energy is precisely what you get back.

- **Don't settle for what you already have because it's more comfortable to do so.** Settling is another word for laziness. Only lazy people settle for less than they can be.

- **Don't let yourself become used to disappointment.** Disappointment should be the exception to the rule, a shock. Life should not be a constant disappointment. Don't accept it.

Remember, too, as you're striving toward your goals, that there can be joy and excitement in challenge. It doesn't have to be drudgery. If you dread change, then it's dreadful. But if you look at change as opening possibilities, then it can be very exciting indeed.

Life really can be an adventure. So can going all out for what you want in that life. It's all in how you approach it.

ACTION PLAN

It's a lot easier to achieve what you want in life when you look and act the part you're aiming to play. Here's how to make sure you always present your personal best:

1. Be impeccably groomed any time you step outside the privacy of your own home. Clean hair, body, nails, and clothes, all neat and in good repair, are an absolute must, in personal as well as professional settings.

2. **Make the most of the looks you were born with.** If your hair is a mousy brown, color it; if your teeth are crooked, get them straightened. There's no such thing anymore as a person who cannot look good.

3. **Smile, smile, and then smile again.** When you smile, you convey self-confidence and a zest for living that few people can resist.

4. **In business situations, act the part of the professional.** Have your résumé and work samples in tip-top shape. Wear conservative outfits, subdued makeup, and discreet jewelry. Be on time, enthusiastic about your work, and unfailingly courteous to your colleagues.

5. **Remember: You attract what you project.** Stand straight and speak forthrightly to project self-confidence, dress for success, and exercise your inner voice daily to convince yourself that you deserve to win whatever prize you're after. Rehearse in front of the mirror until you really feel success within you.

6. **Look for situations where you're likely to meet the kind of people and opportunities you're looking for.** Then go there. When you spot someone you want to know or who might be able to help you, step forward and introduce yourself.

7. **Never dwell on what you can't afford or how life is shortchanging you.** When you put out negative energy, negative results are all you'll get back.

Break the Paycheck-to-Paycheck Habit

Whether you make \$15,000 a year or \$150,000, whether you have a Spartan lifestyle or a tendency to spend lavishly, I bet that your income simply doesn't stretch far enough.

It's a common affliction, of course. I remember reading a survey in *Working Woman* magazine a few years back that asked readers to name their most pressing financial concern. The number one answer was "I'm living from paycheck to paycheck and can never seem to save." That response was cited by nearly two-thirds of the respondents, far outdistancing what I thought would be more common worries, such as being overwhelmed by debt or not having enough money in retirement or being wiped out by a financial catastrophe or even becoming a bag lady. As far as I'm concerned, though, the most telling result from the survey was how universal the inability to save was: Living from paycheck to paycheck was the source of the greatest financial anxiety for these women, no matter what kind of work they did or how much money they made. Whether they were secretaries or CEOs, they all shared the same problem.

Sound familiar to you, too?

Here's the rub: If, as we've seen, all goals in life cost money, then being unable to save means quite simply that you will never achieve your dreams. As far as I'm concerned, that's unacceptable. Completely unacceptable.

So you have to figure out a way to live—and live well—within your means. I don't mean just being able to pay all your bills and buy the things you need without getting into debt. I mean doing all that, plus committing a significant chunk of money to savings, and doing it without sacrificing all the everyday pleasures that make life worth living.

It's easier than you think.

FIGURE OUT THE FLOW

The first step is to determine exactly where all of your money is going now. Just as you put a price tag on your dreams in chapter 3, now you need to put a price tag on your current lifestyle. After all, you can't fix a broken arm if you don't know which bone is broken, or a car that won't run if you don't know whether you have engine trouble or have simply run out of gas. By the same token, you can't plug the leaks in your cash flow and begin to build your savings until you know what you're spending on now—and if or where that spending has gotten out of hand.

I know how easy it is to lose track, especially when someone else is paying the bills. As vigilant as I've had to be since childhood about watching my money, I admit to letting things slide while I was married.

But make no mistake about it, it's a luxury not to have a firm handle on your living expenses. As with every other luxury in life, you pay a price for that lack of knowledge—in this case, it may be the inability to put money away toward your goals or to maintain your lifestyle if your marriage turns sour or something else happens to make you solely responsible for your financial well-being. Only you can decide if that price is too high to pay.

It certainly was for me. Not until Robert's request for a divorce did I sit down and really figure out how much it costs me to live these days. I knew getting the proverbial house in a divorce would be one thing, keeping it would be another. Covering my expenses would be up to me now, and only me, and I found the prospect very scary.

So, after that fateful phone call from Robert came, I sat down with paper and pen and mentally walked myself through my daily life, jotting down how much everything cost. Okay, I said to myself, I have a roof over my head; what do I pay to keep it there? Then I wrote down how much I spend on my apartment, including maintenance, gas, and electric bills. Next, I estimated what it costs me to drive my car; for that I penciled in totals for gas, maintenance, and parking. Health insurance, charitable contributions, clothing, food, makeup, financial support for my family, gifts, caring for my dog, recreational activities (such as going to the movies and the theater)—I duly noted them all. I put in an estimate for travel (two trips a year, ten days each), remembering to include not just what I pay for airfare, hotels, and meals, but also how much spending money I'd need every day. I give a lot of dinner parties, many of them fund-raising events for the center I've founded for abused children and for the political causes I support, so I put in an estimate for those, too.

Of course, I didn't have all of this information off the top of my head, and you won't, either. It takes some research. To help jog my memory (or, in some cases, to inform me for the first time, I'm somewhat embarrassed to admit), I pulled check stubs, bills, and invoices and called the companies involved for copies if I didn't have records of my own. In the case of the dinner parties, for example, I checked my calendar to see how many parties I'd given in the past several months and on what dates, and then pulled the catering bills for a random few so I could estimate the total cost for the year. I called the utility company for copies of my gas and electric bills over the past year. Where there were still gaps, I relied on my own memory for rough estimates.

So whip out your dream notebook now, ladies, and start listing all of your expenses. Set up major categories for the biggest drains on your cash flow—Housing, Utilities, Food, Clothes, and so on. Then put smaller subcategories under each one and perhaps even additional divisions under those so you can analyze in as much detail as possible exactly what costs what.

Let's take a few examples so you can see exactly what I mean. Under the major category Housing, for instance, you'd probably create subcategories for Mortgage/Rent, Property Taxes, Homeowner's Insurance, and Maintenance. Then under each of these subcategories you'd break down your expenses further with individual line items, if necessary. Under the Maintenance section, for instance, you might put entries for home repairs, a cleaning service if you have one, lawn care, and so on. Another major category would be Utilities, under which you'd put subcategories for Gas, Electricity, Telephone, Water, and Cable TV. Under the big category of Food, you'd include groceries, dinners out, lunches out, and take-out meals. Under Clothes, you'd have the clothes themselves, as well as accessories (such as panty hose and underwear), laundry, and dry cleaning.

Create as many categories, subcategories, and line items as you can think of. The more details you know about where your money goes, the better able you'll be to put together a realistic plan for breaking the paycheck-to-paycheck habit. Here are some other categories that I have in my budget—maybe they'll help guide you in putting together yours:

- **Health**, which includes out-of-pocket medical and dental bills, prescription and over-the-counter drugs as well as eyeglasses, contact lenses, and eye exams.

- **Insurance**, which includes premiums for my life, health, and disability insurance as well as what I spend on deductibles and co-payments.

- **Entertainment**, which includes the cost of going to the movies, theater, and other cultural events as well as any dinners and parties that I host.

- **Transportation**, which includes the cost of driving and maintaining my car (which, in turn, includes how much I spend on gas, oil, tune-ups, repairs and parking) as well as taxicabs in and around New York City.

- **Personal Care**, which includes haircuts, coloring, nail polish, makeup, toiletries, and health-club membership.

- **Travel**, which includes airfare, cabs, hotels, restaurants and spending money for the separate subcategories of Business Travel and Personal Trips.

- **Pet Care**, which includes dog food, toys, medicine, and other pet supplies as well as veterinary expenses.

- **Charity**, which includes cash donations as well as the costs involved in my volunteer work (for example, traveling to or from a particular organization).

- **Gifts**, both business and personal, to family, friends, and colleagues.

- **Savings and Investments**, which includes a separate sub-listing of the amounts I'm putting away for every one of my financial goals, short-term and long-term, from some big-ticket purchase I'm planning to make in the near future to how much I'm saving for retirement.

- **Incidentals**, a big catch-all category that covers everything from magazine subscriptions to lottery tickets (yes, I still buy them occasionally).

But don't rely exclusively on my list to guide you. Just as I probably have some expenses that you don't incur, so you may want to include other categories, such as child care, or the cost of cigarettes if you're a smoker. The idea is to make as personal a record of your expenditures as possible.

TRACK YOUR SPENDING

In the end, I'm convinced that last category on my list of expenses—you know, the "incidentals"—is the one that does us all in. A few magazines here, a bagel and a cup of coffee there, all add up until suddenly those seemingly inconsequential expenditures have turned into a serious chunk of change. You may think you know how much you're spending, but I guarantee it: If you take a closer look, you will be shocked—truly shocked—to discover how much money you're frittering away.

Wanda Rains certainly was. Nine years ago, Wanda and her husband Cliff were working sixty hours a week, running their own marine-construction company in Anchorage, Alaska, when they decided to chuck it all and move to a scenic seaside town near Seattle. They wanted to simply kick back and enjoy life for a while, and with a substantial six-figure sum in savings, they thought they had enough money to do just that. They quickly bought a large beachfront home and set out to enjoy their new life of leisure with a vengeance. Within eighteen months, though, they'd run through most of their money and were piling on credit-card debt to pay their way. Soon they were forced to launch another marine-construction business and move to a smaller, inland house just to make ends meet.

Wanda knew that she was spending her dreams away, and made up her mind to reverse course. "I couldn't figure out how we could possibly be going through our money that quickly," she says. "I said to myself, 'Hey, get a grip here.'" To see exactly what was causing the hemorrhage in their cash flow, she carried around a little notebook and wrote down every expenditure she made, big and small and in between, for thirty days. At the end of that period, she says, "It was like somebody hit me upside the head. We were literally spending the equivalent of more than $1,000 a year on espresso alone."

With a written record of her spending habits before her eyes, Wanda found it surprisingly easy to find relatively painless ways to cut back. She stopped browsing the malls and instead began shopping at discount stores and second-hand outlets. She cut down on expensive dinners out with her husband, eliminated impulse purchases altogether and traded their new wheels for a used car, which was a lot cheaper to run and to insure. She also reduced her visits to the local coffee bar from once a day to once a week. "Out here, if you don't drink coffee all the time, you're like a Martian or, worse yet, a Californian without a suntan," she explains. "Now, though, instead of the coffee bar being a habit, it's become a treat again."

The result of all Wanda's efforts? Within two years she was able to cut back her work load from fifty hours a week to twenty, and then, at the ripe old age of forty-six, she retired altogether. She spent the next two years doing volunteer work, taking acting lessons, playing tennis, and working out with a personal trainer. About a year ago, though, Wanda decided to launch a new career as a professional quilter, working roughly twenty-five hours a week out of her home. The business fulfills her creatively, provides some additional spending money, and still allows her time to play tennis, garden, and visit with friends. She notes, "I just wake up in the morning these days and feel totally happy."

To find the little leaks in your own cash flow, follow Wanda's lead. Tuck a little notepad in your pocketbook and jot down everything you spend for a month or two, paying particular attention to those pesky under-$5 outlays that often escape our notice—a pack of mints, a magazine, a muffin on the way in to work every morning. If you find tracking your expenses for this long to be too tedious (or too depressing), try a week or two instead. Alternatively, if you find that you're really getting into it, consider buying yourself a money-management software program, like Quicken, and record your spending there. That's what I do. Within a month or two you'll be able to generate reports showing in elaborate (and sometimes frightening) detail exactly where your money goes.

There's a big bonus to this little exercise, according to all the financial planners I've ever talked with as well as everyone I know who's actually done it: Simply writing down your expenses in and of itself is likely to prompt you to cut your spending by 10 percent to 20 percent or more. When you make yourself accountable to yourself for your spending, somehow you automatically get with the program. Awareness is half the battle.

DEVELOP A SPENDING PLAN

Once you know exactly what you're up against in terms of both your fixed expenses and your personal spending habits, you'll be able to work up a reasonable spending plan—one that enables you to cover all your basic expenditures adequately, with enough left over for savings and at least a few of your favorite luxuries in life.

Let's be honest here. I'm talking about putting together a budget— a little six-letter word that often dredges up four-letter reactions. For a lot of people, I know, a budget connotes going without. It means sacrifice. A straitjacket on your spending. Who in their right minds can get themselves motivated for that experience?

You can, of course—but not if you think of a budget in those terms. In fact, a budget is really nothing more than a planning mechanism, a way of being prepared for the expenses you know you're going to face in life, including the cost of pursuing your dreams. If you learn how to budget wisely, you won't have to go without. On the contrary, budgeting is the best way I know to live as well as you possibly can on the money you've got. Done right, it's a help, not a burden.

Okay, enough of the warm-up. Now let's get down to it.

On a clean sheet of paper or in a new computer file, record your annual income from all sources—your salary (if you work outside your home), your husband's salary (if you are married), any alimony or child support you receive, earnings from freelance jobs, and any interest or dividend income. Now look back over your expenses worksheet, and total how much you're spending in each category. Add in the amount you estimated in chapter 3 that you should be saving toward your financial goals. Then compare your totals for income and outgo (that is, your expenses plus the amount you're aiming to save).

If your income turns out to be greater than your outgo, congratulations. You're entitled to close this book right now, and go out and treat yourself to dinner or a movie or even a new outfit to reward yourself for your superior money-management skills. At the very least, skip the rest of this chapter and move on to the next one.

If, on the other hand, your outgo column is the bigger number—far bigger—roll up your sleeves and get ready to do a nip-and-tuck job on your expenses. Here's how:

- Go back over each of your spending categories to see if any amounts seem way out of line to you. In a new column called Budgeted Expenses that you'll put next to your Actual Expenses column, enter in a new lower figure for the expenses that seem most outlandish to you. For instance, if you see that you're spending several hundred dollars a year on dry cleaning, resolve to stock up on wash-and-wear outfits this year, and slash that amount in half.

- Now take another five percent off every other item and enter those new numbers, too. You'll find that it's usually far easier to squeeze a little something out of everything than to drastically reduce or eliminate whole categories. The sole exception: your savings category. For the time being, at least, regard that expenditure as sacred and don't fiddle with it.

- Run a new total for your budgeted expenses and see how this number compares with your income. If you're now in balance or, better yet, your outgo figure is smaller than your income, you're done.

- If not, go back over each category and lop off another five percent. Rerun the numbers and see where you stand.

- If your expenses are still out of sync with your income, you'll have to take more drastic measures. Maybe you need to consider ways to boost your income (see chapter 14 for tips) or maybe you'll finally have to bite the bullet and rejigger the timetable on one or more of your financial goals to lower the amount you have to save.

- Repeat the last two steps and keep reworking the numbers until your income and outgo totals jibe.

RESOLVE TO STICK TO IT

I followed this process faithfully when I was a young woman without a penny in my pocket, and I follow it today, when (at least for the time being) I have plenty. I know exactly how much I can spend in each expense category, from my clothing to my dog's doctor. I know that if, heaven forbid, my vet bills go over the budget, I have to find that money elsewhere in my budget, maybe by reducing my clothing or travel allowance.

To help keep myself on track, I record literally everything I spend. If I go to the drugstore and buy some toiletries, I bring home that bill and immediately enter it on Quicken. Everything's coded by different lines in my budget, so I can see exactly where I stand at any time. Okay, so maybe I'm a little obsessive. But I'd rather know where I stand than be unpleasantly surprised and run out of money for something I really want.

Then I review my budget once a week to see how I'm doing. I find that sticking to it is easier if I know exactly where I am, and I guarantee you will, too. Say you go shopping and see a dress that you want. The dress costs $125, but you're aware that you have only $75 left in your clothing allowance, so you know you can't afford it. Either you'll have to pass on the dress, wait until it goes on sale, or cut $50 from another category in your budget. What you don't do is buy the dress anyway.

Success in spending less and saving more, as in anything in life, is all about stick-to-it-ness. That's what separates the winners from the losers.

Remember: *AWARENESS IS HALF THE BATTLE*. Awareness will force discipline upon you.

MAKE IT LIVABLE

Don't overdo it, though. That's almost as dangerous as not budgeting at all. Leave room in your budget for the stuff that makes you happiest. Without a few little luxuries and some fun in your life, your resolve to change your financial habits will melt away.

In this respect, budgets are a lot like diets. If you're trying to lose weight but don't allow yourself any of the foods that give you pleasure—say, if you're a bread lover and you eliminate all bread from your diet—you'll never stick to it. The idea is to teach yourself how to limit your consumption. In the case of the bread, for instance, maybe you decide to allow yourself freshly baked rolls with dinner, but only on the weekends.

With budgets, I've found that clothing, food, and personal pampering are the easiest places to reduce spending without sacrificing the experience. For instance, you don't need to eliminate eating out in restaurants because it's too expensive. You simply eat out less often, find restaurants that have specials (for instance, lower prices if you come in before six p.m. or in the middle of the week) or, if you have children, go out only on family night, when the kids can eat for free. You don't stop taking vacations, you just downscale your travel plans—maybe you shorten your stay from, say, seven days to five days or perhaps you drive to your destination instead of flying and stay somewhere with kitchen facilities to save on restaurant meals rather than in a luxury hotel. You don't give up buying clothes, but you do limit your shopping to sale items and discount outlets. (I'll fill you in on some of my other favorite ways to save money when you shop in chapter 11.)

In short, you find creative ways to buy the things that really matter.

That's what registered nurse Dee Paris, thirty-six, does to keep herself and her four children well fed, clothed, and happy on her $35,000 annual income, according to a recent story in *Family Money* magazine. The family, whose income dropped in half following Dee's 1991 divorce from the kids' dad, have learned the value of small economies. The children all pack their own school lunches, every family member is reminded to turn off the lights when leaving a room (the utility bill for their hundred-year-old house in Emsworth, Pennsylvania, rivals the mortgage payment), Dee does many of the necessary repairs on the house herself, and they all love to shop at thrift stores.

Despite their tight budget, though, music lover Dee managed to buy herself a piano recently. To keep the price down, she simply shopped around until she found a used but good-quality upright rather than springing for a brand-new set of ivories. The matter-of-fact Dee doesn't feel gypped, nor does she consider herself particularly heroic for finding creative ways for her family to live within their means. "I know what I make; I know what I have to pay out; I know I have four kids," she told the magazine. "You just do it."

I love Dee's no-bellyaching attitude and wish we could all learn from her example: Don't use a budget as an excuse to deny yourself the experiences you crave; instead simply find less expensive substitutes that will make you just as happy.

LUXURIATE IN CONTROL

The benefit of designing and keeping to a budget is not just financial. You'll experience a huge psychological boost from gaining control over your life and your finances. When we're living from paycheck to paycheck, feeling stretched to the limit (and sometimes beyond) every month, we carry a heavy emotional as well as a financial burden. It's enormously freeing when you finally get your spending under control. Enjoy it.

ACTION PLAN
To break the paycheck-to-paycheck habit and free up some money for your key goals, here's what you need to do:

1. **Make a list of all of your living expenses.** That means line-by-line entries for housing, food, clothes, transportation, and literally everything else that costs you money. Don't rely on your memory alone. Pull check stubs, bill statements, and any other records you need to get a truly accurate estimate of how much it currently costs you to live.

2. **Keep a detailed account of your personal spending for at least two weeks, ideally a month or two.** Carry around a little notepad

in your purse and jot down the item and the amount of every single purchase that you make, from a pack of gum to a magazine.

3. **On another sheet of paper or in a computer file, record your income from all sources.** That includes your salary, earnings from freelance work, child support, or any other income you may receive. If you're married, include your husband's income as well.

4. **Subtract your total household income from your total outgo.** (Outgo includes your major and minor expenses, plus the amount you need to save to reach your financial goals.) The result is the amount you need to trim from your current living expenses to stop living from paycheck to paycheck and really begin to save money.

5. **Go back over your list of expenses, looking for areas where your spending seems really out line.** Enter a more realistic (in other words, lower) figure for those items. Then shave an additional five percent off all the other expenses on your list. Finally, rerun the numbers to see if your income and outgo are now in balance.

6. **Repeat Step 5 until your income and outgo match.**

7. **Be creative in coming up with ways to achieve the savings you've outlined in your new budget.** The idea is to make your spending plan livable. Do not eliminate the pleasures that make you happiest. Instead try to cut back a little or find less expensive substitutes for the experience.

8. **Resolve to stick to it.** Track your progress at least once a week, and make adjustments as necessary. Congratulate yourself for each victory in gaining control over your spending and taking another giant step toward fulfilling your dreams.

Pay Yourself First

*I*t's another one of those financial laws of nature: Your lifestyle will expand to fill the amount of money you have. No matter how much you earn, no matter how carefully you budget, you will spend as much as you take in—unless you learn to pay yourself first.

The concept is simple enough: Don't think of the item in your budget called "saving money" as something you do with whatever cash you have left at the end of the month after all of your bills have been paid. Think of savings as another bill—indeed, your most important bill—and make it the very first one that you pay each month. That's right, the first. Whatever sum you've decided to devote to savings, write out the check for that amount as soon as you get paid and send it off to the savings or investment vehicle of your choice, before you pay your mortgage or rent, buy your groceries, send off your utilities bill, or take care of any of your other monthly financial obligations.

Do this, and I guarantee: You will have money saved by the end of the year and, in all likelihood, a sizable sum at that.

PUT YOUR SAVINGS ON AUTOMATIC PILOT

Actually, there's an even better way to put a pay-yourself-first plan into action than writing the checks yourself: Enroll in an *automatic investment plan*—that is, a program that automatically deducts the amount you want saved from your paycheck or bank account each month and puts the money into investments of your choice.

These plans truly make saving a painless proposition. The chief reason? You rarely miss cash that you've never actually held in your hands and had an opportunity to spend. It's the financial equivalent of an out-of-sight, out-of-mind experience. Then too, after you've arranged to participate, you don't have to worry about disciplining yourself to set money aside anymore; the plan sponsor takes care of the discipline for you. In fact, New York City financial planner Ann Diamond has said, only half-jokingly, "Next to Post-It notes, automatic investments plans are the best invention in the world."

These programs are a piece of cake to set up as well. Literally tens of thousands of banks, brokerages, and credit unions across the country offer them. All you have to do is call the financial institution's toll-free number and ask for an application. On the form, you indicate how much money you want withdrawn from your checking account or paycheck every month ($50 is usually the minimum, although some programs will accept amounts as low as $10 to $25), on what day of the month (the first and the fifteenth are typical choices), and which investment you've chosen to put your cash into (my personal favorites are mutual funds, particularly stock funds; I'll explain why and suggest some solid choices in chapter 13). You can change the amount or the investment you've chosen any time you want or even stop participating altogether, without incurring penalty.

What's the downside? you may be asking. Absolutely none!

To get yourself going with an automatic investment program, I suggest that you start with a modest amount that you're not really going to miss—say, $50 or $100 a month—then slowly ratchet up your contribution every few months until you hit your savings target. It's also smart to up the ante every time you get a raise, directing, say, half of the amount you're awarded to your savings program. In effect, you'll be giving your savings a raise at the same time as you get one yourself.

No matter how much money you put in, though, you'll be amazed at how quickly your savings add up when you're not looking. (It's the financial equivalent of not watching a pot boil.) Say you've arranged with a financial-services firm to have $100 deducted from your checking account every month and put into a mutual fund that invests in blue-chip stocks. If that fund averages the 10 percent a year that stocks have returned over the past seventy-five years, you'll have saved more than $8,000 at the end of five years, amassed over $20,000 at the end of ten, and be sitting pretty with nearly $220,000 in twenty-five. Not bad for $100 a month.

TAKE ADVANTAGE OF FREE MONEY

Tens of thousands of employers sponsor their own automatic savings plans, from programs that allow you to direct your money into U.S. savings bonds to 401(k) and similar accounts that let you build a retirement nest egg by investing in a handful or more of mutual funds, company stock, and other savings vehicles. The concept is the same as ordinary automatic investment plans, but the mechanics of contributing are slightly different. Instead of indicating a set amount that you want withdrawn from your checking account, you direct your company benefits office to automatically deduct a certain percentage of your salary from your paycheck, usually up to 10 percent.

If you're lucky enough to work for a company that sponsors one of these retirement savings programs—and almost all big companies and many medium- and smaller-sized firms do—run, do not walk, to your benefits office and sign up for it right away. Simply put, it's the best investment you will ever make. In fact, it's the closest thing to a guaranteed winner you'll ever find in this life.

Here's why: In the great majority of these plans, employers match a portion of their employees' contributions, typically kicking in 50 cents for every dollar that the employee contributes, up to an amount equal to six percent of their salary. That means you automatically earn the equivalent of a 50 percent return on your account, even if the actual investments you choose don't earn a dime.

But that's not all. You also get two spectacular tax breaks. First, you don't have to pay federal income or Social Security and Medicare taxes on the money that you put into your account until you withdraw the money, presumably after you retire. (In most states you also defer paying state and local income taxes on your contributions.) So every dollar that you put in reduces your taxable-income dollar for dollar in the year that you make the contribution. If you sock away $200 a month, or $2,400 a year, for example, you'd probably shave at least $800 off your annual tax bill, maybe more. Second, you don't pay any taxes on the profits you earn on the investments in your account until you withdraw them, either. That means you not only earn more money on your original investment, but your earnings earn more money as well. The effect, called compounding, is like an application of Miracle-Gro on your savings.

If you translate all those rules into dollars and cents, you'll see exactly what I mean. Say you start saving five percent of your salary when you're twenty-five years old and you put the money into an ordinary taxable investment that earns 10 percent a year. Assuming that when you begin your salary is in the mid-$20s and you get five percent raises once a year, you'll end up with more than half a million dollars by the time you're ready to retire at age sixty-five. Not too shabby, you're probably thinking.

If you invest instead through a 401(k), though, you'll do a whole lot better than that. First off, you'll be able to contribute a little bit more right off the bat without reducing your take-home pay because you don't get any taxes taken out of your contributions. Then too, your savings will grow a lot faster because you won't have to pay taxes on the money you earn on your investments until you're ready to withdraw them. Those twin tax breaks alone will cause your account to grow nearly three times as much as in the ordinary taxable investment, to a cool $1.4 million by the time you're sixty-five. Throw in the typical company matching provision of fifty cents for every dollar that you put in and you'll be looking at roughly $2 million instead, or 400 percent more than in the original example!

Of course, if you're able to sock away more than five percent, you'll do even better than that. If you up the ante to 10 percent of your salary instead, for example, you'll end up with a whopping $3.4 million when you're ready to quit the work force for good—even if your company doesn't match as much as another penny of your contribution.

BEWARE THE SLIGHT CATCH

There is one small caveat to contributing to *a 401(k) or similar company-sponsored retirement plan*: Unlike the all-purpose automatic investing plans offered by mutual fund companies and other financial institutions, these are *employer programs specifically designed to help you save for retirement*. If you take money out of your account before you turn 59½, you'll have to pay a 10 percent penalty, plus ordinary income taxes, on the amount you withdraw. The sole exceptions: withdrawals for financial hardship (say, if you or your spouse has been out of work for a long time) or if you need the money for a medical emergency.

There is, however, a way around the rules, if you really need the money. You can simply borrow against the money in your own account. About three-quarters of the companies that sponsor 401(k) plans allow employees to do so and, unlike hardships withdrawals, the loans are usually approved with no questions asked. The most common reason to borrow against a 401(k) plan is for the down payment on a new home, but you can do so for any purpose. I have a friend who took a $5,000 401(k) loan, for example, to help pay for her own wedding.

Certainly, it's a no-fuss, no-muss way to borrow money. There are no credit checks, and approval is fast: You usually get your money within three weeks. The terms for repayment are fairly painless, too. Like your regular contributions to your account, the loan payments are deducted from your paycheck and usually spread over two to ten years, depending on how much you've borrowed. (If you leave the company before you've repaid the loan, you must either make good on the debt before you go or pay a 10 percent early withdrawal penalty, plus income taxes, on the outstanding balance.) The interest rate is typically far lower than on most personal loans (usually within one percentage point of the prime rate). Best of all, the interest you pay usually goes right back into your account.

Now, I'm not encouraging anyone to use these accounts for anything other than the purpose they were designed for: your retirement. But it's nice to know the money's there for you to use if you really need some.

SET UP A SEP

If you're self-employed or work for a company that doesn't offer a 401(k) or similar tax-advantaged retirement plan, you can set one up yourself through a mutual fund company, bank, or brokerage. Individual retirement accounts (IRAs) are the most popular variety and have become much more attractive lately, courtesy of recent changes in the tax law that have expanded eligibility for claiming a tax deduction for IRA contributions and will allow you to withdraw your money without penalty before age 59½ if you're tapping the account to buy your first home or pay for college tuition.

If you're your own boss, however, you're probably better off setting up an account called a *Simplified Employee Pension*, or a SEP for short. The main reason: SEPs allow you to sock away roughly 13 percent of your self-employment income for retirement (including money earned from freelancing), up to a recent maximum of $24,000. By contrast, contributions to an ordinary IRA are limited to $2,000 a year. Otherwise, though, the two accounts work much the same way. Your contributions to both are tax-deductible, your investment earnings grow tax-deferred, and under most circumstances you'll be slapped with a 10 percent penalty for withdrawals made before age 59½.

The only real drawback to a SEP comes if you employ anyone else in your business. Under current rules, you might have to contribute to a SEP for them, too—even if they work only part-time or have worked sporadically over the past few years. If that's the case, you're probably better off setting up another type of retirement account for self-employed people called a *Keogh plan*. Although the rules governing these accounts are similar to those on SEPs, Keoghs give you more leeway regarding contributions for part-time employees, particularly if you choose the most popular variety, known as a profit-sharing Keogh.

The main drawback—and not an overwhelming one, in my opinion—is additional paperwork, compared with setting up a SEP.

GO FOR THE 10 PERCENT SOLUTION

Just how much is enough to contribute to your retirement savings plan? While any amount is obviously a lot better than none, I strongly encourage you to aim for at least 10 percent of your income.

Think you can't afford to squeeze an additional 10 percent out of your earnings now for retirement, particularly since you're also anxious to save for more immediate, reach-out-and-touch-them goals? Well, I contend if you're determined, you can always find a way.

Former welfare mom Rhoni Smith did, even as she was struggling to get off public assistance and back on her feet financially. When Rhoni, twenty-eight, graduated from Howard University in Washington, D.C., six years ago, she returned to her native Los Angeles to find California in the midst of its worst recession in decades. She also discovered that she was pregnant. The combination made it impossible for Rhoni to find a job in her chosen field (she was a psychology major), or anything close to it. So she patched together a living, working part-time as a bank teller and the rest of the day at jobs she found through a temporary agency. Although she didn't have health insurance (or any other benefits, for that matter) and certainly wasn't making any strides toward establishing a career, she could at least pay her bills, she explained to the *Los Angeles Times* last year—that is, until her son, Baraka, was born five weeks early. "From the moment he was born, I needed to be on welfare," she told the newspaper. "You do what you have to do."

But Rhoni didn't do it for long. Determined to get off of public assistance as quickly as possible, Rhoni pounded the pavement, taking whatever work she could find, as soon as she and Baraka were recovered from his birth. She also cut spending to the bare bone. To save on rent and utilities, she moved into an apartment with her brother, sleeping on the floor because she couldn't afford to buy a mattress. She gave up cable TV, dry cleaning, and even panty hose. But not until she landed a $31,800-a-year job as data specialist for UCLA two years ago was she finally able to support herself entirely on her own again. Only then could she turn her attention to her other financial goals: to pay off the debts she'd accumulated as a student and in her early days in L.A. ($3,800 in student loans and $5,600 on her credit cards) and to buy a house to live in with her son.

Now, here's the really phenomenal part of her story: Even with all of these pressing short-term financial goals on her mind, Rhoni still signed up for an automatic savings plan at work as soon as she was eligible. And she's not contributing piddling amounts, either. She puts 10 percent of her salary into UCLA's 403(b) plan, the equivalent of a 401(k) plan for employees of nonprofit organizations. And another 7 percent of her earnings are automatically deducted and directed into UCLA's employee pension plan. Just two years after getting off welfare, this single mom has over $5,000 in these two accounts. And she's managed to save that amount even while paying off her credit cards, making a dent in her student loans, shelling out tuition for the preschool that Baraka attends while she works and, most recently, setting up an automatic investment plan with a mutual fund company to start putting away money toward her dream house.

If Rhoni Smith can do it, so can you. Do not wait to pass Go or even another minute. Sign up for an automatic savings plan today.

ACTION PLAN
To get really serious about saving money for your financial goals, follow these steps:

1. **Make the mental leap: Stop thinking of saving money as something you do with whatever cash you have left over after you've paid all your bills every month.** Treat your savings as a bill, too, your most important bill!, and resolve to make it the first one you pay every month.

2. **Enroll in an automatic savings program at a mutual fund company, brokerage house, or your local bank.** That way you won't have to worry about disciplining yourself to save. You just tell the

financial institution how much you want to save every month and what investment you want to put the money in, and the amount will be automatically deducted from your checking account until you tell them to stop.

3. **Sign up for your employer's retirement savings plan as well if you're fortunate enough to work for a company that offers one.** Since most employers match at least a portion of the amount that their employees contribute, not taking advantage of these accounts is the same as throwing money away.

4. **If you're self-employed, open a SEP or Keogh plan to start socking money away for your retirement.** These accounts do for self-employed people what 401(k)s do for company employees: provide you with big tax breaks for saving for your retirement.

5. **Start your automatic savings programs with relatively small sums that you won't really miss.** Then periodically ratchet up the amounts—say, every few months or so—until you reach your savings targets. With the company-sponsored plans, aim to put in 10 percent of your salary; if you can't afford that much, contribute at least as much money as your employer will match.

Always Work with a Net

Once you get the hang of saving for your financial goals, it's actually a fun and rewarding process. As you periodically check your balances, see them grow larger and larger, and feel yourself edging closer to fulfilling at least some of your financial goals, you'll be even more motivated to stay the course you've set out for yourself. Although you've got to be careful not to slack off once the initial enthusiasm that accompanies newness wears off, the bigger threat is that some outside event, some circumstance beyond your control, will push you off track. Because life, unfortunately, has an unpleasant habit of pulling the rug out from under you when you least expect it.

We pay lip service to the notion of being prepared for that proverbial rainy day, but rarely take the actions necessary to ensure it. Well, ladies, it's time to change that attitude now. Because the truth of the matter is, women are getting poured on every day. Statistics suggest there will be a nasty thunderstorm in our futures. And we will need a lot more than an umbrella and a raincoat to keep ourselves and our dreams from getting all wet.

Just consider: Three out of every four American households are likely to experience a wrenching change in circumstances—for instance, a layoff, a divorce, a disabling illness, or the death of a family member—that will cause severe financial damage in addition to emotional distress. So says an ongoing fifteen-year study of income dynamics at the University of Michigan. As if that wasn't bad enough, nearly a third of the families in that study saw their incomes drop 50 percent or more—*50 percent or more*!—at least temporarily, as a result of these crises.

Who got hit the worst? Women, of course. The study showed that women were twice as likely as men to fall below the poverty line following one of these financial catastrophes.

To make sure an unforeseen disaster doesn't send your plans and dreams into a free fall, you have to work with a net—a financial safety net, that is. There are three basic components to a financial safety net: an emergency fund, a comprehensive set of insurance policies, and a secret stash of cash that you can tap if your circumstances (or those of a loved one) become truly dire. I'll talk in a moment about the best ways to put together those rainy-day funds and tackle exactly what you need in the way of insurance in the next chapter.

Understand this first, though: Without all three components of the safety net, you are in essence building your house of dreams at the edge of a cliff, hoping that shifting ground or a strong gust of wind doesn't come along to topple everything you've worked for over the brink.

I don't know about you, but I'm not about to leave my financial security up to luck or a twist of fate. I say build that net, and build it *now*.

START A RAINY-DAY FUND

Could you handle an unexpected bill for $1,000 without hardship? If you're like more than half of the women who responded to a recent survey in *Money* magazine, the answer is no. Some 55 percent said they'd find it difficult to come up with a thousand bucks to pay an unplanned bill. Only a third of the men, by the way, said they'd be similarly pressed.

Ouch.

Unfortunately, expenses of that size—and a whole lot larger—come up all the time. If the roof springs a leak or the car breaks down or, worse yet, you suddenly lose your job, you don't want to be forced to sell investments you've been building for your long-term goals or borrow money at exorbitant rates to get over the hump. Having sufficient cash on hand is also crucial if you or your spouse becomes ill or dies to tide the family over financially until long-term disability kicks in or the estate is settled or you get a check from the life insurance company. That's why financial planners routinely suggest that you keep enough money tucked away in the bank or some similar safe haven to cover three to six months of your living expenses.

I made sure that I had that much cash handy right after I separated from Robert. When I was unexpectedly hit with an outsized tax bill on one of my investments a few months later, I was mighty glad that I had.

The easiest way to build your emergency fund is the same way you're saving for all the rest of your financial goals: Enroll in an automatic savings plan at a bank, brokerage, or mutual fund company and have a little bit of cash (say, $50 or $100 a month to start) deducted from your checking account. Only in this case, instead of directing the financial institution to put the money in a long-term investment like a stock fund, choose a super-safe, highly liquid vehicle like a bank or brokerage money market account or a money market mutual fund. Like an ordinary passbook savings account at a bank, money market accounts and funds are designed with one purpose in mind: to protect your principal. In plain English, that means that you can't lose money. That's critical because with an emergency fund you need to be sure your savings will be easily accessible and completely intact if and when you need the money.

I prefer to use a money market fund for my own emergency cache because I hate to have a lot of money languishing in the bank, earning a skimpy one to three percent in interest. Rates on money market funds typically run at least two to three percentage points higher than those on an ordinary bank account, and you can write checks against your fund much the same way you can with your ordinary checking account. (The major difference between the two types of accounts, from the consumer's point of view: You usually can't write small checks from your money fund, since most companies impose a minimum check amount, typically around $250.) While they're not federally insured the way that a bank account is, no money market fund has ever lost a penny in their nearly thirty-year history. Given the money funds' far higher rates, that track record is good enough for me.

SECURE A SOURCE OF CREDIT

If you're too strapped for cash to put aside three to six months' living expenses—or even if you're not—you should also open up some lines of credit now that you can tap later if you need to. After all, no reputable lender will extend credit to you *after* you lose your job or suffer some other serious reversal in fortune. If you were a banker, would you lend money to someone under those circumstances?

The absolutely best kind of credit to get if you own your own home is a *home-equity line of credit* with your local bank or mortgage company. This credit line allows you to borrow money against the equity you have in your home simply by writing a check for the amount you need. In one sense, it operates a bit like an ordinary credit card since you pay no interest and little or nothing in the way of fees unless you actually use your home-equity line. But the interest rate on home-equity lines is usually far lower than on most other loans—at least five points lower than the typical rate on a personal loan, for example, and ten or more percentage points below the finance charges on the average credit card. And unlike ordinary credit cards and other forms of borrowing, the first $100,000 in interest that you pay on a home-equity line is typically tax-deductible, so the net cost of borrowing is even cheaper.

While you're at it, try to pay down the outstanding balances on your credit cards and push your charge limits to the max. (For more suggestions about managing your credit cards, including how to nab a lower rate, see chapter 11.) The idea is to create as much room on those cards as possible so if you are truly strapped for funds, you can charge what you need until the emergency is over.

Let me be very clear here, however: Taking a cash advance on your credit card should be your last line of defense in a financial emergency because it's one of the most expensive ways on earth to borrow. The average finance charge on cash advances, after all, is around 22 percent. But if you're really pushed to the wall, it's good to know that the money would be there.

ESTABLISH A SECRET STASH

Can you hear the drum roll? Here comes the single most important, most practical tip I will pass along to you in this book: In addition to your family emergency fund, you must keep some money of your own tucked away in a safe place, a private stash of cash that absolutely no one else knows about. Private means private. Do not tell anyone that this stash exists—not your mother, your sister, your best friend, your husband, not even your hairdresser. Just as you do with your household emergency fund, try to add to your secret stash on a regular basis. And continue to build it every chance you get.

The reason for secrecy is simple: Whenever anyone knows that you have money around that doesn't appear to be earmarked for a specific purpose, someone has a crisis that warrants using it. And yet this private emergency fund does have a very distinct purpose: It will give you the financial means to survive, even thrive, if you suddenly find yourself in an untenable personal situation—for example, if your husband leaves you without warning, if he threatens you physically or emotionally, if your marriage otherwise breaks down irretrievably, or if you or someone you love is in a life-or-death situation and money can help solve the crisis.

What you *do not do* is tap this money for a new pair of earrings that your husband would object to you buying. You don't use it to go on the fantasy vacation that you've always wanted to take or to buy the dream car that you've always wanted to drive. You save for those goals, and you use your savings to buy them when you reach your target. No, you use your secret stash only in a bona fide catastrophe: a divorce or some other unraveling of your life in which having money is key to your survival.

Think of it as private catastrophic insurance for women—the single most important insurance policy every woman must have.

After all, if you lived in a flood-prone region, you'd take out flood insurance; if you lived in an area susceptible to earthquakes, you'd take out earthquake insurance. Well, statistics tell us that marriages are among the most fragile structures around. Even if your relationship is sound now, you cannot be sure of what lurks around the corner. You must, *must*, MUST protect yourself.

GET OVER THE EMOTIONAL HURDLES

I know that some of you will cringe at the idea of squirreling money away in a secret place, feeling as if you would be committing an act of deceit. Honesty is the very foundation of a good marriage, you want to tell me, and you and your husband do not keep secrets from each other.

Well, I say to you, God bless and good luck. I would have said the same thing of my relationship with Robert Mosbacher. And, like millions of women before me, I was proven wrong. My ex-husband certainly managed to hide from me the unhappiness that prompted him to file for divorce, and in the months that followed I discovered that he'd kept other information from me as well. It was such a clichéd situation but then, clichés exist for a reason. Stuff like this happens unfortunately, heartbreakingly, all the time.

Should you too wake up one day to find that your honest-as-the-day-is-long husband has secrets from you, deep secrets that may cause your marriage to crumble, should you be forced to go from a nice house to an efficiency apartment, from a comfortable lifestyle to just scraping by, you may live to regret the decision not to give yourself the financial means to rebuild your life.

Creating a secret stash has nothing to do with deceit and everything to do with being practical, with preparing for life's curveballs, with ensuring your security.

One last thought: Sometimes we worry that if we put a system of financial safeguards into place, we will somehow precipitate the dissolution of our marriage or whatever relationship we happen to be in. Even if we're happy now, maybe *especially* if we're happy now, we become concerned that by the very act of creating a secret stash, we'll create a situation in which we have to use it. In short, we're afraid we'll jinx ourselves.

···

Creating a secret stash has nothing to do with deceit and everything to do with being practical, with preparing for life's curveballs, with ensuring your security.

···

Get past it. If the relationship is strong, having some money on the side will not threaten it. If anything, not feeling tied to the relationship by financial dependency should only make all other aspects of the relationship stronger. And if the relationship weakens for other reasons, you'll applaud yourself a million times over for giving yourself the means to get out of it, in your own way, on your own terms.

DO WHAT YOU MUST

So much for the philosophical underpinnings of the secret stash. Now let's get down and dirty about exactly how you come up with the money in the first place.

To paraphrase the poet Robert Browning, let me count the ways:

- **Siphon off a part of your paycheck.** If you earn your own income, it should be relatively simple to shift a small part of your pay whenever you receive a check—say, five, ten, twenty dollars, or whatever other amount won't be missed—and tuck it under your equivalent of the mattress. Ideally, you should keep the money in a safe, liquid, interest-bearing account like a money market mutual fund, just as you do with your regular household emergency fund. But if you think that a separate account in your name will be discovered—say, if you think your husband will find the statements or notice the extra interest you declare when you file your taxes—don't risk it. Simply keep the money physically in your possession—say, in an old pocketbook stuffed in the back of your closet or an emptied-out sachet bag in your lingerie drawer—and consider the fact that you're not earning any interest on it to be the cost of your freedom, if you need it. If you're loath to keep too much cash in the house, you might instead rent a safety deposit box at a local bank (not the one where you and your husband maintain a joint account, if you have one) and stash the cash there.

- **Divert raises and bonuses.** If your husband has your take-home pay memorized to the penny, you'll have to be a little more creative. That shouldn't be a problem if you qualify for a year-end bonus or some other form of incentive pay. Just keep the news of your professional reward to yourself, and put the cash in your private account.

- **Sign up for company spending accounts.** Another possibility is to sign up for your company's flexible spending accounts, if your employer offers them—you know, those accounts that reimburse you for your medical or child-care expenses. You can then pay the bills out of household funds and use the reimbursement check when it comes to add to your secret stash.

- **Skim from your allowance.** If you're a full-time homemaker, the easiest way to come up with funds for your secret stash is simply to divert a small sum from your allowance every week—that is, assuming you get one. If the husband is the sole financial provider, I firmly believe that the wife is entitled to some discretionary money, what I call mad money, that she can use to buy herself a little something or go out to lunch with a friend or go to the hairdresser without having to ask for permission or otherwise account for the money. Given all that wives do to take care of the house and the kids and to facilitate their husbands' lives, I think that's a fair request. In this case, though, instead of going to lunch or getting your hair done, why not invite your friends over to your place for a bite or do your hair yourself, and save the money for your stash?

- **Hoard small change.** Routinely collect all the spare coins you find lying around on dresser tops as you clean up or when you empty pockets before taking clothes to the dry cleaners as well as the change you receive from shopkeepers as you run your daily errands. While the individual amounts are small, spare change can really add up over time.

In fact, no amount is too small to use for your secret stash, if that sum is all you can manage, even it's just a buck a week that you take from the milk money. I know it may sound as if a dollar a week could never make any difference in your life, but it's a whole lot better than nothing. A buck a week will add up to $52 by the end of the year, and that will buy you a bus ticket out of town, or a room at a Holiday Inn, if you need them. If you have a husband who comes home one day and starts beating you or your kids, that $52 may end up saving your life.

GIVE YOURSELF OPTIONS

Above all, though, what your secret stash buys you is choice. As long as you have some money of your very own, you have options about how to go forth with your life, a choice about whether to stay in a relationship or leave it based on the merits of the relationship itself rather than your financial dependence on it. And that is extraordinarily liberating—even if you choose not to make any changes at all.

That's certainly what Delia Delveccio* discovered after painstakingly building a secret stash for years. Delia was just twenty-nine, and her two sons were one and three, when she realized that her relationship with her husband, a paper-goods salesman who was struggling with addictions to alcohol and pills, was deeply troubled. But Delia felt trapped in the marriage by her dependence on her husband's $60,000-a-year salary. Her post–high school education was limited to secretarial school, and she'd held only low-paying part-time clerical jobs since getting married. Delia wanted to go back to school to earn her college degree, which she believed would give her the skills she'd need to support herself and her two sons comfortably if she decided to leave her shaky marriage. But her husband adamantly refused to help with tuition.

Angry but undeterred, Delia began building a secret stash. Each time she took one of her sons to the pediatrician—and with two small children, she was at the pediatrician's office a lot—she would write a check for the visit from the general household funds. Then when she received a check from their health insurance company reimbursing them for the visit, Delia would deposit the money in a private account in her name only. When the account grew large enough, she enrolled part-time at a local college. It took eight years, but Delia finally got her bachelor's degree in communications. She now works in the human resources department of a university in New York and is working on a master's in cross-cultural communications. Only these days she no longer needs to use her secret stash for school since the university offers full tuition reimbursement to its employees.

Yes, by the way, she's still with her husband. While the marriage isn't yet on completely solid ground, the relationship has been slowly improving—in part, Delia believes, because of her newfound sense of independence. "Keeping some separate money was part of learning how to take care of myself, and understanding that I really can take

---

*This is an assumed name, but the story is real.

care of myself has helped make me a stronger person," she says. "Now I don't *have to* stay married, I *choose* to stay married. Now that I have my education, I know I could leave and support myself if I wanted to." As for her secret stash, she has no second thoughts. "The money I took wasn't ever missed and never hurt our family in any way," Delia notes. "I cannot regret investing in myself."

ACTION PLAN

To make sure you have systems in place that will enable you to cope financially with unforeseen emergencies, follow these steps:

1. Understand that circumstances beyond your control usually pose the biggest threat to your long-term financial security. Unless you take preventive measures, an unexpected layoff, a disabling illness, a divorce, or a death in the family—events that three-quarters of all U.S. households experience—can easily wipe out the savings you've been working so hard to build.

2. **To be prepared for that proverbial rainy day, keep enough money on hand to cover three to six months of your living expenses.** Put this cash in a safe, easily accessible account, such as a bank or brokerage money market account or a money market mutual fund. If you don't have that much money available now, enroll in an automatic savings plan at a reputable bank, brokerage, or mutual fund company and let them shift a modest amount from your checking account every month into a money market vehicle to get your emergency fund up to speed.

3. **Secure a line of credit that you can tap in a financial emergency if necessary.** If you own a house, your best bet is a home-equity line of credit. Although credit cards should be your absolutely last line of defense, you should always have one or two cards handy with plenty of room to charge—just in case.

4. **Keep some money of your very own tucked away in a safe place that you can tap if you suddenly find yourself in an untenable personal situation.** Having private money readily available may make all the difference to your financial survival if your husband leaves you without warning, if he becomes abusive, if your marriage otherwise breaks down, or if someone you love has a personal emergency.

5. **Add to your secret stash on a regular basis, just as you do with your ordinary household emergency fund.** Routinely divert small sums from your paycheck, bonuses, reimbursement accounts, household allowance, or even spare change in order to build your personal balances.

6. ***Do not feel guilty!*** Understand that maintaining a secret stash is not an act of deceit but a critical act of self-protection for women. Statistics strongly suggest that you will need this money one day to survive. Ignore this ultimate act of financial security at your own peril.

Cover Your Assets

A key component of your financial safety net is a comprehensive group of insurance policies. We're talking health, life, disability, a homeowner's or renter's policy to cover the place you live in, and if you own a car, auto coverage, too.

Yes, I know insurance is a subject too tedious for words. Yes, I know, figuring out what kind of coverage you need seems like an over-whelmingly complex prospect. Yes, I know you'd rather go to the dentist for a root canal than tackle it. And yes, I know, that if you don't just knuckle down and do it, you're cooking up a recipe for pure disaster.

Margaret McGinnis learned this lesson the hard way. Nearly a dozen years ago Margaret's husband Bill, an otherwise healthy man of fifty-eight, complained of a headache while the couple were out running errands around their hometown of Rockford, Illinois. They headed home and Bill lay down on the living room couch to rest. A few min-utes later, Margaret, who was forty-five years old at the time, heard her husband scream and ran into the room to find him lying lifeless. An aneurysm had ruptured in his brain, killing him within seconds.

As if his sudden passing wasn't heartbreakingly difficult enough, Margaret soon discovered that her comfortable lifestyle had died along with her husband. In the twenty-two years that they'd been married, Margaret had been content to let Bill handle the family finances. In all that time she'd not so much as stepped into a bank to make a deposit, let alone inquire about such seemingly mundane matters as how much life insurance he had. As it turned out, the answer was none. In the space of a day Margaret went from easily managing the household on Bill's $60,000-a-year salary as an electrical engineer to barely supporting herself and her two daughters, a twenty-one-year-old college junior and a fourteen-year-old just entering high school, on her $11,000-a-year salary as a department-store cashier. If not for the fact that they owned their house outright, she'd never have been able to manage. Still, it was tough enough. "Every penny I earned went to pay for food, clothing, heat, and electricity," she recalls. "We couldn't do anything for entertainment, not even the movies."

TAKE STOCK OF WHAT YOU HAVE

If you don't know what kind of insurance your family has and what's covered under those policies—or, indeed, if you even have any insurance in the first place—find out and find out *now*.

I confess that, like Margaret McGinnis, insurance is one of the areas that I let slide over the course of my marriage. The longer that Robert and I were together, the more assets we acquired and the more complicated our insurance situation became. I just didn't keep up with what coverage we had and what modifications were made over the years. When our marriage ended and I had to deal with my insurance myself, I was completely overwhelmed. I didn't know if I had private health coverage (that is, a policy independent of the coverage I'd gotten through Robert's work), life insurance, or disability protection. I knew I had homeowner's insurance, but I didn't know what was covered under the policy and what wasn't. And when I started to investigate my insurance options, I was stunned at how much everything cost.

After that wake-up call I found out in a hurry what protection I had, what I still needed, and how to cut costs—and you can, too.

Start by taking inventory of the policies you have. You'll have an easier time sorting everything out if you write it all down. Grab a pad and down the left side of the page, jot down each of the major kinds of insurance: Health, Life, Disability, Homeowner's/Renter's, and Auto. Then across the top, make two columns, one labeled What I Have and the other labeled What I Need, so you'll be able to make easy comparisons. (Feel free to create your inventory on computer if the high-tech route is more your style.)

Now you're ready to take stock. If you work for a company, haul out your employee-benefits handbook to see precisely what kind of coverage your employer provides. You'll probably find that you at least have health insurance and possibly some life and disability coverage, too. Look at what's included as standard in your benefits package, then check to see if you're able to buy additional coverage if you're so inclined. For instance, many employers include a life insurance policy with a death benefit equal to one or two times your salary as part of their basic benefits package, then give workers the opportunity to buy additional coverage of up to five times their salary at the company's group rates. Some employers even throw in the chance to buy cheap protection for other family members, too. These are usually great deals because group life insurance rates are commonly far lower than premiums on individual policies.

If you're married, be sure to go through the same exercise with your husband's employee-benefits package, too. If he claims he has no idea where the handbook is, simply call his company benefits department or the personnel manager, explain who you are, and ask to have another one sent to you directly or to have someone call you with the information you need.

Finally, go through your personal financial papers at home—hopefully, you or your husband keep them in a central place—to locate any individual insurance policies you have and make note of the key provisions in your ledger. The most important factors to look for: what your *deductibles* are (that is, the amount you have to pay out of your pocket when you file a claim before your insurance kicks in), what your *premiums* are (that is, how much you're paying for the insurance itself), what your *co-payments* are (that is, the portion of each claim that you're expected to pay), what the waiting period is before you qualify for benefits, and what specifically is included and excluded in your coverage.

Now, with your What I Have column complete, you can compare the coverage you have with what you need. Herewith, Georgette's crash course in the insurance protection every woman needs.

YA GOTTA HAVE YOUR HEALTH

Given the skyrocketing cost of medical care these days, everybody—man, woman, child, android—must have *health insurance* to pay the lion's share of your expenses if you or a member of your family becomes ill. Young or old, healthy or sickly, rich or poor, trust me, you need it. Whether you get coverage through an employer (your company or your spouse's, if you're married and he has the better plan) or must buy an individual policy, I strongly advocate going for the most comprehensive coverage you can afford.

If you can deal with restrictions on your choice of doctors and the bureaucratic hassles of getting referrals and prior approval for just about every medical procedure you need, you'll probably get the best all-around deal by going with a *managed-care plan* (such as a *health maintenance organization*, also known as an HMO, or a *preferred provider organization*, called a PPO for short) rather than a so-called *indemnity policy*. Your premiums (remember, that's the amount you pay for the insurance coverage itself) will be roughly the same either way. But just about everything else about managed care is cheaper: You'll probably pay only $10 to $15 for each doctor visit and prescription drug you buy, while hospitalization, checkups (both physicals and gynecological exams), mammograms, vaccinations for your children, and other routine care will be completely free. Under an old-fashioned indemnity plan, on the other hand, a typical family might pay between $400 and $1,000 in annual deductibles, 20 percent of all covered medical costs (the plans picks up the rest of the bill) and 100 percent of all uncovered expenses, which typically includes most kinds of preventive care. Particularly for families with young children, who seem to spend half their time in the pediatrician's office for checkups, immunizations, ear infections, and other assorted childhood maladies, managed care is almost always the way to go.

There is one exception: If you have a long-standing relationship with a particular doctor or doctors and those practitioners are not among your choices in the managed care plans available to you, you might consider a traditional indemnity policy to keep your health care in familiar hands. Increasingly, though, many managed-care plans—specifically, PPOs and so-called point-of-service HMOs—are allowing their members to go outside the network for treatment. You're simply charged more to do so (typically, the patient has to pay 20 percent to 50 percent of the bill, versus the standard low, flat rate). PPOs have one other advantage over HMOs: You do not have to go through a primary doctor for referrals to specialists every time you need to see one; you can make an appointment directly with anyone in the network you want.

If, like me, you were covered under your husband's company policy and have recently separated or gotten a divorce and you either don't work, are self-employed, or work for a company that doesn't provide health insurance, don't despair. Even if your husband tries to cut you off, you may still be able to retain coverage for yourself, as long as you have children and they're also covered under the plan, according to Violet Woodhouse, a top-notch family attorney and financial planner in Newport Beach, California. Just call your husband's benefits or personnel office and find out what the company's policy is. In any event, as long as the firm employs at least twenty people, you're entitled by federal law to keep your coverage for up to thirty-six months after your divorce, as long as you're willing to pay for it yourself.

Be warned, though: Corporate-group plans, which are among the most comprehensive policies you'll find, can be very expensive once the company is no longer subsidizing the premiums. So you should regard this only as a short-term solution and start shopping immediately for a lower-cost replacement policy. Your best bet is to join a trade or professional association that offers group coverage for its members; while the policies are usually a lot less comprehensive than the Cadillac plans offered by big employers, they're usually a whole lot less expensive as well. Alternatively, you might seriously consider going to work, at least part-time, for a company that provides subsidized health coverage to anyone on its payroll.

If you have children who were on your husband's health plan, by the way, don't worry about their coverage. Under a 1993 federal law, your ex-husband cannot remove them from his plan just because he no longer has custody or lists the children as dependents on his tax return. In this regard at least, the kids are safe.

TAKE A LOOK AT YOUR LIFE

Unlike health insurance, everyone does not need life insurance. The crucial test is whether you or anyone else in your family depends on the income or services of a particular member of the household; if so, you need a life insurance policy on that person. A couple of simple questions can help you figure out who needs what. To see if your family needs a policy on you, ask yourself: If I died tomorrow, would my family's finances change materially as a result? To determine if you need a life insurance policy on your husband, ask: If my spouse died tomorrow, could I continue to support myself and my family in the style to which we've all become accustomed?

Here's how the answers to those questions are likely to play out in real life:

- If you're single and you don't have kids, you probably don't need life insurance. The big exception: If you're currently or may soon be caring for an aging parent or other relative who would suffer financially if you die, consider a policy with that family member named as your beneficiary.

- If you're married, nearing retirement age, and you've already built up sizable assets, neither one of you is likely to need life insurance.

- If you're married with children living at home and both spouses work, you probably should have a policy on both spouses.

- If you're married, you both work, and you don't have any children, you may need life insurance only if there is a big discrepancy between your incomes. The spouse with the lower salary may not need coverage for herself (sorry, but that's usually going to be the woman). But a policy on the higher wage earner is essential for the survivor.

- If you're a married homemaker, you absolutely, positively must have a life insurance policy on your husband. If you have young children, you should probably have a small policy on your own life as well to cover the cost of child care and any housekeeping services your husband might need or want to hire.

How much is enough? The right way to figure out just how big a life insurance policy you need for yourself and your husband, if you're married, is to figure out how much each of you contributes to your current living expenses (that is, the mortgage, food bills, utilities, etc.), large future bills (such as saving for college tuition for your kids, if you have any), and the running of the household. Then you multiply the resulting amount by the number of years the household would be dependent on that income and those services to come up with the amount you need the policy to cover.

As a rough rule of thumb, though, figure that a policy on each wage earner that will pay a death benefit equal to five to eight times their annual salary should do the trick. Or so my financial-planner friends tell me. That means you're probably talking about a policy ideally worth at least $250,000 and possibly $500,000 or more. If you're a full-time homemaker, a $100,000 to $200,000 policy on you will probably be enough—or however much you figure it will cost your husband to replace the child-care and housekeeping services (cooking and cleaning and so on) you now in all likelihood provide free of charge.

Don't be surprised if your husband balks at taking out a policy quite that large for himself. My accountant calls this the Red Mercedes Syndrome, also known as the dancing-on-my-grave theory. A man who suffers from this condition worries that after he dies, his wife will become wealthy from the proceeds of his life insurance policy, promptly meet another man, and then shower the new boyfriend with gifts, including the biggest, reddest Mercedes that Daimler-Benz makes. In reality, of course, we know that widows are a lot more likely to be on the bread line than they are to be rolling in the dough.

So stick to your guns and insist that your husband get the financial protection that you (and your children, if you have any) need. Point out that you don't have to break the family bank to pay for it, as long as he chooses term insurance rather than a far more expensive cash-value policy. A *term policy* offers no-frills insurance protection (a death benefit to your beneficiaries if you die, and that's it) and, as coverage goes, it's dirt cheap: A forty-year-old non-smoking man, for instance, can easily find a $250,000 ten-year term policy for under $250 a year or buy $500,000 worth of protection for between $500 and $600 annually, or less than $50 a month.

On the other hand, *cash-value insurance*, which combines insurance protection with a savings or investment account, typically costs ten times as much as term. Sold in varieties known as *whole life*, *universal life*, or *variable life*, the stiff fees and commissions on these policies undercut the profits you can earn, making them an unappealing investment proposition. To my way of thinking (and that of just about every financial pro I know, except the insurance agents who sell these policies), you're almost always better off buying term and putting the money you save on lower premiums into investments that you choose yourself. Or, perhaps better yet, use at least some of that money to buy an even bigger insurance policy than you could afford with a cash-value plan.

If you outlive your husband—and statistics tell us that most women do—the extra cash may mean all the difference between just scraping by in your new solo life, as Margaret McGinnis was forced to do, or making a real go of it. Eight years ago, Carolyn Stolz was a forty-two-year-old full-time mom with two sons, aged eleven and thirteen, when her husband died suddenly of a heart attack. As heart-wrenching as his death was for everyone, the family did not suffer financially because Carolyn soon received a sizable six-figure sum in benefits from her husband's life insurance policy. She used the money to support her family while she got back on her feet and to pay for her tuition at Tulane University, where she went to earn an M.B.A. As she told *Working Woman* magazine, "I went from reading *Town & Country* to *The Wall Street Journal*." She now works as a financial adviser at American Express, and has this wisdom to pass along to other women: "Don't wait for a crisis to get your financial act together."

DEFEND YOUR INCOME

A life insurance policy on your spouse is the most important coverage a woman needs if she's married and doesn't work outside the home or earns a lot less than her husband. But if you're single or married and earning a comfortable income of your own, *long-term disability insurance* is the truly critical component of any sound financial-emergency plan. A disability policy will pay a substantial portion of your salary if you can't work for a lengthy period of time (usually more than ninety days) because of illness or an accident. Unfortunately, the day may come when you really need it: Up until age fifty-five, a person is five times as likely to become disabled as they are to die. And the odds facing women, who typically file two to three times as many claims as men, are even tougher.

You may think you're already protected against this contingency, either through your benefits plan at work or government programs, such as workers' compensation and Social Security. Think again. While most big companies do provide some long-term disability coverage, most women work for small companies, which typically do not. Meanwhile, a growing number of women are self-employed and almost entirely on their own when it comes to protecting their income—the rules that govern collecting Social Security when you're disabled are so strict that about two-thirds of those who apply are turned down, at least the first time that they try.

Moreover, even if you do have a disability plan through your employer, chances are the coverage is too skimpy to do you much good. Most employer plans will pay you for only five years after you become disabled—what are you supposed to do if you haven't recovered by then? Then too, because the company is paying the premiums, the benefits are taxable, which reduces the amount you get to keep. If you pay the premiums yourself instead, you get to keep every dime. Last but not least, most group plans put a lot of restrictions on the conditions under which you can collect benefits. For example, many plans will pay you for the first two years if you can't work in your own field, but after that will pay only if you can't perform any job at all.

By all means, sign up for disability if it's available to you at work. Then supplement that coverage with a private policy of your own. And if you don't have any disability at all, bite the bullet and buy a policy now.

Here's what to look for:

- Ideally, you want a policy that will replace 60 percent to 70 percent of your income at least until you turn sixty-five, possibly for life.

- The policy should have an "own occupation" provision, which means it will pay if you can't work in your field, not just if you can't work at all.

- Look for "residual benefits," which will cover you even if you work part-time.

- The waiting period before benefits kick in should be no longer than ninety days.

I won't kid you. Unlike term life insurance, this disability stuff is expensive. For a private policy that provides a $4,000 monthly benefit, a 35-year-old woman might pay more than $2,000 a year, a 45-year-old woman will probably shell out $3,000 a year, and a 55-year-old woman might have to fork over $3,700, judging by some sample premiums quoted to me recently by one of the biggest disability insurers.

Don't let the cost stop you from buying the protection you need.

Shop around among several insurers to get the best prices (I'll fill you in on some other ways to cut the cost of disability and other kinds of insurance down in a moment), and do whatever you can to come up with the money for the most reasonable one. If the amount you need is still out of reach, then just buy as much disability as you can afford. Some is better than none. It's *that* important.

ALWAYS CARRY AN UMBRELLA

If you own your home and a car, in all likelihood, whether you know it or not, you already have *homeowner's insurance* and auto coverage, too. Most lenders won't approve you for a mortgage unless you take out a homeowner's policy (the bank wants to protect its investment, and you should, too). And almost all states require that you at least have *liability coverage*—that is, insurance that will pay any financial claims against you if your car injures someone in an accident—before they'll allow you to drive.

Whether the coverage you have is enough, however, is another question entirely. For instance, many homeowner policies pay only the current cash value of any property that's stolen or damaged as a result of fire, heavy rain, wind, or other common risks to your home's well-being. That's means if, say, a tree crashes through your dining room window during a heavy storm, destroying the table, some chairs, and a breakfront full of china you received when you got married, the insurance company would pay what it estimates a ten-year-old table and some old dishes are worth, not the cost of buying a new dining room set and china. To do that you have to ask for what's known as *guaranteed-replacement coverage*, which gives you enough money to buy new items that are comparable to your old ones—the coverage is more expensive than the standard practice, but well worth it.

Most homeowner's policies also limit the amount that they'll reimburse you for certain (typically expensive) kinds of property. Take jewelry, for example. Most standard policies cover jewelry to a maximum of $2,500. The same holds true for artwork and luxury rugs and carpets as well. The limit on computers and other home-office equipment is typically $5,000.

If you have lots of antiques, furs, collectibles, or other valuables that you want protected, you can increase your coverage by adding what's known as a *floater*, or an addition to your basic policy that specifically insures that class of property. Floaters can be expensive, however, particularly if you're adding more than one to your policy. So you have to decide if the additional coverage is really the best use of your money. For instance, after I priced floaters to add my jewelry to my homeowner's policy, I concluded it was just too expensive and decided to go without it. Then I used some of the money I saved to upgrade my home-security system so that I wouldn't have to worry about my jewelry being stolen in the first place.

By the way, you may think you're off the insurance hook if you rent the place where you live rather than own it. But you're not. True, when you rent, you don't have to concern yourself with the possibility of damage to the building in which you live. That's the landlord's responsibility. But you still have personal property that you need to protect from fire and theft and all the other disasters, natural and unnatural, that could imperil your furniture, clothes, jewelry, stereo, TV, computer, and other worldly possessions. And you can still get sued if someone slips and falls in your apartment. That's why you need *renter's insurance*, with most of the same clauses that homeowners need in their policies.

Just a word on *auto insurance*. If your car is more than five years old, seriously consider saving some big bucks on your premiums by dropping your *collision* and *comprehensive coverage*—that is, the part of your insurance that will pay for repairs if your car is damaged in an accident or replace it altogether if your wheels are stolen. Of course, the most you can get from the insurer if you put in a claim is the cost of replacing your car with a comparable used car. If your car isn't worth very much, meaning that you'll never collect very much, why waste money on the premiums at all?

What may well be worthwhile in today's lawsuit-happy society, however, is a so-called *umbrella liability policy*. This add-on to your homeowner's or auto policy protects you from financial ruin if you're held responsible for someone else's losses or injuries—say, if someone breaks a leg stumbling over a loose plank on your porch. The policy will pay not only for the losses themselves but also for your legal defense if you're sued as a result. Although standard homeowner's and auto policies have liability coverage, the amounts are usually quite small in this era of multimillion-dollar judgments—typically just $60,000 per accident on an auto policy and $100,000 on home-owner's. You can pick up $1 million worth of additional coverage for just $100 to $300 a year—a relatively small sum, considering the potential consequences if a claim is ever filed against you.

KEEP THE COSTS REASONABLE

A comprehensive insurance package isn't cheap. But if you shop smart, there are ways to keep the costs down. These are some of my favorite strategies:

- **Comparison shop.** There can be several hundred dollars' difference between seemingly identical policies issued by different insurers. It pays to check with several companies to see who can give you the best deal. The easiest way to do this is to use a free price-quoting service. You give them your profile and your policy requirements—for example, you might say I'm a forty-two-year-old female who doesn't smoke and I want $300,000 worth of term life insurance with guaranteed premiums for ten years—then they produce a list of the best-priced policies that fit the bill. Companies that offer this service include **Insurance Quote Service** (800–972–1104; www.iquote.com), **Quotesmith** (800–431–1147; www.quotesmith.com), **SelectQuote** (800–343–1985), and **Termquote** (800–444–8376). If they don't cover the kind of policy you're looking for, hit the yellow pages instead or call your state insurance commission and ask for the names of local companies that specialize in the coverage you're looking for.

- **Buy direct.** Several insurance companies conduct business by selling their policies directly to the public, typically through a toll-free
  number. By eliminating the middle man—in this case, the commission-hungry insurance agent—these policies tend to be a lot
  less expensive than those sold through the traditional agent system. The only caveat: The qualifying standards are usually strict (in
  other words, they really want you and your property to be in tip-
  top shape). But they're certainly worth a try. For auto and home
  insurance, check out **American Express** (800–842–3344),
  American Mutual Insurance (800–242–6422), or **GEICO**
  (800–841–3000; www.geico.com). For life and disability insurance,
  call **USAA** (800–531–8000) or the **Wholesale Insurance Network**
  (800–808–5810), a service that sells policies from several companies. For life insurance, **Ameritas** (800–552–3553) and **American
  Life of New York** (800–872–5963) may also be worth a try.

- **Raise your deductibles.** One of the simplest ways to cut your premiums is to raise your deductibles. For instance, you can save as
  much as 30 percent on your car insurance premiums by raising
  your deductible for collision from $100 to $500. Increasing the
  deductible on a traditional health insurance plan from $1,000 to
  $1,500 for a family of four might drop the price by 25 percent or
  more. Hiking the deductible on your homeowner's policy from,
  say, $250 to $1,000 could chop your bill another 15 percent to 20
  percent a year.

- **Negotiate a discount.** An insurance agent probably won't volunteer the information, but there are lots of ways to qualify for price
  breaks if you know what to ask for. Take the matter of security
  measures. If you have dead bolts on your door, a burglar alarm,
  smoke detectors, fire extinguishers, or live in an apartment building with a doorman stationed out front, you could nab a discount
  on your homeowner's policy ranging from 5 to 20 percent.
  Consolidating your home and auto coverage with a single insurer
  could be worth another 5 to 15 percent.

If you use these tactics, you can save hundreds of dollars a year on your insurance premiums, and maybe a lot more, without too much hassle. I remember reading in *Family Money* magazine about a woman named Denise Allen, who lopped nearly $1,200 off her insurance costs in one year alone. Allen, a forty-five-year-old widow with a ten-year-old son, admitted that she and her late husband had chosen their coverage in haste. Working with two financial planners, Allen set out to undo those mistakes. First, she shopped around for a new home-owner's policy. After reviewing several possibilities and agreeing to increase her deductible from $250 to $1,000, she found one that offered broader coverage at a cheaper price: She added guaranteed replacement coverage and $1 million worth of umbrella liability protection, and still saved $57 a year. Shopping around also netted her new auto and term life policies that cost $246 and $385 less than her old policies respectively, without giving up any coverage. Finally, the planners advised her to drop a $480-a-year cash-value life insurance policy with $50,000 in death benefits that she'd held for several years, deeming it unnecessary. Denise's total savings: $1,168 a year.

DON'T FALL FOR SALES PITCHES

If you took the advice of the insurance industry, you'd be covered against every possible calamity known to womankind—not just the possible death of a spouse or your own sickness or disability, but against plane crashes, credit-card fraud, hurricanes, floods, and maybe pestilence and a few other deadly plagues as well. You'd also be broke within a year or two of paying the exorbitant premiums.

Here are some commonly sold insurance policies that you really don't need:

- **Dread-disease insurance.** If breast cancer or heart attacks or some other terrible disease runs in your family, you may be scared enough to consider buying an insurance policy designed to cover the costs of that specific illnesses. Don't do it. The guidelines on so-called dread-disease policies are often complicated, and the benefits are difficult to qualify for and limited, at best. For example, many policies pay a flat dollar amount for procedures like chemotherapy or angioplasty; if the price runs higher where you live, you'll have to pay the difference out of your own pocket. Most important, you should already be covered for these diseases under your general, comprehensive health plan. Why pay for duplicate coverage?

- **Credit insurance.** You're a rare woman if you haven't yet gotten a pitch from a bank, mortgage lender, credit-card issuer, or car dealer offering to sell you insurance that will pay off the balance due on your mortgage, car loan, or credit cards if you become disabled or die. Sounds reasonable enough on the surface, but in fact this overpriced insurance is one bum deal. If you become disabled or you're laid off, these policies typically pay just the monthly minimum on your debt, and they usually do so for a fairly limited time, such as a year; in the meantime, the interest due keeps piling up and you end up even further in debt than you were before. If you die, your spouse or your children can simply use part of the proceeds from your life insurance policy to pay off your debts. (That works, of course, only if you buy adequate life insurance.)

- **Flight insurance.** Your chances of slipping and killing yourself in the bathtub are just as great as the possibility of dying in a plane crash, but you don't see insurance companies peddling tub policies. That's because no one is afraid of the dying in the bathroom, but lots of us are fearful of flying—and flight insurance preys on that fear, not the statistical chances that we'll be killed in the air. Yes, it's cheap, but it's still not worth it. In any event, you may already be covered: If you charge plane tickets on your credit card, many issuers give you automatic flight insurance at no charge.

- **Life insurance for your children.** No matter how hard an insurance agent tugs on your heartstrings, never, ever, under any circumstances, be talked into buying a life insurance policy on your kids. Not only are the odds against a young child's death much too slim to warrant this coverage, but unless your little darling is the next Macauley Culkin, it's not as if you have to worry about replacing his income if tragedy does strike. No amount of money will ever compensate you for the loss of your child. Period, end of story.

ACTION PLAN

To make sure you have the insurance coverage you need to protect yourself and your family from financial ruin if disaster strikes, follow these steps:

1. Find out exactly what kind of insurance your family has and what's covered under it. Start by checking your company handbook to see what policies you get in your benefits package, and if you're married, check your husband's benefits plan, too. Also look at any individual policies you may have, such as homeowner's or renter's insurance and coverage on your car.

2. **Make sure you have the basics covered.** That means health insurance, disability (if you work outside your home or are self-employed), life (if you have children or other family members who rely on your income or your contribution to the family as a homemaker) and property/casualty protection (homeowner's or renter's insurance, plus auto insurance, if you own a car). If you find gaps, start shopping for policies to fill them immediately.

3. **If you're married, make sure your spouse is well covered, too.** For homemakers, the single most important protection you can have, after health insurance, is a substantial life insurance policy on your husband. Don't let him convince you otherwise: The chances are great that he'll go before you will.

4. **Do some legwork to bring the price of your insurance coverage down.** Get price quotes from several companies, consider buying from an insurer that sells directly to the public to avoid paying commissions to an agent, and always ask for discounts. To bring costs down even further, consider raising your deductibles, which can shave 20 to 30 percent off most common kinds of insurance coverage.

5. **Don't be talked into buying insurance you don't really need by commission-hungry insurance agents.** Among the commonly sold policies that you should avoid: so-called dread disease insurance, which covers you for specific illnesses; flight and credit insurance; and life insurance for your kids. When the agent comes calling to peddle any of these policies, emulate Nancy Reagan and Just Say No.

Don't Be a Damn Fool

A fool and his money are soon parted, the old saying goes. Experience tells us the words are true. My advice is simple: Don't be a damn fool.

Of course, none of us ever think of ourselves as damn fools when it comes to our money. Nevertheless we find ourselves doing damned foolish things with our money every day. To see what I mean, take a moment to give yourself my Damn Fool Test and see where you come out. Quick, without thinking hard, answer yes or no to the following five questions:

- Do you often find yourself giving money away to people who are a lot better off than you are?

- Do you routinely work hard at jobs for which you refuse compensation?

- Do you accept everything you're told at face value?

- Do you regularly pay an additional 15 to 20 percent more than the stated price on the things you buy?

- Do you get a kick out of throwing money in the garbage?

Chances are you said no to all of these questions. But don't go patting yourself on the back just yet.

Think about this: If you earn considerably less than your husband or boyfriend, yet split the household expenses or the costs of dating, you are, in fact, giving your money away to someone who's a lot better off than you are. If you're married or living with someone and you do more than half the household chores, yet don't ask for and get an allowance, you're doing hard work for which you receive no pay. If you hand over whatever the price tag says when you make a purchase without bothering to see if you can get a better deal, you're accepting whatever you're told at face value. If you don't pay off your credit cards in full every month, you are inflating the price of everything you buy by 15 to 20 percent. And if you let your savings get eaten away by various fees and surcharges at banks and on your credit cards, you're literally throwing your money away.

I work too hard for my money to treat it so disrespectfully.

LET CHIVALRY REIGN

Let me tell you a little story to illustrate my point.

A few years back, when Joan Rivers still had her TV talk show, I made an appearance with two other high-profile women as part of a segment on "Power Couples." At the time I was still married to Robert, who was then Secretary of Commerce, while I was CEO of La Prairie. Like me, the other two women on the show were well-compensated, high-level professionals who were married to high-powered, high-profile men. Among other questions, Joan asked each of us how we divvied up expenses in our respective households.

The first guest proceeded to tick off who paid for what. She said: I pay for the groceries, he pays for the maid, I pay for my clothes, he pays for the children's clothes—except for the kids' clothes that I charge on my credit cards because I take care of my own credit cards, and so on and so forth. The audience listened politely. The second guest had a similar but somewhat simpler system. She said: He moved into my house when we got married, so I just continued to pay all the expenses for the house, but he picks up everything else, except that we each take care of our own personal expenses and gifts for our respective families. Again, the audience listened politely.

Then Joan came to me. I said: I pay for nothing. He pays for everything. The audience perked up.

Joan pressed on. What about personal items, like your clothes and makeup? she asked. He pays, I replied. What about Christmas presents and birthday gifts for members of your family? she followed up. He pays, I replied. No matter what specific expense she questioned me about, my answer remained the same. The rule is simple, I explained, and it operates twelve months a year, seven days a week, twenty-four hours a day: Whatever the expense is, *he pays*.

The audience cheered wildly.

Now, at this point I know that some of you are starting to prickle about how unfair my policy seems, particularly since by that time in my life I could definitely have paid my own way. Well, let me remind you that Robert Mosbacher, being a multimillionaire, could well afford our arrangement. If I were married to a man who could not easily manage to carry the financial load, I'd willingly and unquestioningly live by different rules. Even in my own marriage, if there had been something that Robert and I had wanted to buy that we couldn't afford unless we used our joint incomes, I would have been willing and happy to pool our resources.

But since Robert's income and assets were far, far greater than mine, that wasn't the case. And while women these days are certainly earning more than they ever have before, that still isn't the case in most relationships. As in my situation, the majority of women have far less in terms of financial resources than their husbands and boyfriends. And the financial risks we face if we divorce, or our husbands die or we take time out of the workforce to raise our children or care for aged relatives, are far greater. To split expenses under those circumstances, out of some misguided sense of equity or in a superficial show of independence, is not just unfair, it's downright foolhardy. Let's be really clear here about the message that financially independent women ought to be sending to their men. In my opinion, it is this: Just because

I don't need your money doesn't mean I don't appreciate your generosity, especially if generosity is well within your means. It certainly doesn't mean that we should throw chivalry out the window.

···

Just because I don't need your money doesn't mean I don't appreciate your generosity

···

DON'T FEAR THE WRONG FEAR

Some women may feel guilty about letting a man pay if they are earning comfortable salaries themselves. I say, as long as he can afford it, let the guilt go. I, for one, enjoy the feeling of being taken care of and cherished. It makes me feel special, and it has made the men in my life feel good, too. If everyone involved enjoys the arrangement, I don't see what the debate is about.

Some women may worry that letting a man pay will somehow undermine their power and independence in the relationship. Hey, this is the nineties! Just because a man picks up the check doesn't mean you are beholden to him or somehow subservient. Girls, it's time to get it right! The notion that you're somehow giving up your freedom because your husband is paying for your clothes is ridiculous.

No, the danger in letting a man pay is not that you somehow compromise your self-worth or that you won't be able to say no to him or that you will give up your power and voice in the relationship. The real danger is that you'll be lulled into a false sense of security so that you won't take the steps you need to look out for yourself financially. The danger is that you assume the circumstances you're in now, that permit someone else to pay the bills, will be eternal. You still have to follow the Girl Scout motto and BE PREPARED.

Women get caught up in the wrong argument about this issue all the time.

GET AN ALLOWANCE

How much would it cost to hire a wife on the open market? By my conservative estimate, at least $80,000 a year.

Look at it this way: The average cook makes around $13,500 a year, according to the Bureau of Labor Statistics; the average cleaning woman earns maybe $12,000; the average child-care worker brings home roughly $10,000; a typical psychiatric counselor might charge around $75 an hour; and business consultants clear a minimum of $100 an hour (it's more like $200 in most big cities, but I'm low-balling things here). If you figure (again, conservatively) that the average wife probably puts in five hours a week on the consultant part of the job (5 hours times $100 times 52 weeks equals $26,000 a year) and at least an equal number on the counseling part (5 hours times $75 times 52 weeks equals $19,500 a year), you're looking at another $45,500 between the two. That brings the grand total to $81,000— and that's without even trying to calculate charges for all the other aspects of the job, such as meeting planner, schedule coordinator, chauffeur, travel agent, and (if you have more than one child) referee.

Is your husband paying you that much?

I thought not.

Now, I know many women (and even more men) would argue that you can't really put a price tag on the contribution that a wife makes out of family duty, responsibility, and love. Well, guess what? People do it every day. Evaluating the contributions of marital partners is what keeps divorce lawyers in business. That's how attorneys and accountants come up with the numbers in pre- and postnuptial agreements. And let me tell you, if you wait for someone else to put a price tag on what your contribution is worth to your marriage, you can bet it's going to be a lot lower than the value you'd place on it yourself.

Now, I'm not actually suggesting that you ask your husband to pay you eighty grand a year, or whatever you estimate the full monetary value of your work as a wife may be. I went through this exercise merely to suggest that what we do as wives is worth a lot more than any of us would be likely to guess. But I do strongly believe that, unless you earn a lot more than your husband does, you should get some discretionary money, outside the money set aside to run the household, that is for your use and your use alone. I call it an allowance; if that term bothers you, put any name on it you wish. But whatever you call it, insist on getting it—a set amount each week or month that you do not have to account for in the family budget, that is yours to do with as you see fit, without having to explain or defend your reasons.

....

If you wait for someone else to put a price tag on what your contribution is worth to your marriage, you can bet it's going to be a lot lower than the value you'd place on it yourself.

....

BELIEVE IN YOUR ENTITLEMENT

Given all the uncompensated work that wives do to run their households, an allowance is a small and eminently reasonable request. In my opinion, just about every married woman is entitled to one.

If you're a full-time homemaker with no outside source of income, though, an allowance is not just a fair request, it's an absolutely essential one. Men may defend their right to control all the money, using some variation on that old line, "I work hard all day to put food on the table." Well, if I were a full-time homemaker and my husband said that to me, I'd answer, "No, you don't. You work hard all day to get the money to buy the groceries. I put the food on the table. I have a right to get paid for my work, too."

Don't get me wrong. I have no quarrel with a woman choosing a traditional role in marriage as long as she finds that fulfilling. What we have to change, however, is how we think about the work we do in those traditional roles. We have to be willing to put a monetary value on it and demand fair compensation. And we shouldn't feel bad or guilty or embarrassed about that or think that by doing so, we're somehow challenging our husbands or undermining them. We're simply insisting on a fair deal.

I also believe that wives who work outside the home are entitled to an allowance, even though they have an independent source of income. Unless your household arrangements are highly unusual and evolved beyond most, the chances are you really hold down two jobs—the professional one for which you earn a salary and your unpaid domestic position as cook-cum-housekeeper-cum-child-care provider. Sure, many men these days—particularly those in the baby-boom generation and younger—are doing a whole lot more around the house and with their kids than their fathers did. But doing more and doing an equal share are vastly different propositions. You deserve some compensation for the additional work you take on, even though you do it out of love for your family (and love of clean clothes and hot food and sanitary living conditions, which you probably wouldn't get with any regularity if you weren't the one providing them).

Although I earned a handsome salary during my years running La Prairie, I did get an allowance from my husband during that time. I feel no embarrassment in admitting it, but rather proud of myself for asking for and getting something I deserved. I earned every penny of what Robert gave me and then some, running the household, organizing and acting as hostess for the myriad social and political functions that were necessary in his position, and acting as his consultant and sounding board in his various business deals as well as in his political life.

Now, I'm not saying the asking part was easy. Each time I used the straightforward approach: I sat down and explained that I wanted some spending money that I didn't have to account for, that I didn't want to explain or beg every time I needed money, that I felt it was demeaning. Then I'd suggest the amount. Of course, he bridled at the concept initially because to men, giving up money means giving up power, and men never easily give up power, particularly to women. In the end, though, he agreed, as long as I was willing to compromise on the amount. It was always a negotiation, even though Robert could easily have afforded what I first asked for. But the sum we ultimately agreed on was comfortable enough, and that's all I needed or wanted.

....

To men, giving up money means giving up power, and men never easily give up power, particularly to women

....

STAND UP FOR YOUR RIGHTS

On the way home from a business trip recently I struck up a conversation with a flight attendant named Angela, who was mighty steamed about her husband's spending habits. As it turned out, every time her work took her away from home for a two- or three-day layover, her husband would spend money from their joint account in some wildly extravagant way. Angela wasn't quite sure whether he did it to punish her for being away so much or because he thought her absence was an ideal time to get away with such antics. She didn't much care either way. She did, however, care passionately about the fact that he was wasting their money on what she considered unnecessary luxuries and big-ticket items that they'd not talked about together and agreed to buy beforehand. When she came home from her last trip to find that he'd put down $10,000 on a new BMW, she determined to put an end to his foolishness once and for all.

Angela's solution was to devise a penalty for her husband: He was to give her $200 a week, payable in two new crisp hundred-dollar bills left on her dresser every Wednesday, for the rest of his life, or for as long as it takes to make up the money he frittered away on the car, whichever comes first. (Don't worry, he could afford it.) She put the agreement in writing, included additional financial penalties if he was ever late with a payment, and had him sign it. "It was the lack of respect that drove me to it," she told me. Although the couple were only a few weeks into the payback system when I spoke with Angela, she really felt her solution was improving their relationship. "I have to be able to trust my husband with our money, and this way he'll think twice before he pulls another stunt," she said. "I want to be a real partner in this marriage, half of the decision making in our household."

....

No matter how much money you make (or he makes), you should be a fifty-fifty partner in the financial decision making in your marriage because you are half of that relationship

....

I loved Angela's story and not just because of the ingeniousness of her solution. I loved it because she stood up for her financial rights in her marriage, demanded that she be treated like an equal partner and took concrete steps to ensure it happened. Angela didn't care that, as a flight attendant, she earns a lot less than her husband, who happens to be the president of a dry-dock company that repairs ships. No matter how much money you make (or he makes), you should be a fifty-fifty partner in the financial decision making in your marriage because you are half of that relationship.

Financial accountability in marriage—or in any serious relationship—is a two-way street. "Men need to be answerable for how they spend the joint money in a marriage, the same way that women do," says the divorce lawyer Violet Woodhouse. "Like it or not, marriage is a financial partnership as well as a romantic partnership, and the real problem is not recognizing that fact. We should, but don't, talk about how we plan to spend our money and come together on our financial goals. But this part of the relationship is as fundamental to its success as being of the same mind about whether to have children or having similar attitudes about sex or any other intimate element of being a couple. When spouses don't share common financial goals, their risk factor for divorce goes way up."

GET IT IN WRITING

Ideally the time to sit down with your husband or boyfriend and talk about how you'll handle money and what financial goals you'll be working toward is before you get married or the relationship gets serious. But if you didn't do it then, now is certainly better than never. "It may not be romantic, but neither is doing the dishes or taking out the garbage, and that's part of our lives, too," Violet points out. The more financial stuff you can work out ahead of time, before real problems crop up, the better off you'll be in the long run.

You may even want to put your agreement in writing, particularly if either one of you earns a hefty income or is bringing sizable assets into the relationship. Only about five percent of the 2.4 million American couples who get married every year sign a prenuptial agreement, I'm told, and even fewer sign post-nups. But family lawyers and financial planners routinely urge more people to do so. Certainly before we got married, each of my three husbands requested that I sign a prenup spelling out our financial responsibilities to each other and how our assets would be divided in case we divorced. I readily admit that I found the whole process distasteful, but I understood why they thought it was necessary. And now that I have considerable assets of my own, I also will ask for a prenuptial agreement if I ever choose to marry again.

Please, please, *please*, if you do find yourself in a situation where you'll be drawing up a prenuptial agreement, retain the services of a good independent lawyer and financial adviser who can help you look out for what's fair and best for you. Never, ever let his lawyer cut the whole deal. To find a savvy and trustworthy adviser, your best bet is to ask friends and colleagues who already have been down this road for referrals. You can also get names of qualified professionals in your area by contacting the appropriate professional associations. For legal counsel, try **The American Academy of Matrimonial Lawyers** (150 North Michigan Avenue, Suite 2040, Chicago, IL 60601; 312–263–6477); for financial advice, you can get names from the **Institute of Certified Financial Planners** (800–282-PLAN) or the **National Association of Personal Financial Advisors** (888-FEE-ONLY).

I don't want to leave you with the impression, though, that prenups are for men only or the rich only or rich men only. They're not, particularly these days when women are earning more than they ever have before, are opening businesses at record rates, and are more likely than ever to be marrying for a second (or third or fourth) time. Certainly, if you have your own business, however small it is, you should have a legal agreement establishing that business as a separate asset so that your spouse cannot claim a piece of it should you divorce. And since 60 percent of second marriages end in divorce, remarrying without a prenuptial agreement is downright dumb, particularly if you have children from a previous marriage whom you want to protect. Among the issues you need to resolve: whether and how to share financial responsibilities for those children (and his, if he has any); how your assets will be divided between your spouse, the children, and other loved ones if either one of you dies; whether to merge your assets and liabilities; and how to divide property you each acquired before and after the marriage in case you get a divorce.

DON'T LOSE YOUR WILL

While you're in the mood to get everything down on paper, turn your attention to writing a will, too. Like many women, you may not think you (or husband or companion) need one, particularly if you don't have children or much in the way of assets. If you're married, for instance, you probably figure you'll just inherit whatever your husband has if he should die first (as is likely, unless you're not in good health or are considerably older than your spouse), and vice versa.

Well, maybe, but then again, maybe not. It's true that if you're married and your husband dies, you'll almost certainly get any property that the two of you owned jointly as well as any of his separate assets that named you as the beneficiary. But the rest of his estate will be divided according to state law. If the two of you have children, that means the kids probably will get from one-half to two-thirds of his property (divided equally among them)—even if they'd be likely to fritter the money away at age eighteen or if you need it to support them—and you'll get the rest. If you don't have children, you may get all of your husband's property, or the state may divide his assets between you, his parents (if they're still living), and perhaps his siblings. And if you're not married but have a companion of long standing who dies without a will, his parents or children (if he has any) will inherit whatever he owns; you'll be left with nothing but your memories.

And what happens if you're married with young children and both you and your husband die together in an accident? Without a will that names a guardian who'll look after your little ones, their fate will rest in the hands of a court-appointed judge who knows nothing about them. Similarly, what happens if you're divorced and you die before your ex? The court will probably award custody to the children's biological father, even if one of the reasons you divorced him was because he was a lousy dad or if you've since remarried and the children have developed a strong, loving bond with their stepdad and prefer to remain with him.

There's not a single scenario that I've outlined here that I would be happy with, and I suspect you wouldn't be, either.

So stop the excuses, bite the bullet, and have that long overdue argument with your spouse about who should inherit the antique silverware your parents gave you for your wedding and whether Aunt Rose or Brother Leon would do a better job of raising your kids. Then get yourself into an estate or family lawyer's office (ask for referrals from friends, or call your state or county bar association for names of attorneys in your area), do the dirty deed, and get your significant other to do the same.

Expect to pay anywhere from $100 to $1,000 or more for your will, depending on how simple or complicated its provisions are. But you can cut those costs substantially by doing much of the prep work yourself—perhaps even drawing up the will itself—using any one of several good will handbooks now on the market or a software program, such as Quicken Family Lawyer (800–223–6925) or Nolo WillMaker 6.0 (800–992–6656).

As with prenuptial agreements, drawing up a will is especially crucial for anyone who is remarried with children from a previous union they want to protect. When you remarry, your new mate automatically becomes the beneficiary of your pension plan, individual retirement accounts, 401(k) plan, and any other retirement accounts you have (unless he has relinquished his claim in writing). So it's up to you to make sure your children get some, if not most, of what's left by spelling out your wishes in your will—even if your new spouse has pledged to provide for your kids as if they were his own. Maybe he will, but I wouldn't let their future hang on a promise.

Only a damn fool leaves herself and her children unprotected financially. Again, my advice is simple but imperative: Whatever else you do, *Don't be a damn fool!*

Action Plan

All too often we women unwittingly make mistakes in how we manage money in our personal relationships that can cost us dearly in the future. Here's what you need to do to protect yourself:

1. **Remember that just because you may not need his money shouldn't mean you don't appreciate it.** If your husband or boyfriend can afford to handle the lion's share of the expenses in your relationship, let him. The cardinal rule, wherever and whenever possible: let him pay!

2. **Let go of the guilt.** If you enjoy being taken care of by a man and he enjoys it, too, go for it.

3. **Insist on being an equal partner in the financial decisions in your household.** Never yield any of your power or independence in a relationship just because your husband or boyfriend may pay the bills or earn more than you do.

4. **Don't be lulled into a false sense of security.** Just because your husband pays the bills today doesn't mean he'll be around to pay the bills tomorrow. Continue to take appropriate steps to secure your own financial future independently.

5. **Whether you have a job outside the home or are a full-time homemaker, insist on getting some discretionary money of your own, apart from the cash you use for household expenses, to spend or save as you see fit.** Consider it partial compensation for all the unpaid work you do to keep your family and household running smoothly.

6. **Seriously consider getting a pre- or post-nuptial agreement to protect your money.** If you're getting married and you earn a substantial salary, own your own business, have a fair number of assets

or children from a previous marriage, it's particularly important to take measures to safeguard your livelihood and the people you love most in case the new union doesn't last.

7. **If your prospective groom instead asks you for a legal agreement protecting his financial interests, make sure to hire a top-notch independent lawyer or financial counselor to help you look out for what's fair and best for you.** Don't think it's a done deal just because you've signed on the dotted line. Revisit the arrangement periodically, and insist on updating it as your needs change and circumstances warrant.

8. **Draw up a will if you don't already have one—and urge your husband to do the same.** Specifying how you both want your property divided if and when you die is essential to making sure that you both receive your fair share of the assets you own and that your children are adequately provided for.

Respect Your Money

*I*t's not only in our personal relationships that we routinely make foolish, unthinking, *expensive* mistakes with our money. Remember my Damn Fool Test in the previous chapter? As my questions about purchases, credit cards, and bank fees suggested, we also make these kinds of mistakes every day when we buy something without trying to negotiate a better deal, when we pay exorbitant finance charges on credit cards, and when we don't pay attention to the nickel-and-dime fees on bank accounts and ATM withdrawals that eat up our money bit by bit. We don't make any of these mistakes on purpose, of course; we don't even make most of them consciously, but nevertheless we make them all the time.

I call this being disrespectful of money. If I had my way, it would be the eighth deadly sin.

Now, my *Webster's* defines *respect* as holding something in high or special regard or with particular esteem. That's certainly the way that I feel about my money. I work too hard to get my money to fritter it away thoughtlessly. I'd rather put all my efforts into keeping as much of it as I can.

LEARN THE ART OF THE DEAL

To me, the cardinal rule about treating money with respect is not to pay a penny more for anything I buy than is absolutely necessary. Over the years I've learned that almost everything is negotiable. Almost anything that you want to buy can be had at a lower price than the one that's advertised. But you'll never get the better deal if you don't ask for it.

When I go into a store and see an item that I want, I always ask the salesperson when that item is going on sale. Then I ask if she can give me the sale price in advance. I can't tell you how many times that simple, straightforward request has been successful, whether I've been in a boutique or a department store, whether the establishment is lowbrow, upscale, or somewhere in between.

If the salesperson says no, however, I don't just drop the issue. I push a little further to make sure that I'm not getting a stock response. I'll ask, Can you please speak to your supervisor and see if there's something she can do? If that request proves fruitless, too, I'll then ask the salesperson if she can keep her eye on the item for me. When she realizes that I really won't buy the article unless I get the sale price, she often becomes more motivated to see if she can get the price dropped now. If she still can't or won't give me the discount, I really will give her my phone number and ask her to call me when the item finally goes on sale. And when I get the call (as I do at least half the time), I go and buy it. One way or another, more often than not, I end up getting the item at the price I wanted in the first place.

The problem that most people have with negotiating is that they're afraid to ask. They're embarrassed. But what's the worst thing that can happen to you? The salesperson will say no, or maybe say no *and* laugh at you or add a snide remark. I say, so what? A little attitude won't kill you and is certainly worth risking for the chance to save some money or acquire some coveted item that you otherwise couldn't afford. In my experience, though, I've found that most merchants are pretty good-natured about customers looking to make a deal, as long as you make your request graciously.

If you take the attitude that there's nothing that you can't live without, that you either get what you want at your price or you'd rather not have it at all, that attitude alone will give you the courage to ask for a discount. As a bonus, this approach disciplines you not to buy something you can't afford—you either get it at the price your budget allows or you don't get it. You never let yourself fall in love with anything to the degree that you can't walk away.

HONE YOUR TECHNIQUES

It's also a good idea to develop and build relationships with people who can regularly save you a bundle. If there's a store where you particularly like to shop and a saleswoman there who often serves you, find out when her birthday is, remember to send her a card to commemorate the date, and be sure to give her a little gift at Christmas, too. In turn she'll remember to call you when some item she knows you'll like is about to go on sale. Develop that relationship, be loyal to that person, and she will serve you well.

It helps too if you have a mental price in mind for whatever it is you're buying and then resolve to stick to that price. I know of an Atlanta housewife named Laurie Smith who had budgeted $55 a night for lodging during her family's vacation in Florida without booking in advance. While they were there, she and her husband and kids stopped at a hotel, and as they waited at the front desk for service, they overheard the clerk tell the couple ahead of them that rooms went for $75 a night. The couple walked away, disappointed. When Laurie got to the counter, she said forthrightly, "I'll pay you fifty-five dollars a night. That's all the money I have, but we want to stay in this hotel." The clerk said okay, and that was that.

Knowing the real value of the item or service you want helps you set that mental price. That in turn means being an educated consumer, which in turn means doing some research about whatever that article is selling for on the open market before you ever set foot in the place where you want to cut your deal. Check out the store's newspaper ads (particularly during sale times), look up the item in *Consumer Reports* or another buying guide, comparison shop to see what it's selling for elsewhere, and ask friends what they've paid for similar stuff.

Before I went to trade in my old car last year, for instance, I first looked up the model and the year in the *Blue Book*, the bible of used-car prices, to see what my wheels were worth. When I got to the dealership to do the trade-in, I then tacked on an extra thousand dollars because the car was in perfect condition. And I just stuck to my guns. When the person on the other end of the negotiation sees your determination, you have the advantage. There's a certain attitude that you project when you're sure of the ground that you're standing on, and that attitude makes all the difference between getting a yes or a no at the other end.

Did I get the blue-book price, plus $1,000, you may be wondering? You bet I did!

KNOW YOUR AUDIENCE

Of course, you have to know where you can negotiate and where you can't. Where you can, fortunately, is almost anywhere. No matter how upscale the store or sophisticated the service, they're usually willing to play Let's Make a Deal. Just to cite a few examples, I've negotiated at Macy's, A&S, the Gap, Radio Shack, Sears, Saks Fifth Avenue, Tiffany's, Bergdorf Goodman, and several designer boutiques, as well as with my accountant, caterer, doctors, and lawyers.

I remember reading in *Family Money* magazine about a San Antonio veterinarian named Melissa Greenwood who even cut a deal at the butcher's. She was in the shop buying prime rib for a holiday dinner when she noticed that many other meats were on sale. So she asked the manager if he'd mind extending the sale price to her roast. He did, saving her about $25, or 30 percent off her order.

And don't shy away from pressing for further discounts just because an item's already on sale. In fact, that's when you can get some of the best deals of all, because there's extra pressure on the sales staff to move the merchandise out the door. Your best bet: Shopping in consignment stores, thrift shops, sample sales, off-price outlets, factory outlets, and second-hand designer clothes shops. That's how Elizabeth Ferrarini, a public relations executive in Boston, puts together the fashionable wardrobe she needs for her job. "I've negotiated Burberry raincoats down to $20, Armani skirts to $30, and I had a great run recently, where I walked away with an Ann Taylor suit, two wool dresses, a pair of shoes, and new leather gloves, all for $128," she recounts gleefully.

Last, don't be afraid or embarrassed to barter for something you really want but can't quite afford. If you're an excellent seamstress, for example, maybe you could offer to alter clothes for a painter friend in exchange for getting a fresh coat for your kitchen. If you have an expensive suit that's nearly brand-new but no longer fits, or some toys that your child has outgrown but are still in mint condition, you might offer to trade with a friend who could make use of your stuff and happens to have stuff of her own that you want but she no longer needs.

Not that you have to confine your bartering to people you know well. If you adore fine wine and have up-to-date office skills, for instance, maybe you could offer to do some clerical work for your local wine merchant in exchange for a few free bottles. I have a friend who every week puts in several hours of filing and computer work for a tony nursery school in her neighborhood. In exchange, the school director lets her three-year-old daughter attend free of charge two days a week.

LOOK FOR THE HIDDEN COSTS

When I'm in the midst of a business deal, I always look for the hidden costs—that is, any covert or unexpected expenses that will destroy my cash flow and undermine my business plan. In the corporate world, that's known as *due diligence*. I practice it as faithfully in my personal life as I do in my professional one.

Remember: It's the hidden costs that'll kill you every time.

Say you want to take a ski vacation. So you scout out nice, reasonably priced ski resorts, figure the cost of your airfare, lodging, and meals, save that amount, and figure you're all set. But what about the price of renting skis if you don't own them? And ski lessons? And lift tickets? Will you have to buy appropriate clothes if you don't already own a parka, ski cap, goggles, and all the other accessories of the sport? What about spending money? By the time you're done, these "little" incidentals could easily put you over your vacation budget by an extra thousand dollars or more.

It pays to be aware. With every product or service you buy, with every dollar that you spend, try to figure out in advance what the hidden costs will be. Do what you can to minimize or eliminate them, but if that's not possible, at least incorporate them into your budget so that you are not constantly being hit by unexpected expenses. Hidden costs that are unaccounted for can undermine your savings goals faster than Häagen-Dazs can melt a dieter's willpower.

....

Hidden costs that are unaccounted for can undermine your savings goals faster than Häagen-Dazs can melt a dieter's willpower.

....

WATCH THOSE NICKELS AND DIMES

Of all the hidden costs I can think of, probably none are more insidious than the nickel-and-dime fees on bank accounts and credit cards. A dollar here, two dollars there, five dollars somewhere else, and by the end of the year you're probably a few hundred dollars or more in the red. One banking-industry consultant I know recently calculated that since 1991 the number of different types of fees and service charges that banks can nail customers with has risen from 96 to 270.

The amounts are rising, too. These days you'll get hit with $1 to $2 in charges every time you use an ATM that doesn't belong to your own bank. If your balance dips below the minimum needed to maintain free checking, you're probably looking at an extra $6 in monthly fees, at least. Bounce a check and you'll get dunned for $20, maybe even $30. Innocently deposit a rubber check that someone else gave to you, and you'll probably see a $5 to $6 processing fee on your next statement. A lot of banks these days are even charging $2 if you use a real-live teller instead of a machine—even if you're just depositing your own money.

Talk about throwing money away!

Here are some of the ways you can fight back:

- **Comparison shop.** Roughly a third of all banks in a recent survey by Consumer Action, a consumer-advocacy group based in San Francisco, offered free checking accounts, and plenty of others have minimum balance requirements well below the nearly $1,000 that's typical nationwide. Call several banks in your area to see which one has the lowest fees. Don't rule out smaller institutions. Since small local banks can't compete on convenience, they're more likely than their bigger brothers to promote value to attract customers.

- **Switch to a credit union.** If you have access to a credit union through your job or a professional association, join now and switch your banking there. Yes, you'll sacrifice a bit in convenience without a bank branch or affiliated ATM on every street corner. But you'll more than make up for it in the pocketbook. Not only do credit unions usually have far lower fees than banks for virtually every service they offer, but they also typically have lower interest rates on loans and higher interest rates on savings accounts.

- **Kick the ATM habit.** The average bank customer uses a cash machine seven times a month, or nearly twice a week, typically to make withdrawals. At $1 to $2.50 a pop if you're not using your own bank's system, you could be spending as much as $200 a year or more just to gain access to your own money. Do a better job of planning your cash needs in advance so that you don't need to make as many trips to the ATM; setting an amount for the week and then using only that much and no more will also help you rein in your spending. And when you do have to visit an automated bank branch, make sure it's one of your own bank's machines rather than a competitor's, even if you have to travel a little bit out of the way to get there.

- **Don't write rubber checks.** Fees for bouncing a check range from $10 to $30 per transgression around the country, making them the nastiest of all bank levies. The average consumer writes two bad checks a year. Don't be one of them.

BORROW SMART

How do millionaires get to be millionaires? One way is that they don't borrow money. In fact, two-thirds of all millionaires don't have any debts at all. The rich know that every dollar you pay in interest to satisfy some immediate desire is one less dollar that you have to invest or otherwise put toward your most important long-term goals.

I'm not going so far as to say that all borrowing is bad. Sometimes it's the only way to get something you really need; sometimes you have no choice. But you do have to be smart about why and how you do it.

To my mind, there are basically only two sound reasons to borrow money: to buy or attain something that has great emotional meaning for you or to achieve a big-ticket milestone in your life—that is, something that will greatly enhance the quality of your existence or that of someone you love. Borrowing to buy a new house or to add a bedroom after you've had a child makes sense to me. So does borrowing to buy a second car if that will make life more convenient for your family or enable a non-working spouse to get a job and bring additional income into the household. Borrowing a modest sum and repaying it in a timely fashion—for instance, charging a few small items on a credit card and making regular payments on the balance—can also help you establish a solid credit record. And I'd certainly advocate borrowing to put your aged, ailing mother in a high-quality nursing home if that was the only way you could afford it.

You do not, however, borrow just to buy a new dress or eat out at a nicer restaurant than you can afford. You don't borrow to take a fancy vacation or for any transient event or perishable item that you'll still be paying for months or even years after the experience has passed and long since faded from memory.

You also have to be smart about *how* you borrow money. Never, ever finance major purchases from your credit card; finance them (if you must) from the bank or some other cheaper source of money, such as a home-equity line of credit or a loan against the balance in your 401(k) plan at work. (You'll recall I talked about how those two kinds of loans work in chapters 8 and 7, respectively.) At two to three times the interest rates that banks charge, I regard the finance charges on the average credit card as nothing short of obscene.

··

Credit cards are potholes on the road to financial security, and they're deep and damaging.

··

Credit cards are potholes on the road to financial security, and they're deep and damaging. Learn this lesson and practice it routinely: *You do not spend money in your wallet that you do not have.* If you want to buy some makeup and it costs $5 and you have only $4, *you do not buy it because you do not have the money*. You do not whip out a hot piece of plastic and take it home anyway.

I do not mean to come across as holier-than-thou on this issue. It's sheer pragmatism. Like most people—no, let me be honest here, probably *more* than most people—I like to buy stuff and acquire beautiful things. But if I charge them today and run a balance on my credit cards, the interest that I'll accrue and eventually have to pay means that I won't be able to buy the things I want tomorrow—or at least I won't be able to buy as many of them as I could have if I wasn't still paying interest on the things I bought yesterday.

I simply refuse to do that. And you should, too.

GET PLASTIC SURGERY

I know that for many women this advice recalls the old cliché about shutting the barn door after the horse has gotten out. With credit-card sponsors sending out 2.4 million separate offers for new cards each year, it's easy to see how so many of us get sucked into today's gotta-have-it-now culture. These days, the typical American family holds fourteen different credit cards, according to credit-card tracker RAM Research of Frederick, Maryland. And households that don't pay off their cards in full every month have an average outstanding balance of more than $7,000, the Consumer Federation of America reports. The price of that charging habit, at the average interest rate of around 18 percent: nearly $1,300 a year.

So what can you do to pay down those balances and get rid of those interest payments forever? Here are my suggestions:

- **Use credit cards for convenience only.** Pledge that from this moment on, you will not charge another dime on your credit cards unless you'll be able to pay off the entire amount as soon as the bill comes in. I do use credit cards occasionally to avoid carrying large amounts of cash while I shop, but I pay my balances in full every month. And I've done that all my life, even when I barely had enough money to pay my rent and buy food. Whenever you're tempted to whip out the plastic, repeat to yourself the mantra of reformed chargers everywhere: I refuse to spend on interest what I could be spending to buy myself something else.

- **Carry two cards, maximum.** That's right, all you need is two: one for personal purchases and one for business use. (Separating the two makes figuring out your deductible business expenses at tax time a lot easier.) Pick the two all-purpose cards with the best terms—that is, American Express, a lower-than-average rate Visa or MasterCard, or similar cards that can be used virtually everywhere, as opposed to plastic issued by specific retailers. And chop up every other card you have.

- **Pay more than the minimum required.** If you pay off as little as possible each month, you'll be paying off those cards forever. When getting rid of those balances, every little bit—$5 more, $10 more, whatever—really helps.

  Say you're carrying a balance of $1,900 on a card that charges 18 percent in interest. If you never charge another nickel but make only the standard minimum payment of $15 a month, it will take you 23 years to get rid of that debt, and you'll wind up paying $4,097 in interest, or $5,997 in all. If you kick in just $10 more toward your payments each month, you'll instead pay off that card in five years and spend $1,019 in interest. Total savings: $3,078.

- **Pay on time.** If you think the fees associated with ordinary bank accounts are outrageous, wait until you get a load of what your credit-card issuer has in store for you. Miss your due date, sometimes by just a single day, and some issuers will slap you with a penalty of as much as $20 to $30. One or two months of late payments also prompt many companies to hike your interest rate by anywhere from three to ten percentage points. If you unwittingly charge beyond your credit limit, even by a lousy buck, you may get hit for another $20 or so. The most outrageous of all: Some issuers are punishing cardholders who seldom charge or who pay their balances in full every month with an "inactivity" fee. If that happens to you, cancel immediately.

- **Switch to a lower-rate card.** Why pay 18 percent in interest (more like 21, 22 percent or more if you're using a department store or other retailer's plastic) when you can pay 12 or maybe even 10 percent or possibly even single-digit rates? No reason that I can think of. Plenty of card issuers these days offer low-rate plastic. While you need a spanking-clean credit record to be approved for the really cheap deals, you have nothing to lose by applying and hundreds of dollars a year in saved interest payments to gain.

  You won't have any trouble finding these deals. In addition to the solicitations that probably already flood your mailbox, you can get a list of the best low-rate cards by sending away for a copy of the newsletter "CardTrak" ($5; RAM Research, P.O. Box 1700, Frederick, MD 21702; 800–344–7714). If you're comfortable navigating the Internet, you'll also find free information about good low-rate card offers at the site operated by the newsletter "Bank Rate Monitor" (www.bankrate.com) and at "CardTrak" (www.cardtrak.com).

- **Negotiate a better deal.** There's also a very simple way to get better terms on the credit card you already have: Just ask. Competition is so fierce within the credit-card industry that issuers are increasingly willing to lower your interest rate or slash fees rather than lose you as a customer. Simply call the toll-free service number on your monthly statement, ask for a lower rate, and tell them—nicely, of course—that you're prepared to transfer your balance to a competitor's card unless they cooperate.

- **Get help if you need it.** Sometimes you just can't do it alone. If more than 20 percent of your income goes toward paying off your credit cards and other debts (excluding your mortgage), if you can make only the minimum payments required (and sometimes not even that), if you've borrowed from one lender to pay another, if you're constantly taking out cash advances, or if you're often charging perishable staples (like your groceries), you may well be in too deep a debt hole to climb out on your own.

You may be able to negotiate a more reasonable repayment plan by calling your credit-card issuers and explaining your troubles. After all, it's in their best interests to figure out a way for you to pay your debts, too, rather than risk you paying erratically or defaulting on your payments altogether.

For fees ranging from nothing to $25 a visit, depending on the location, you can also get help from a professional credit counselor. One of the biggest and probably best in the business: the nonprofit **Consumer Credit Counseling Service** (800–388–2227). With more than 1,100 regional offices, this service assigns you a counselor who sits down with you to review your spending habits, suggests ways to change them, devises a smart strategy to repay your debts, and, if necessary, negotiates with creditors on your behalf.

That's how Sharon Hoffman, a hospital manager in Atlanta, managed to reduce dramatically the $15,000 in debt she accumulated a few years ago. As Sharon told *Working Woman* magazine a while back, she had no debts at all in 1990, when she decided to move from Orange County, California, to the suburbs of Atlanta, ironically enough, to escape the Golden State's high cost of living. But by the time she finished paying for the move, buying a place to live, and decorating it, she'd fallen so deeply into debt, she was forced to sell her house just to meet her loan payments. That's when Sharon turned her accounts over to the Atlanta branch of the Credit Counseling Service. She cut up all her cards, and slowly but steadily over the years paid them off, account by account, starting with her highest-rate credit-card debt first. At the time of the article she was still not completely debt-free, but was well on her way. She noted proudly, "These days I pay cash for everything."

Now, that's what I call treating your money with respect.

ACTION PLAN

Don't rob yourself of the money you need to live well and to achieve your long-term goals by overpaying for purchases, frittering your money away on hidden costs or getting in over your head with debt. To make sure you're treating your money with the respect it deserves, take these steps:

1. **Never pay full price for anything without first asking if you can get a better deal.** Remember everything, absolutely everything!, in this life is negotiable.

2. **Have a mental price in mind for any product or service you intend to buy, and resolve to pay that amount and no more.** Do some research before you shop to make sure you know the true value of the item. When you project the attitude that you're sure of the price ground you stand on, you've already won half the battle.

3. **Consider bartering.** Trade something you own but no longer want or a skill you can put to good use in order to acquire a product or service that you really want but can't afford.

4. **Always try to calculate the hidden costs before you spend your money.** Among the most insidious: the nickel-and-dime fees on banks accounts and credit cards. To avoid them, shop around for the best deals, don't use a cash machine that's not on your bank's system, and consider joining a credit union to take advantage of its low-cost credit and banking deals.

5. **If you must borrow money, borrow smart.** Stay away from credit cards and instead look for lower-cost sources of financing, such as a home-equity line of credit or a loan against the balance in your company 401(k) plan.

6. **When you're shopping and see something you really can't afford, learn to just say no.** Steel your resolve by telling yourself: I refuse

to spend money on interest that I could be spending to buy something wonderful for myself or saving for my future goals.

7. **Get plastic surgery**. Take steps immediately to get yourself out of the credit-card hole. Pay off new purchases in full every month, switch to a lower-rate card, cut up your high-rate ones, and write checks for more than the minimum balance every month. And if you're in too deep to get out of debt on your own, don't be too embarrassed to seek help.

Step 12:
Always Have Something to Sell

*T*o make real money, you have to have something to sell at the end of the day. As important as it is to steadily sock away a portion of your paycheck every month, you cannot rely on your salary alone, regardless of how high that salary is, to lead you to financial security. Remember that financial law of nature—you know, the one that says your lifestyle expands to fill your paycheck? Since you cannot count on being able to squeeze large amounts of money out of your salary, the only way to grow a substantial nest egg is to build equity in something that you can ultimately sell in exchange for a lump sum—preferably a *big* lump sum.

The only surefire way to do this is to invest in stocks.

Historically stocks have beaten the pants off every other kind of investment around. They have been the *only* investment to consistently and handily beat inflation over time. If you do not invest in stocks with at least a portion of the money you're setting aside for the future, the consequences are clear and they are stark: Your savings will not grow fast enough to outpace rises in the cost of living or the amount grow big enough to allow you to fulfill your financial dreams. You risk having to work the rest of your life just to make ends meet or having to seriously scale back your lifestyle as you grow older. And you can kiss those dreams of a bigger, better life good-bye.

Think of it this way: Stocks are your ticket to financial freedom.

OPERATE ON FACTS, NOT FEAR

I know, I know—it's a scary proposition for those of you who haven't yet ventured into the market. But if you take a moment to dissect why the prospect of investing in stocks is so unappealing, I suspect much of your distaste may melt away.

Among women who do not invest, the single most important reason is lack of money. At least that's what 58 percent of the female non-investors claimed in a recent survey by OppenheimerFunds, a major mutual fund company. Not knowing where to begin and fear of losing money came in second and third, respectively.

Let me tackle the lack-of-money bugaboo first.

It's simply not true. For as little as $25 a month, you can launch a comprehensive investing program. For between $100 and $1,000, you can instantly acquire a well-diversified, professionally managed portfolio with hundreds of stocks in it. With $5,000 you just might parlay a stake in stocks to a cool million or more.

If you don't believe me, consider the story of Anne Scheiber, a former auditor for the Internal Revenue Service who never earned more than $3,200 a year in her life. In the twenty-three years that she spent poring over other people's tax returns, Anne learned one very powerful lesson, the same lesson, in fact, that I'm trying to impart to you now: The best way to get rich in America is to invest in stocks. When she retired from the agency in 1943 at the age of forty-nine, she took that lesson to heart and invested $5,000, the bulk of her life savings, in the stock market.

Anne didn't do anything fancy. She simply bought small stakes in leading brand-name companies, whose products she liked and whose industries she understood—companies like Coca-Cola, PepsiCo, Bristol Myers (makers of Excedrin, Clairol hair coloring, and Windex, among other consumer products), Columbia Pictures, Paramount, and Loew's (she was a real movie fan). Then she held on to those shares, in good times and bad, never selling in a panic when stock prices temporarily headed south. When Anne Scheiber died in 1995 at the ripe old age of 101, her portfolio was worth more than $20 million. That works out to a 17.5 percent annual return, roughly five percentage points better than the average stock's 12.4 percent return over the same period and a good enough showing to match or best many of Wall Street's most renowned investors. Still, Anne Scheiber's story might never have come to light if not for one key, publicity-stirring development: Upon her death she left her entire fortune to New York City's Yeshiva University, with the money specifically earmarked to help educate young women.

Now, I can't guarantee that, like Anne Scheiber, you'll make millions in the market. But I can guarantee that if you just stick with stocks, you too can parlay a small stake into a substantial sum. Even if you invest only $100 a month and do no better than average on your stocks, you'll still end up with roughly $100,000 in your pocket after twenty years. Bump that up to $200 a month (less than $2,500 a year) and earn slightly better-than-average returns, and you'll be looking at a cool quarter-million after twenty years instead.

You really don't need much to get started. As of this writing, there are more than 5,000 mutual funds that allow you to open an account with $1,000 or less, and over 1,500 funds that require as little as $100 to $500 initially. In addition, hundreds of fund companies will waive the minimum-investment requirements for customers who sign up for their automatic-investment programs, promising to have at least $25 to $100 a month transferred from their bank accounts into one or more of the company's funds. Many brokerage houses have their own no-minimum versions of the fund companies' automatic-investing programs, and some have even eliminated minimums on their ordinary accounts as well.

The bottom line: Not having a lot of money to invest now is no impediment to making a bundle on your investments later.

RECOGNIZE THE REAL THREAT

Men are interested in making money. Women are interested in not losing any. That's the stereotypical view of the difference between the sexes when they're investing. And it's easy to see how we get our reputation as risk-averse wimps. In survey after survey on the subject, far more women than men report that they are unwilling to take risks in order to make big gains. Furthermore, they strongly favor keeping their money in "safe" investments like bank accounts and certificates of deposit, even if that means settling for far lower returns than they could get elsewhere.

Bad call, ladies. The biggest threat to a woman's long-term financial health is not losing money. It's inflation. That's right, inflation—even at the historically tame rates of the past few years. Even at the super-low 2 percent rate recorded in 1997, inflation will still cut your purchasing power by a third in twenty years. That means for every $10 you have now, you'll only have the equivalent of $6.66 twenty years down the road. If inflation rises to a still moderate but more typical 4 percent rate, that $10 will be worth only $4.50. That's a 55 percent decline in its value! Let's not even think about what would happen if inflation ever really rises again, let alone gets back to the double-digit levels of the late seventies and early eighties.

The danger here, of course, is that you will outlive your money. You won't have a prayer of building your savings to fulfill your financial goals. You won't even be able to live as well as you do now when you retire. And eventually, if you live as long as the average woman does, you'll simply run out of money. Does the term "bag lady" hold the same horror for you as it does for me?

There is only one sure way to avoid this ugly scenario: Invest a portion of the money that you're setting aside for long-term goals in stocks—preferably a big portion. Over the past fifty years the average stock has gained nearly 12 percent a year, versus 5.4 percent for the typical bond and just 4.8 percent for Treasury bills (which are a pretty good reflection of the rates on short-term certificates of deposit and other bank products), according to Ibbotson Associates, an investment research firm in Chicago. Inflation, meanwhile, averaged 4.4 percent during that period.

We've been led to believe that if we keep our money in the bank, it will be safe. I say the time has come to redefine safe. When it comes to money, no risk is just too risky.

In the long run, in any case, it turns out that stocks are not nearly as risky as most of us think. True, on a year-to-year basis they can suffer dramatic price swings. Historically, one out of every four years is a loser in the stock market, and some of those down years have been real doozies. But if you stick with your stock picks for the long haul—and that's the only way to do it, in my opinion and that of nearly every other financial adviser on earth—the risk of losing money declines dramatically. Over the past fifty years, investors who held on to their stocks for at least five years had less than a 5 percent chance of losing money, Ibbotson reports. And none of those who held on for ten years or longer lost even a penny; most instead made double-digit gains.

My motto: PATIENCE MAKES PROFITS.

REMEMBER: IT AIN'T ROCKET SCIENCE

A friend of mine who's a financial planner passed along the following anecdote to illustrate the different attitudes that men and women bring to investing. She notes: "If I have a male client who invests in a stock that subsequently loses 50 percent, he will angrily blame the market or his broker or the idiot on the golf course who gave him the hot tip in the first place. If I have a female client who buys the same stock with the same result, she will blame herself."

....

My motto:
Patience makes profits.

....

In all aspects of our lives, women have an exaggerated fear of making mistakes, a fear that we will not be able to master what we don't already know, a fear of looking stupid. When it comes to managing our money, those fears can be crippling. In a 1994 study by the Center for Women and Retirement Research, three-quarters of the women surveyed said that lack of knowledge about how to select the best stocks, bonds, and mutual funds for their needs stopped them from becoming more active investors. More than half of them said they'd postponed financial decisions for fear of making a mistake—and frequently second-guessed themselves after they'd finally made a choice.

It's time to get over it.

Yes, there is some risk associated with investing in stocks and bonds. But certain fears you can get past only by doing whatever it is you fear and gaining the knowledge firsthand that you have nothing to be afraid of. Sometimes we just have to bite the bullet. We're always looking for psychological crutches that will somehow help us to do the right thing, that will allow us to feel totally comfortable about whatever challenge we're about to take on. Well, we don't have that luxury when it comes to our money. Some actions we just have to take because all of our research, all the facts before us, tell us that it's the most prudent action, even though we're still not comfortable with it. There is no magic potion, no magic wand that I can wave that will make it okay. It just takes courage. You're not going to get ahead in this life without courage.

....

It just takes courage. You're not going to get ahead in this life without courage

....

That includes getting over the fear of being embarrassed about what you don't know about investing or being afraid to ask questions that might make you look stupid. When I first started to invest, my broker was always talking about PE ratios. I thought PE stood for Phys. Ed. or physical education—you know, what we used to call gym class when I was in school. I couldn't imagine what gym had to do with my stocks. So I went out and bought myself a book on investing and learned that in the financial markets, PE stands for price-to-earnings ratio, and it's a way to calculate whether a stock is cheap or expensive to buy. These days, if my broker uses a term that I'm not familiar with, I just ask him what the heck he's talking about.

The point is, what you don't know about investing is easy enough to learn—particularly if you just drum up the guts to ask someone what they mean every time they use some Wall Street jargon to describe what inevitably is a very simple concept.

In fact, investing needn't be a complicated process, and it's not particularly hard to learn. Honest. Of course, you can make it difficult and complex if you want to, and plenty of people on Wall Street do just that every day. But the truth is that almost none of them end up making more money on their investments than the average Joe—or, in this case, the average Jane. No, the folks on Wall Street make the big bucks from the salaries and bonuses and commissions they earn by convincing people like you and me that we need them to manage our money for us. You don't—at least, not for the basics and the basics are all most of us need.

MASTER THE BASICS

So I'm now going to give you a crash course in those basics. Don't worry, it's easy and will be over quickly—you might even find it fun. And if, as you become more proficient at investing, you want to learn more and make the whole process more sophisticated, you can certainly do so (and I'll pass along some tips for those of you who do in the next chapter). But if you don't want to do more than the basics, you don't have to—ever. Do just this, and you'll do just fine.

Okay, here we go:

Basic Concept Number One: Don't put all your eggs in one basket.

Financial planners and other investment professionals routinely dress up this very simple notion with fancy names like *diversification* or *asset allocation*. All it means in plain English is to spread your money among different types of investments. That way, if one of those investments has a temporary setback, at least one or two of the others are likely be doing okay and will cushion the blow.

You have basically only three types of investments to choose from: (1) stocks; (2) bonds; and (3) cash (*cash* is the catch-all name given to any investment in which your principal is virtually guaranteed to be safe, such as money market accounts and funds, certificates of deposit, and Treasury bills). It's smart to have at least some money in all three since each one behaves differently under various economic conditions.

When you buy a *stock*, you are in essence buying a partial ownership in a company. You stand to gain the most when the economy and the business you're in are growing. When you buy a *bond*, you are instead making a loan to a company; you earn money from the interest that the company pays to you on its loan. If you sell before the bond matures, you may also make money if interest rates have fallen since you first bought it. That's because other investors would be willing to pay more for your bond than you did because it pays higher interest than new bonds on the market. Cash tends to do best when the other two are faltering.

Study after study has shown that you can cut the risks of investing in stocks dramatically without sacrificing that much of your potential gains by putting some money into each of these three investment categories. Judging by history, for instance, if you put 60 percent of your savings into stocks, 30 percent into bonds, and 10 percent into cash, you'd earn roughly 80 percent as much as you would with an all-stock portfolio while cutting the risk of a major loss in half. I like those odds.

To further temper your risks, it's also smart to spread the money you're allocating to stocks among different types of companies. Again, you have three basic choices: (1) large, well-established U.S. companies; (2) small, up-and-coming U.S. companies; and (3) foreign companies. Big American companies should be the basic building block of your portfolio since they're the safest kind of stock investment you can make. But historically the returns have been better on small U.S. companies, so it pays to have at least some money in them, too. And foreign companies often do well when U.S. stocks are flagging, so they are a good way to hedge your bet on the American market.

Basic Concept Number Two:
Choose your investments based on
when you'll need your money.

Again, financial pros have a high-falutin' term for this concept—they call it your *investment time horizon*. Forget the jargon, but remember the idea: You choose which investments make the most sense for you depending in large part on how soon you will need that money. The sooner you need to tap the account, the more important it is to be sure your principal will be intact when you withdraw your money. Conversely, the more time you have to reach a particular goal, the more you can focus on earning the best returns and the more you can afford to take some short-term risks to do so.

Here's how that advice plays out in real life:

- **Short-term money.** Savings that you may need to tap within a year or so—say, the money you've earmarked for your emergency fund or your child's first year of college and that child is now a high school senior—belongs 100 percent in cash. You must be sure that every dollar of that stash is there when you need it. Only cash offers that kind of guarantee.

- **Medium-term money.** If you're saving to buy a house or a new car or for any other big-ticket goal that you hope to achieve in roughly three to five years, you still need to play it relatively safe. "Relatively" is the operative word here. While you should still keep a hefty chunk of this money in cash, you can try to jazz up your returns by adding some bonds to your mix. Your safest bet: Bonds that mature in five to seven years (known in the investment world as intermediate-term bonds), which over time have provided the most return for the least risk. If you're not the nervous type, you might also consider putting a small portion of this money—say, no more than 20 percent to 30 percent—into stocks. The small risk of a loss over a five-year period is probably more than offset by the potential for even higher profits—particularly since the other 70 percent to 80 percent that you have in cash and bonds are practically guaranteed winners. For goals you hope to achieve in five to ten years, bump up the percentage you commit to stocks to at least 50 percent—and perhaps as much as 75 percent.

- **Long-term money.** Put as much of the money you're saving for goals that are at least ten years away into stocks as your stomach can handle. If, for instance, you're investing through your 401(k) or some other account earmarked for retirement and you're in your twenties, thirties, or even forties, it's okay to put 100 percent of this money into stocks—if your nerves can stand it. Even in your fifties and early sixties, it's still a good idea to keep most of your retirement savings in stocks. At that age, the average woman will probably live another twenty to thirty years. That's plenty of time to ride out any temporary losses in the stock market and plenty of time, too, for inflation to lay waste to your savings if you choose overly conservative investments instead.

Basic Concept Number Three: Reinvest your profits.

There are two ways to make money on stocks. The first is if the prospects for your company are good enough that other investors buy more shares, pushing the price of the stock higher. Profits from a higher stock price are known as *capital gains*. The second way, known as *dividends*, is if the company distributes a portion of its profits to its shareholders, including you.

When most people think about making money in the market, they focus on the first way, routinely checking the ups and downs of their stock's price to see how well their investment is performing. But in reality the truest path to stock market profits is dividends, which will build and compound to a small fortune over time, if you'll only let them.

Just consider: An investor who put $100 into big blue-chip stocks in 1926 would have earned close to $7,000 by the beginning of 1998, assuming she's spent all her dividends along the way. But if she'd instead reinvested those dividends, she'd have amassed more like $150,000.

The lesson is obvious: Always reinvest your dividends.

Basic Concept Number Four:
The secret of investment success is not
genius or even luck, but discipline.

There used to be an advertisement for the New York state lottery that went like this: You gotta be in it to win it. Well, the same is true of the stock market and, believe me, it's a lot surer bet than playing the lottery (odds of winning the grand prize in New York's Lotto: 1 in 12 million; odds of being struck by lightning: 1 in 600,000).

But "being in it" means staying in it, virtually all the time, rather than trying to figure out when stocks will do well and buying your shares at that point, then trying to figure out when the market is about to tank and dumping those shares before the trouble hits. I say: Trying to build wealth by trying to time the stock market is a fool's game. No one can predict in advance with any certainty when stocks will climb and when they will fall—not all the pundits on Wall Street, not your Uncle Lou the broker or your colleague down the hall who's been playing the market for years or anybody else who tries to convince you that they know the inside scoop. If you stay on the sidelines waiting for the best time to invest, chances are you'll miss the boat.

....

Trying to build wealth by trying to time the stock market is a fool's game

....

Here's why: The history of the stock market shows that gains typically come in short, sharp spurts. By the time anyone realizes that an advance has begun, the best part of it is over. A study by the University of Michigan illustrates the point. Looking at the period from 1963 to 1993, the researchers found that the best stock market advances of that three-decade stretch had been randomly scattered over ninety days. If you'd invested $1,000 in stocks in 1963 but missed those ninety days, your money would have been worth only $2,100 at the end of the period, or less than you would have earned in a safe, dull investment like bank CDs. But if you'd stayed fully invested during that period, your grand would have grown to a cool $24,300.

Now, I know that sticking with your stocks when the market is in a tailspin is a tough proposition from an emotional standpoint. It's nerve-wracking to watch your hard-earned savings shrink, no matter how much or how often your head tells you the loss is temporary. Even after all my years of investing, of watching my portfolio bounce back after market downturn after market downturn, I am not immune. When stock prices start to tumble, my stomach churns; I find myself obsessively watching the financial news and wondering if I should get out and get out quickly. The crucial point here, though, is that *I do not act on those fears*. Instead I get reassurance where I can find it and sit tight.

In the fall of 1998, for example, when turmoil in Russia and ongoing troubles in Asian economics sent the U.S. market into a sharp decline, I got on the phone immediately. I called all my advisers. I called friends who were knowledgeable investors, people whose talent for making money I admired and respected, and I asked them how they felt about what was going on in the market and what they were doing with their own money. They would say, "This is a bad one, Georgette, but it will turn around." They were sitting tight with their own investments. That gave me some comfort and the reassurance I needed about the long-term outcome.

The bottom line: Once you find an investment mix that you can live with, stick to it. Tell yourself that there are going to be ups and downs and then ups again in the market so that you don't sell in a panic. And keep reminding yourself of that fact as often as you need to hear it. Place Post-Its all over your house and office saying the equivalent of "This too shall pass." Get comfort wherever you can find it. But whatever you do, don't turn a paper loss into a real loss by selling when stock prices fall.

Remember: Patience makes profits.

KEEP YOUR EYES ON THE PRIZE

Conceptually, that's all you need to know. I can sum it up in a few short sentences:

- Keep the bulk of your long-term savings in stocks.

- Always reinvest your dividends.

- Split the rest of your savings between bonds and cash, favoring cash for any money that you'll need within the next three years or so.

- Then be patient, sit tight, and be prepared to ride out any temporary setbacks in the financial markets.

- Enjoy the sight of your money growing.

That's it. That's all. Really.

Action Plan

The only way to grow your savings fast enough to achieve your financial goals is to invest at least a portion of your money in the stock market. The following steps can help you launch a simple investment program that doesn't require tons of time, research, and money, and won't cause you to lose sleep at night:

1. **Understand the most important fact about investing**: The biggest threat to your long-term financial health is inflation, not losing money. Even at recent low rates, inflation will cut your purchasing power by one-third to one-half in just twenty years.

2. **Understand the second most important fact about investing: Only by investing in stocks do you have a prayer of growing your money faster than inflation over time.** Over the past seventy-five years, stocks have been the only investment to earn significantly more than inflation. All other investments—including so-called safe financial products, like bank CDs and money market accounts—have barely kept pace.

3. **Push yourself to get past your anxiety about investing and *just do it*.** Only firsthand knowledge will show you that you really have nothing to be concerned about. Start with a relatively small amount that you'll barely miss, so you won't constantly worry about losing your money, then keep adding to your stake as your confidence about investing grows.

4. **Always spread your money among several different kinds of investments.** Put some into stocks (preferably a mix of big and small companies and even some foreign funds), bonds, and cash investments, such as money market mutual funds. That way, if and when one of your investments stumbles temporarily, one or more of your other investments will likely be doing just fine and can cushion the fall.

5. **Match your investments to how soon you'll need to tap these accounts.** Any money that you'll need within a year or so should be 100 percent in cash investments. For goals that are three to ten years away, a mix of cash, bonds, and stocks works well; the closer you are to the goal, the greater the proportion that you should put in cash and bonds. For goals that are ten years or more away, put as much money into stocks as your stomach and nerves can stand.

6. **Always, always, always reinvest your dividends!**

7. **Stick with it.** Waiting for the perfect time to buy or sell is a fool's game. No one can do it right in the long run—not the pros on Wall Street and certainly not the average Jane or Joe.

8. **When the market dips temporarily, as it inevitably will, turn to more seasoned investor friends and advisers for comfort.** Then sit tight and wait for the bad times to pass, as they virtually always do. Selling after prices have already dropped only turns a loss on paper into a real loss.

9. **Remember my motto and repeat to yourself as many times as you need to hear it: Patience makes profits!**

Step 13:

Keep It Simple

Now you're ready to put the investment concepts you've just learned into action.

I promised you it would be simple, and now I'm going to make good on that promise by telling you about a single investment that can do it all for you, if a single investment is all you're inclined to make. That's right, with just one smart investment you can assemble a well-diversified portfolio of stocks that has consistently outperformed three-quarters of professionally managed funds over the past thirty-five years or so. And you can make this investment for as little as $1,000—even less if you invest through an individual retirement account (IRA) or an automatic-investment program.

The investment is called an index fund (don't worry, I'll explain exactly what it is in a little bit), and it ought to be the basic building block of every smart woman's portfolio. Just look at the facts: An investor who put $10,000 into a typical professionally managed diversified U.S. stock fund ten years ago would have had an investment worth $45,190 by mid 1998 compared with $17,041 if she'd just kept her money in CDs, according to Morningstar, Inc., a Chicago research firm that monitors fund performance. That's good, but still nearly 15 percent less that she would have earned by simply buying shares in the granddaddy of all index funds, an investment called the Vanguard

Index 500, which would have would be worth $51,639. And the more recent record of big-company index funds is even better. Over the past three years the indexers have beaten the average U.S. stock fund by about six percentage points (rising an average 31 percent a year versus 25 percent) and by nine percentage points in 1997 alone (33.4 percent versus 24.5 percent).

Now, that's my kind of investment. And I'm betting it's your kind of investment, too.

FOLLOW THE CROWD

But let's backtrack for just a minute to talk about exactly what an index fund is. An index fund is a type of *mutual fund*, which to my way of thinking is one of the best investment vehicles ever created. When you buy shares in a mutual fund, you are pooling your money with thousands of other investors to buy securities—stocks, bonds, cash investments, or a combination of all three. A professional money manager picks the specific investments for the fund and then oversees them; with so much money at his or her disposal, the manager is able to build a portfolio with dozens, often even hundreds, of different securities. The upshot is that you get a professionally managed, well-diversified portfolio for a fraction of the price you'd pay to assemble it on your own and then hire a pro to watch over it for you.

Sounds like a pretty great deal, right?

And it is. In fact, mutual funds are such a terrific way to invest that it seems like just about every Tom, Dick, and Harriet with a few hundred dollars to spare is investing that way, too. Over the past ten years the number of mutual fund investors and the amount of money they've poured into these portfolios have exploded beyond anyone in the investment world's wildest imagination, so that mutual funds now collectively hold a stunning $4.5 trillion—yes, that's *$4.5 trillion*—of investors' money.

And as investors' appetite for funds has increased, so has the number and types of funds on the menu. There are now over 6,800 funds, almost triple the number available a decade ago, in every flavor imaginable. In addition to plain-vanilla stock and bond funds, there are funds specializing in big companies, medium-sized companies, and small firms; U.S. stocks and foreign securities; particular industries like high technology or energy or health care; socially responsible investments (including one fund that only buys companies with a good record of hiring and promoting women); long-, intermediate, and short-term bonds; U.S. bonds and foreign bonds; corporate bonds as well as government issues; gold and other precious metals and . . . well, you get the idea.

And therein lies the rub: With so many mutual funds now on the market—there are almost as many mutual funds out there as individual companies to invest in—how in your hurried, harried life can you possibly find the time to do the research necessary to pick the ones that are right for you?

There's another sticking point as well: Although I daresay most individual investors will do better by investing in mutual funds than they could by picking individual stocks themselves, the funds themselves rarely manage to do as well as the general market. Over the past five years, for instance, the stock market has earned an average 20 percent a year, while the average stock fund has gained 17 percent. Sure, there are individual funds that have managed to beat those averages handily. But the list of those winners is constantly changing. For instance, if you look at a list of the top ten mutual funds over the past one year, three years, five years, and ten years, none of the names remain the same.

Enter index funds, which are about as no-fuss, no-muss, no-bother an investment as you're ever likely to meet. An *index*, by the way, is simply a way to measure the ups and downs of a particular type of investment. The most famous index is probably the **Dow Jones Industrial Average**, more popularly known as the **Dow**, which measures the stock performance of 30 of the biggest companies in the United States, outfits like IBM, McDonald's, and General Motors. The index most closely watched by knowledgeable investors, however, is called the **Standard and Poor's 500-stock index**, usually just referred to as the **S&P 500**. It tracks the performance of 500 leading companies, and when people talk about how "the market" is doing or how the average stock has performed, they're usually quoting statistics about the S&P 500. There are also indexes that track small stocks, foreign stocks, bonds, and just about any other kind of investment you can think of.

Now, here's the really important part about index funds: Unlike most other mutual funds, **index funds** don't try to do better than the stock market averages. The manager of an index fund just buys all the stocks of a particular index, or a representative sample of them, so that the fund's performance mimics the performance of that index as closely as possible. Since over time the market as a whole (rather than any one particular stock or fund) has proven to be the best investment of all, investing primarily through index funds should prove to be the winning-est strategy of all.

It's also the easiest since you don't have to do a lot of research to pick the best index fund—they're all pretty much alike in terms of the investments in their portfolio. You simply pick the index you want to follow—or better yet, several of them—and you're mostly there.

DEVELOP YOUR GAME PLAN

Enough groundwork. Get ready for Georgette's Basic Investment Plan I—the only investment plan you'll really ever need.

Remember the first rule of investing from the last chapter—the don't-put-all-your-eggs-one-basket rule? Practically speaking, you'll recall, that means you want to spread your money between stocks, bonds, and cash, with most of the savings you have earmarked for long-term goals in stocks. Then, if and when you can afford to, you want to further diversify your stock investments by spreading the money you're putting in stocks among big companies, small companies, and foreign firms.

You can easily put together this kind of portfolio using mutual funds—even working entirely through the same company for convenience, if that suits you. Money market mutual funds are the best way to go for your cash investments because they offer the highest yields. Stock and bond index funds can take care of the rest.

I'd start with a big-company index fund as the foundation of this portfolio, one that tracks the S&P 500. If you never made another investment besides this one, you'd do just fine in the long run. Of course, I'm the type that wants to do better than "just fine," so as soon as I could afford to diversify, I'd branch out into small-company stocks, again with an index fund. When I could afford to diversify some more, I'd add a foreign-stock index fund and, finally, a bond index fund. And then I'd stop and have myself a beautifully diversified portfolio that I could stick with for a long, long time to come.

It's that simple.

You can buy index funds directly from the mutual fund companies that sponsor them (Vanguard, Fidelity, and T. Rowe Price are some of the big names in the business) as well as from discount brokers who offer what are known as mutual fund supermarkets—that is, programs that allow you to buy funds from many different companies in a single place (Charles Schwab, Fidelity, Waterhouse Securities, and Jack White are the leaders, each offering hundreds of funds with no commissions and more than 1,000 others at nominal fees). Since the index funds in each category are virtually all alike in terms of the investments they hold, I believe in choosing them based on cost and convenience. Vanguard (800–523–2566; www.vanguard.com), which offers the greatest variety of index funds and has been in the index business the longest, also charges the lowest management fees by a wide margin: only 0.19 percent for its S&P 500 fund, which works out to about $5.70 for each $3,000 you invest. (By comparison, the average stock fund charges about 1.5 percent, or about $45 per $3,000 investment.) But if you can't afford the $3,000 minimum initial investment required for Vanguard's index funds or you prefer the convenience of having many other no-commission funds to choose from, consider buying your index funds from Charles Schwab, which requires only $1,000 to get your foot in its index fund door.

CONSIDER THE NEXT LEAP

While I believe that index funds should be the foundation of your portfolio, as you become more comfortable with mutual funds and the investing process, you may want to try your hand at picking *actively managed funds,* whose managers research specific companies and invest

only in those stocks that they believe have a good shot at outperform-
ing the market averages. This makes sense particularly for money that
you want to put into small-company or foreign stocks, both categories
in which index funds have a fairly short history and have not outperformed actively managed funds by a really wide margin.

If and when that happens, here are some guidelines to help you
make your choices:

- Limit yourself to no-load funds. A load, in mutual fund parlance,
  is simply another term for a commission. When you buy a load
  fund, you pay a commission to the broker or other middleman
  who sells it to you, supposedly in exchange for his help in select-
  ing the fund that's best for you. But these days there are so many
  good free or low-cost ways to get fund recommendations that it
  makes little sense to pay a broker to pick for you. (My "homework" section just below mentions specific places you can look for
  information and advice.) And there's no evidence at all to suggest
  that load funds earn more than the no-load or no-commission
  funds that you can buy yourself directly from the companies that
  sponsor them or from the mutual fund supermarkets run by discount brokers like Schwab, Waterhouse, and Jack White.

  Why pay good money for something you can get for free? No
  smart reason that I can think of.

- **Do your homework.** The business sections of virtually every major
  newspaper in the country periodically run features recommend-
  ing mutual funds for just about every taste and temperament, as
  do personal-finance magazines like *Money, Smart Money*, and
  Kiplinger's Personal Finance, and general-interest business magazines like *BusinessWeek* and *Forbes*. You can also get free educational material about funds and low-cost fund directories from
  groups like the **American Association of Individual Investors**
  (their directory, called *Individual Investor's Guide to Low-Load
  Mutual Funds*, costs $25; their address: 625 North Michigan

Avenue, Suite 1900, Chicago, IL 60611; 312-280–0170; www.aaii.com) and the **Mutual Fund Education Alliance** (their directory, *Investor's Guide to Low-Cost Mutual Funds*, costs $5; their address: 1900 Erie Street, Suite 120, Kansas City, MO 64116; 816–471–1454; www.mfea.com). There's also a wealth of free fund information available on the Internet. Two of the best sites, run by **Quicken** (www.quicken.com) and **Morningstar** (www.morningstar.net) even have screening services that allow you to plug in your investment criteria (for example, the minimum investment needed, the type of fund you're looking for, and the level of performance you want), and then will produce a list of funds that meet your requirements.

To my mind, Morningstar (800–735–0700), a Chicago investment-research firm that specializes in tracking the fund industry, is the single best source of information about mutual funds around, whether you're talking about their print materials, their software, or their website. One of their most popular and useful products, called *Morningstar Mutual Funds*, is a binder filled with comprehensive single-page reports on more than 1,600 stock and bond funds, giving you the lowdown on each fund's prospects in plain English (or, at least, as plain as these things get) so you don't have to be some Wall Street wizard to figure out what they're talking about. Most libraries carry Morningstar in their reference or business sections, or you can get your own three-month trial subscription, updated every two weeks, for $55, or $45 for a version that focuses exclusively on no-load funds. (At more than $400 a year, I don't think a full subscription to either version is worth it for anyone but truly dedicated fund investors who get a real kick out of this stuff. Possibly worth a full subscription if you find yourself really getting into the fund-picking process is the company's newsletter, "Morningstar Investor," which offers useful general articles about picking funds, along with performance and other data on 500 leading funds for $79 a year.) If you're comfortable surfing the Net, though, you don't really have to pay a dime for Morningstar's expertise; just log onto their website, where plenty of useful information is yours for free.

- **Look for a proven track record.** Just because a fund has performed brilliantly in the past is no guarantee that it will be a stand-out in the future. Still, I'd rather place my bet on a proven performer in the hope that it will continue its winning ways than gamble on a dog of an investment in the hope that it will reverse course and have its day in the investment sun.

  Focus your search for winning funds on ones that have been around for at least five years, with the same manager at the helm. (This requirement alone, by the way, will narrow your investment choices by more than 50 percent, because so many new funds have been created over the past few years and so many portfolio managers have switched jobs.) That's a long enough period to see how well the fund has fared in both good and bad markets and to tell if a year or two of sizzling returns turned out to be a flash in the pan. Then among these older funds, favor those that have consistently earned more than the average fund with the same investment mission. (In other words, you want to compare apples to apples, which in the fund world means, big-company funds to big-company funds, foreign funds to foreign funds, and so on.)

  This strategy probably won't lead you to the kind of funds that will produce chart-topping gargantuan gains in a single year. But it may well do you one better by pointing you toward funds that produce consistently superior gains over longer periods.

- **Favor funds that are cheap to own.** All funds impose fees for managing your money. All else being equal, the lower those fees are, the higher your investment returns will be. Here's how it works: The average stock fund nips 1.5 percent a year from your account to cover its expenses (funds specializing in small-company stocks and foreign shares typically cost a bit more), while the average bond fund charges just under 1 percent. That means that if your stock fund earns 10 percent a year and charges standard fees, in reality you earn only 8.5 percent. Find a fund that earns the same returns but charges just 1 percent, and your return jumps to 9 percent, with no additional risk. Sticking with low-fee funds is about the easiest, safest way that I can think of to boost your returns.

By the way, the *expense ratio* is the formal name for the amount that a fund charges in annual fees, and is expressed as a percentage of the amount you've invested. This percentage must be clearly stated in the sales literature that the fund sponsor sends to you (also known as the *prospectus*, which also discloses the fund's investment philosophy, performance history, and other pertinent details to help you evaluate if it's an appropriate investment for you). Expense ratios are also routinely listed in reports by Morningstar and other fund researchers.

- **Opt for an investment style you can live with.** Some funds are Steady Eddies: Year in and year out, they provide solid, if somewhat unspectacular, gains. Others give you a roller-coaster ride: thrilling ascents, occasionally interrupted by stomach-jolting declines. Neither style is inherently better or worse than the other. The trick is to find a level of risk and volatility that you feel comfortable with, so you won't toss and turn at night worrying about just how much money you're losing (even if you understand intellectually that those declines are probably temporary) or be tempted to bail out of the fund and turn those paper losses into real ones. After all, the point of investing in funds is to make yourself some serious money, not to lose a bundle or turn yourself into a nervous wreck on the way to wealth.

To find your fund comfort level, take these steps:

- Ask yourself how big a loss you could live with before you'd be seriously tempted to sell. Would you stick with a promising fund if it fell 5 percent in value? What if the fund dropped 10 percent? How about 20 percent?

- Once you've determined your "panic number," look over the fund's year-to-year performance record in Morningstar to see if the fund has ever come close to hitting it. If so, steer clear.

- If you know you're a nervous Nellie, also check to see how dramatically the fund's returns change from year to year and how well the fund held up during recent downturns in the market (specifically, that means checking the fund's performance in 1987, 1990, and 1994, when the average fund lost 1.2 percent, 6.0 percent, and 1.3 percent, respectively). If your candidate swings wildly from year to year, or fell much more than the averages when the market slid, it's probably not the right fund for you.

- **Keep tabs on your fund.** Sure, you should buy a fund with the intention of sticking with it for the long term. That doesn't mean, though, that you should never consider selling—particularly if the circumstances that led you to buy the fund in the first place change. If a manager with a winning track record leaves, for instance, you might consider heading for the exits as well. Or if the fund's performance lags behind the average fund in its category for a protracted period—say, a couple of years or more—that also may be a sign that it's time to say good-bye.

GO FOR THE GUSTO

You don't *need* to invest in anything other than mutual funds to have a winning portfolio. But there may come a time when you *want* to.

Buying individual stocks is the logical next step.

Buying shares of individual companies has one basic advantage over investing exclusively in mutual funds: The chance to make some really

Big Money, to hit upon a stock (or two or three) that delivers a 30 or 40 or 50 percent gain or more in a single year, perhaps even doubling or tripling the cash you put into it in a year or two. When you invest in a mutual fund, your money is spread among so many different stocks that even if one or more of them hits it big, the effect is diluted by the far lower returns on the many other investments in the portfolio.

Of course, the main disadvantage of buying individual stocks is the flip side of this happy scenario. What if the stock you pick turns out to be a clunker? That happens sometimes, even if you've done your homework on the business, because you can't possibly predict every turn of events in a company's fortunes or other investors' reactions to those events. Maybe an upstart competitor will come out with a hot new product that destroys your company's market share; maybe the CEO turns out to be a crook—sometimes it's just impossible to know in advance. If your stock does prove to be a dud (or worse), you stand to lose a bundle—at least as much as you stood to gain—and unlike investing through a mutual fund, you won't have a big bunch of other stocks in your portfolio to cushion the fall.

Make no mistake: No matter how seductive the potential gains are, investing in individual stocks is a riskier business than investing through mutual funds. Consider doing it only *after* you've created a solid investment base with mutual funds *and* if you have the temperament to stand sometimes dramatic price swings without selling in a panic or developing an ulcer. What also helps is having saved enough money to buy at least a few different stocks so that you don't have *everything* riding on a single pick.

If this describes you, get ready for Georgette's Basic Investment Plan II.

USE YOUR INSIDER'S EDGE

The strategy behind my system for picking individual stocks couldn't be simpler: Invest in what you know. In the course of your everyday life, just take note of any particularly impressive products that you come across or much needed services delivered with unusual skill.

Then follow up your hunches with some basic research to see if the company behind those products and services is publicly traded and has true investment potential.

If you work for a computer software company, for instance, you may be among the first to hear about a rival firm's exciting new CD-ROM that seems destined for mega-sales. If you're in the health-care field, you may learn early on about a new drug that could help significantly in the treatment of some common illness. If your child is constantly begging for a particular toy, and so are all his friends, perhaps the manufacturer is worth a look. Or maybe you've noticed that everyone you know suddenly seems to be shopping at a particular store or sipping a particular drink or wearing a particular line of clothing. Any or every one of these situations may yield a stock that eventually tops the charts.

Investing in companies whose products and services personally have impressed me is how I've found many of my biggest stock-market winners. I'm by no means alone. Anne Scheiber, the millionaire IRS auditor whom I told you about in the last chapter, used this strategy, too, and so does legendary investor Peter Lynch, who guided the popular Fidelity Magellan mutual fund to a record-setting 31 percent average annual return during his thirteen-year tenure as manager in the 1970s and 1980s.

Lynch rarely invested in the high-tech stocks that were the darlings of that period (he claimed he didn't understand them), but instead filled his portfolio with familiar consumer-oriented companies whose products he'd come across and enjoyed in his own life. Among his greatest hits: Hanes (his wife liked the convenience of buying the company's L'eggs panty hose in the supermarket), which increased six-fold (600 percent) before the company was bought by Sara Lee; Dunkin' Donuts (its shops were always crowded and the coffee tasted great), which increased more than ten-fold during the time he owned it; and La Quinta Motor Inns (he liked the fact that they offered Holiday Inn–quality rooms at 30 percent less than Holiday Inn prices), which increased eleven-fold over the ten-year period that he owned it before suffering a downturn. Toys R Us, Wal-Mart, Subaru, Stop & Shop, and

McDonald's were all in his portfolio at one time or another, and all of them were what Lynch refers to as "tenbaggers"—that is, stocks that appreciate 1,000 percent or more.

But you don't have to be a Wall Street pro like Lynch to make extraordinary profits this way, as Anne Scheiber proved. Indeed, Lynch himself, in his 1989 book *One Up on Wall Street*, contended that the average person comes across potential tenbaggers at least two or three times a year. All you have to do, he noted, is look close to home—if not in the backyard, he said, then at your place of work or down at the shopping mall.

In fact, I confess to cruising the malls regularly for investment ideas. Sometimes my sister Lyn and I will just sit in the food court of whatever mall we happen to be shopping in and observe what kind of shopping bags the passersby are carrying. That's what first tipped me off to the fabulous investment potential of the Gap, the $5 billion retail chain whose casual clothes for men, women, and kids have become a staple in so many wardrobes over the past few years. Every time I'd go to a mall, every person I saw seemed to be carrying a Gap bag. I'd never shopped there myself, so I decided to check the store out. The place was packed, and I could see the appeal right away—well-made, comfortable, reasonably priced casual clothing that I would definitely wear myself and could see just about everybody else I knew wearing as well. The stock has gained more than 50 percent a year over the past three years (77 percent in 1997 alone), more than tripling in price over that period.

Then there was Bombay Company. Around the time that I bought this stock, I was moving to new offices and needed to furnish them. But I didn't want to spend a lot; I preferred to put my money into the business itself. So I shopped around and, while at the mall again one day, wandered into Bombay, which had traditional-looking furniture at considerably lower prices than the average furniture dealer. I did my entire office with furniture from Bombay, and when I was done buying the desk and the lamps and the chairs, I decided to buy the stock, too. The price shot up from $13 a share when I bought the stock in mid–1993 to $32 a share by mid–1994 when I sold it—a 146 percent gain in just over a year.

Of course, the business you really know best is your own. If you work for a publicly traded company and you think the management is fabulous and the product or service you put out is terrific, buying shares in your own firm may be a terrific way to dip your toe in investment waters. That's particularly true if your employer is among the thousands that offer a *stock-purchase program*, which allows employees to buy shares at a more advantageous price than those shares sell for on the open market.

DO YOUR HOMEWORK

Mind you, I'm not suggesting that you just run out and buy shares in any company whose products you love. Use your knowledge to tip you off to good investment ideas. Then do some research to find out if that company really is a good investment.

In this sense, shopping for stocks is just like shopping for any other item, from clothes to appliances. The cardinal rule: Be an educated consumer. Always understand what you're buying. Know the facts about the company before you shell out a dime.

Fortunately, just as with mutual funds, there is a wealth of solid, easy-to-access information out there for stock pickers, whether you're a novice or an experienced investor. For an overview of any company that you're considering as an investment, you can consult the *Value Line Investment Survey*, which contains one-page data-packed profiles on more than 1,700 companies. (You'll find *Value Line* in most libraries, or if you find yourself really getting into the stock-picking spirit, you can get a ten-week trial subscription for $55. Phone: 800–577–4566.) If you're working with a broker, ask for any research the firm has on the stock—even many discount brokers these days make stock research available to their clients, either free or at a fairly nominal cost. Then go on-line to check out the company further. (If you're going to invest in individual stocks, you really *have* to bite the bullet and learn how to navigate the Internet!) One of the first sites I visit for the lowdown on individual companies is Hoover's Online (www.hoovers.com), which has company profiles; balance-sheet data, such as sales and profit figures; news about competitors, and the general outlook for the industry. Hoover's also provides lots of links to other websites with useful information, such as research reports, recent news stories in which the company was mentioned, and earnings estimates from Wall Street analysts. You can also get information on individual stocks at Morningstar's website (www.morningstar.net), organized much the same way they put together data on mutual funds.

....

Shopping for stocks is just like
shopping for any other item.
The cardinal rule:
Be an educated consumer.

....

Whatever sources of information you choose to tap, here are the basic facts and figures to focus on:

- **Product mix.** Find out if the product or service that has caught your attention contributes to the bulk of the company's sales. If not, find out if the firm's other products look like winners as well. After all, XYZ Company can make the best widget in the world, but if the widget operation is the smallest of XYZ's fifty divisions, it probably won't have a great impact on the company's fortunes. On the other hand, if XYZ's three largest divisions also make superior products, the stock may be still a good buy, with widgets simply the icing on the investment cake.

- **Earnings prospects.** Check out whether Wall Street analysts expect the company's sales and profits to grow at a strong pace over the next several years. Projections of at least 10 to 15 percent annual increases are a good sign.

- **Management prowess.** To me, management is everything. You can make the best product in the world, offer the best service, and own the most up-to-date factories and equipment, but if you don't have the people in place who can build the business and make things happen, the company won't go anywhere—and neither will your investment. Read all you can about your company's CEO, president, and other key officers, learn as much as possible about their vision and strategy for the business, and see if your head and your instincts tell you that they have what it takes for success.

- **Insider trading.** I always check out insider buying and selling patterns before I invest—that is, whether the top officers of the company are buying or selling shares of the firm's stock. When a company's management puts its own money on the line, they're indicating that they have a lot of confidence in the business and its prospects. That's a very good sign because they're the ones who know the company best, and they're the ones who have to make it happen.

Conversely, if I discover that insiders are selling big blocks of stock, I want to know why: Have they lost confidence in the business? Are sales and earnings going to be worse than anticipated? Do they know of some new competitive threat that the general public hasn't learned about yet? Until I find out the reason behind the sales and am satisfied that the answer doesn't reflect real problems at the company, I won't buy the stock.

Information about insider trading patterns is not as readily accessible as other facts about individual companies. Although corporate officers are required by law to disclose their trades, not many investment-research groups track the patterns. Two websites that I've found particularly helpful in this regard are www.cda.com and www.insidertrading.com, both of which specialize in following and interpreting insider transactions.

- **Industry domination.** I prefer to invest in companies that dominate their field, particularly if that field is small. If all the competition in a particular business is between two companies and you own shares in both companies, it's pretty hard to go wrong. Take the auction business. Basically there are only two companies in the auction business, Sotheby's and Christie's, which between them completely dominate the market. I own both, and that's a pretty safe bet. In fact, Sotheby's stock has gained 24 percent a year over the past three years, while Christie's is up 32 percent in the eighteen months that I've owned it.

- **The stock price.** Sometimes, no matter how fabulous the prospects are for a particular company, the price of its stock is simply too high to pay. A stock that is selling at or near its all-time high, for example, makes me nervous; I figure it may not have much further to rise—at least in the near term. Just as I would with an expensive dress that I'd like to own, I prefer to wait for a sale before I buy—that is, to hold off investing in the stock until its price drops (as will happen to any stock from time to time, no matter how stellar its long-term prospects are) and use that (hopefully) temporary dip as an opportunity to pick up some shares at bargain prices.

Among seasoned investors, the most popular way to evaluate if a stock price is reasonable is to check out its *price-to-earnings ratio*, called *P/E* for short (pronounced just by the letters, Pee-Ee). Now, don't get intimated by the jargon. A P/E is nothing more than a number, figured by dividing the price of a stock by its earnings per share, that's used to determine how cheap or expensive a stock is. The higher a stock's P/E, the more you are paying for its earnings and the more expensive that stock is considered to be. You'll find P/Es listed, along with share prices, in the stock tables that run in the business sections of daily newspapers, as well as in research reports, which often help you evaluate whether a particular stock's P/E seems high or not, given its recent earnings and long-term prospects. One common way to judge is to compare the stock's P/E to its projected growth rate over the next several years. A stock with a P/E lower than its growth rate is considered cheap; conversely, a stock with a P/E higher than its projected growth rate may be on the expensive side.

I know this probably all sounds terribly complicated if you're new to investing, but believe me, it gets a lot easier with a little bit of time and experience. And remember, you don't *have* to delve into individual stocks at all, unless the spirit moves you to do so. If you don't get a kick out of picking stocks, stick with mutual funds, and you'll do just fine.

KNOW WHEN TO FOLD

Poker players have a saying: You have to know when to hold and when to fold. The same is true of investing in individual stocks.

If your stock's performance trails that of similar companies for six months to a year or longer—that is, if the shares lose more money than the average stock during a market downturn or don't make as much money as the average stock when prices overall are rising—it's probably time to reevaluate the investment. Do some additional research to see if the problems besetting the company are temporary or if there's been a fundamental change in the circumstances that led you to like the company in the first place. (Use the same techniques and sources you used for picking the stock in the first place, as I outlined in the preceding section.) If it looks like it's a short-term glitch in a happily-ever-after story, hang on and wait for the good times to roll again. If there's been a more permanent change, get out immediately. If you're not sure either way, consider selling a portion of your shares—say, 50 percent. That way you won't lose everything if the stock continues to fall, and you still have a shot at a comeback if there's life in the old investment yet.

There also will come a time to pack it in simply because you've already made so much money on a stock. Why risk losing a piece of that spectacular gain? A perfect example for me was a company that you may be familiar with, called General Nutrition Company, a retail vitamin and health-food chain better known by its initials, GNC. I'd first taken an interest in the store when I was shopping with a friend who stopped in at GNC to buy some vitamins. I thought the idea of a one-stop shopping center for all your vitamin and nutritional needs was smart. So I followed up, did some research, and bought the stock. In one year I made 70 percent on my investment. At the end of the year I said to myself, I don't need to make any more than 70 percent, so I sold my shares—even though my broker was convinced the stock would continue to rise and advised me to hold on. But I was happy with my 70 percent, so I sold anyway. The company subsequently had some problems with inventory control, and while the stock didn't crash, it certainly gave back a lot of its gains.

Greediness will get you every time.

Of course, sometimes it's not greediness but rather emotion that makes us hold on to a stock that's already delivered substantial gains. We form an attachment to a company that's been so good to us by making so much money—and the attachment is all the greater if we genuinely like and use its products and services in our personal lives. An investment adviser I know suggests breaking this emotional attachment by changing the way you think about your investments. "I always tell my clients that if they treat a stock like a friend, they'll end up in trouble," he says. His advice? "Treat an investment like a disposable razor: Use it until it's served its purpose, then get rid of it."

To help me keep this perspective, I calculate a mental price at which I will sell my shares when I first buy a stock. I have in mind a gain that would satisfy me and a loss that would really bother me. I write both numbers down in a ledger, where I also record the name of the investment, the price at which I bought it, the date of the transaction, and the number of shares involved. Then I periodically check those target prices. Unless circumstances have changed in a dramatic enough way to make me recalculate them, I sell my shares when the stock price hits the target, in either direction.

Never sweat getting out with a profit—even if the stock continues to rise after you sell. That to me is the definition of a real loser: Someone who wins, but is unhappy because she didn't win bigger. That attitude will not only get you into trouble—your stock is as likely to go down after you've reached your target price as it is to go up—but it also makes life miserable. Don't let yourself be consumed by "if only . . ." If you've made a profit, you're already a winner; just enjoy it.

....

The definition of a real loser: Someone who wins, but is unhappy because she didn't win bigger

....

RELISH THE PAYOFF

Making money in the stock market really *is* an enjoyable experience. And that's the great surprise about investing for most women after they've been at it awhile: It's fun.

Yes, I know that may seem impossible to believe now, if you're among those who haven't yet jumped on the bandwagon. But it's true. Once you see that it's fairly easy after you get going, once you understand that *you really can do this*, once you start to see that you're really making money—serious money—it's empowering. You will like it.

Successes, in investing as in the rest of life, hurl you forward. But you can't have those successes unless you take the first step.

Go for it.

ACTION PLAN
To put together a well-diversified investment portfolio that doesn't require a lot of money and effort, follow these steps:

1. **Stick with mutual funds for the lion's share of your investment dollars.** For a relatively small amount of money, you'll get instant diversification among scores of securities and professional money management. All in all, a great deal!

2. **Make index funds the basic building block of your portfolio.** Start with a fund that tracks the performance of big, leading U.S. companies, known as an S&P 500 fund. Then, as your investment stake grows, add funds that follow the performance of small U.S. companies, foreign firms and, finally, bonds.

3. **As you get more comfortable with the investment process, consider adding an actively managed mutual fund or two, particularly for the money you're allocating to small-company and foreign stocks.** Favor no-commission funds (known as *no-loads*) with a proven success record, low expenses, and the same manager at the helm for the past three to five years.

4. **If you find that you really enjoy investing and are eager to make even more money, consider investing in individual stocks as well.** In picking stocks, follow one simple rule: Invest in what you know. In other words, stick with companies that provide products and services that you're familiar with and really understand. That's the only way you can make a reasoned and reasonable judgment about the company's long-term investment potential.

5. **Do your homework.** If you're investing in mutual funds, read newspaper and magazine articles about promising candidates and consult Morningstar and other good sources of fund info. If you're investing in individual stocks, learn everything you can about the company and its management.

6. **Never marry an investment.** If the positive circumstances that led you to buy the stock in the first place change, be prepared to sell.

7. **Don't be greedy.** If you've already made as much money on an investment as you anticipated—or more, much more—think about selling at least a portion of your shares. Why risk losing a portion of that spectacular gain?

8. **Enjoy the power that learning how to invest bestows on you.** Check your account balances periodically and relish the payoff!

Step 14:
Maximize Your Earning Power

*W*hen you come right down to it, there are only two ways to get more money: Spend less or earn more. Given a choice, I'll always opt to earn more. Maybe it has to do with the relative poverty that marked my childhood, maybe it's just my personality, but the very idea of seriously cutting back smacks of deprivation and stagnation to me. I'd much rather move forward, achieve more, grow—myself and my money.

Now, there's no getting around the fact that women face some pretty serious obstacles on the road to higher earnings. Despite tremendous progress in the fight for equal pay in recent years, the average woman still earns only 76 cents for every dollar that a man brings home. And the older the average woman gets and the further she advances in her career, the wider that gender gap typically gets. Small wonder then that, according to a 1996 survey in *Money* magazine, four out of every five women believe they aren't earning what they're worth.

As important as it is for all of us to collectively fight the injustices that still face working women, I strongly believe that the greatest progress in the workplace today is made on an individual basis. No employer in today's tight labor market can afford to lose hardworking, talented people to a higher-paying company. Real progress is made by doing the job, doing it well, and taking appropriate steps to ensure what's rightfully ours. Progress is made by projecting the confidence that we can do the job every bit as well as our male colleagues. Women have paid lip service to the idea that we are just as capable as men, but only recently have we begun to project a real sense of inner security about that fact. When you know inside yourself that you're really good at what you do, you reflect it. And that confident attitude, that pay-me-because-I'm-good-or-someone-else-will air about you, will do more toward ensuring you're paid fairly than rabble-rousing ever will.

··

Women have paid lip service to the idea that we are just as capable as men, but only recently have we begun to project a real sense of inner security about that fact

··

Ultimately employers will have to pay us what we're worth because they won't get the work out of us that they need otherwise. Progress will be made by the sheer reality of the fact that there are so many more women in the workforce now and we're better educated, better trained, and more experienced than at any time in history.

In this sense, the times really *are* on our side—if only we know how to seize the opportunities and make the most of them.

GET A FRESH START

The surest, fastest way to earn more money is to land a new, higher-paying job. Once you're on the payroll, it's a lot harder to raise your salary substantially because employers base annual raises on your current wages. If you think your pay is low now, chances are you won't be happy with your raise, either. Judging by the past several years, the average employee can expect to get a raise equal to about four percent of her base pay. That's not much more than annual increases in the cost of living, so you probably won't feel like you're really putting more money into your pocket. When you're negotiating salary for a new job, however, you start with a clean slate—any amount, within reason, goes.

Moving from job to higher-paying job to highest-paying job is how twenty-four-year-old Sally Black, a public relations executive in New York City, managed to more than double her salary in just three years. After graduating from college in 1994 with a degree in communications, Sally started out modestly enough, working for a small PR firm in Boston, earning $24,000 a year. Eager to learn the trade, she worked long hours, including many nights and weekends, with duties ranging from high-level account work to grabbing sandwiches for the staff. As she puts it, "Basically I just did anything anyone wanted me to do."

A year later Sally was due for a promotion and a raise. Given her starting salary, she knew the most she could expect was an additional $4,000 a year. When a friend landed a job paying $38,000 a year with another PR firm, Sally (at the friend's suggestion) lined up an interview at that company for herself as well. She got the job, asked for the same salary as her friend, and got that, too—an increase that was more than three times the maximum raise she'd anticipated from her old firm. The result was a salary over 50 percent higher than what she'd been earning before. Just as important in Sally's view, the new job came with more responsibility and shorter hours at a company with a better future.

As it turned out, Sally loved her new position and, within a year, found herself on the verge of another promotion. Around that time, though, her fiancé moved to New York City to go to business school, and Sally decided to move with him. To find work, she asked everyone she knew if they knew of any interesting opportunities for her in New York. She also asked colleagues whom she respected to give her an honest assessment of her value in the job market, so she'd know how much money she could reasonably ask for. Their advice? Shoot high, and request a starting salary of $60,000 a year. Acting on their suggestions, Sally landed eight interviews in rapid succession after arriving in New York and ended up with four job offers, all in a salary range of $57,000 to $60,000. She ultimately accepted a position for $58,000—not the highest offer she received but the job she considered the best fit in terms of corporate culture and career opportunities. And, of course, considering the salary was 240 percent higher than what she'd been earning just three years before, the pay wasn't too shabby, either.

KNOW THE DRILL

Sally's story is almost a textbook study of smart ways to maximize your earnings. Here's my take on what she did right—and how you can do it, too:

- **Know what you're worth.** Before you walk in the door for your first interview, do some research to get a good sense of the salary you can command in the current job market. Most people focus on what they want in terms of pay rather than what they can get. But the number you think you need to live on may be much too high or too low compared to what the market is paying for your skills and experience. Deal with the reality of the situation, not false hopes or expectations.

  Like Sally, talk to friends and colleagues in comparable positions to find out how much they earn. If you're close to anyone in a supervisory position, ask for their honest assessment of how much your skills are worth in the workplace. Sally also consulted executive recruiters, commonly known as headhunters, who really have the lowdown on what various jobs pay and can help you with other aspects of your job search as well. And don't forget more traditional sources of information, either, like salary surveys in trade journals as well as the classifieds.

- **Network, network, network.** Like Sally, the vast majority of people find their jobs through someone they know—or someone who knows someone whom they know.

  Cast as wide a net as possible, and be forthright about what you need. I can't begin to count the number of times I've called a friend or colleague and said directly, "Do you know so-and-so and can you make an introduction for me?" or "Can I use your name to get my foot in the door at ABC Company?" If I were job hunting, I'd also make a point of attending professional meetings and trade shows as well as local get-togethers sponsored by my college alumni association. Once there I'd make a point of chatting with anyone who might be in a position to help, whether I knew them or not. And I'd do the same at social functions—you never know where a lead will turn up.

  Try not to let fear—of rejection, humiliation, or any other negative reaction—keep you silent. I, for one, am not afraid to go up to someone I don't know well and make my pitch, and this is why: Sometimes the person may look at me like I'm crazy, but the look doesn't kill me. It may make me uncomfortable for a second, but even if it does, I'm not paralyzed for life, I'm only paralyzed for a second. Sure, I may feel foolish, but I've felt foolish before and lived to tell the tale. It's not fatal. You get past the moment and move on. And maybe, just maybe, the payoff for that fleeting feeling of embarrassment will be an opportunity that transforms my life. That's a risk worth taking.

- **Sell yourself.** "There's nothing wrong with being bold about what you bring to the table," says Sally, who came to each of her interviews prepared to discuss specific ways in which she had contributed to the success of key accounts at her previous jobs. In fact, it's always a good idea to first give prospective employers a good sense of the kind of job you can do and the skills you bring to the job, so they really want to hire you before the subject of compensation ever comes up.

Before going on any interviews, make a list of your skills and accomplishments, and jot down a few examples that illustrate these strengths, so they'll readily trip off your tongue. Don't limit yourself to on-the-job achievements. If you've been a full-time homemaker for the past few years, for instance, and you chaired several successful fund-raising drives for the PTA, use this achievement to demonstrate your marketing and communications skills. Also think about how some of your skills might be adapted to different needs. Sally, for example, convinced her new employer that the experience she'd gained doing public relations for technology firms in her previous jobs would be ideal for her new job, which involved refurbishing clients' images following a corporate crisis.

In preparing, also make sure to learn as much as you can about the companies you're going to interview with. Know the history of the company and their business goals, then think hard about how you can enhance what they do. Employers like people who do their homework and who have taken the time to think about where they fit into the organization. And rightfully so.

- **Think in terms of the total package.** Salary is only one part of your compensation. Some jobs may give you the opportunity to earn more through bonuses or overtime. Some jobs offer sterling benefits that would cost thousands of dollars to buy on your own. Some jobs may offer a degree of flexibility in your work schedule that's worth a lot to you. You need to calculate it all.

Sally, for instance, chose the job that she believed offered the best package, although the salary was $2,000 less than her highest offer. In particular, she believed that the company she chose offered the best opportunities to learn and advance, which in turn held out the promise of even more money down the road.

- **Make it a win-win.** I don't believe in playing games when discussing your salary requirements. Specifically, I don't believe in naming a figure much higher than what you want just to give yourself bargaining room. Negotiating salary isn't the same as going to a flea market, where haggling is the norm. Go in asking for what you really want and feel you're worth in the marketplace.

That's not to say you shouldn't be prepared for some give-and-take. Always have a range in mind that you would be satisfied with. Think about what you'd be willing to give up without feeling that you're being taken advantage of—that's not a good attitude with which to start a new job—and what other kinds of compensation you could ask for to keep you satisfied. To help offset what she was giving up in cold cash, for instance, Sally negotiated more generous vacation time, adding three days' paid vacation to the standard two weeks that her new employer offered. Some of the other things you might ask for include: an accelerated salary review (for instance, in six months instead of the usual one year), a signing bonus, an annual bonus or other cash compensation tied to your ability to achieve specific goals, or a more flexible work schedule.

Be prepared to make some concessions so you appear to be flexible, too. Ideally both parties in a negotiation should come away from the table feeling that they have won. After all, you want to start off your working relationship on a good note—and they should, too.

HEAD FOR HIGHER GROUND

Of course, you can't spend your career job-hopping forever. At some point you'll want to settle down with a single employer, partly for your own sense of comfort and security and, more pragmatically, to accrue the retirement benefits you'll need to live on once you quit the workforce for good. At most companies, you must be on the payroll for five years to qualify for full retirement benefits (for example, a pension or the company's contributions to a 401(k) plan), a process known as *vesting*. Yet the average woman leaves after 4.8 years—just a few months shy of that magic date.

How do you keep your salary climbing once you've found the company you want to stick with? In this era of skimpy raises, the key is to get yourself promoted to a higher-paying position or to negotiate incentive pay or—if you're really smart—both.

Easier said than done, I know, particularly for women. In fact, one key reason that women end up making so much less money than men over the course of their careers is not that they're paid less for comparable work but rather that they are not promoted as often into the high-profile positions that pay the most. Now, don't shoot me for saying this, but sometimes the fault is ours. We assume that our boss knows that we want that position, that we're fully qualified to do it, and that we'll work hard once we get it. We assume that rewards naturally follow hard work. We assume that if we're skilled enough and experienced enough and patient enough, we'll get what we deserve.

Lesson Number One: *DON'T ASSUME ANYTHING!*

The biggest mistake women make is expecting other people to read our minds. Too often we keep our expectations a secret, believing that the outcome we're looking for will just naturally evolve. We expect people to know what we want. Well, you know what? They don't. It's up to you to communicate what you're trying to accomplish, to make clear that you want to move to the next level and that you expect the position to be yours when the time is right. You have to be aware of what that next position is, when it's going to open up and to actively campaign for it.

Lesson Number Two: *IF YOU DON'T ASK, YOU DON'T GET.*

Start by stating your goal explicitly at your next performance evaluation, then ask for a frank assessment of your chances and what you have to do to make it happen. Don't let the fear of being turned down, of being told you're simply not good enough, stop you. Chances are, your boss will be happy to hear that you're ambitious and eager to get ahead, and will be willing to offer guidance. Even if not, though, you're better off getting a clear picture of where you stand and how you're viewed so you can take steps to get your career back on track or, if need be, move to a different company where your prospects will be better.

The next step is to follow through—that is, to perform so brilliantly that your boss would be a fool not to give the next promotion to you. Indeed, when Catalyst, a New York career research and consulting firm, asked female executives to name the key strategies that had enabled them to advance in the workplace, virtually all of them named the ability to consistently exceed performance expectations as a critical (77 percent) or fairly important (22 percent) factor in their success.

Here are some other ways you can show your boss what you're really capable of, get a leg up on the competition and, ultimately, put more dough in your pocket:

- **Volunteer for high-profile assignments.** Seek out important or difficult projects that will raise your visibility to key people within your company—that is, as long as you know you can deliver. Some 94 percent of the female executives in the Catalyst survey named this technique as critical (50 percent) or fairly important (44 percent) to their success. After all, they can't promote you if they don't even know who you are.

- **Go beyond the job description.** Stay late, without being asked, if your division is on a tight deadline for a project. Send a memo to your department head outlining your ideas for improving sales or productivity (and if you don't have any ideas, put your thinking cap on). Attend a professional seminar and report back on what you learned. Volunteer to fill in temporarily for a sick colleague.

In short, always do more than is expected of you. Everybody likes a team player who, at least occasionally, puts the company's interests above her own. Especially bosses.

- **Suggest a pay-for-performance plan.** While most employers these days are Scrooges when it comes to raises, many are increasingly willing to part with incentive pay—that is, bonuses, stock options, and other alternative forms of compensation that are linked to achieving specific goals. In the past such incentives were strictly an executive perk. Not anymore. Roughly half of the large companies in a recent survey by Towers Perrin, a New York City benefits consulting firm, granted incentive pay (averaging 7.5 percent of salary) to non-executive employees, up from just 25 percent in the early 1990s, and another 26 percent were considering doing so.

  Employers like incentive pay because there's a payoff in it for them as well the employee—you must contribute something measurable to the company's prospects in order to earn it. So think of some way in which you can make such a contribution, then make your pitch to the boss. Maybe you can devise a strategy to raise revenues in your department by 10 percent, with a 10 percent bonus attached if you reach your target. Maybe you can develop and implement a plan to cut costs by 5 percent, with a 5 percent bonus as your reward.

- **Toot your own horn (softly).** Being good at what you do is often not enough to get ahead. You have to make sure everyone else knows you're good, too. In performance evaluations, don't be afraid to give yourself high marks where you deserve them. Keep a written log of your accomplishments so you can cite specific examples if needed. Keep your supervisor updated on your progress on assignments that are important to the company with written memos and copy *his* boss as well.

A lot of women are uncomfortable with this kind of self-promotion; they regard it, at best, as a crass game that men play. But trust me, false modesty—a more typically female than male trait, I'm sorry to say—won't get you anywhere. There's a world of difference between artful self-promotion and over-the-top testosterone-induced bragging. After all, if you're not in your own corner, how can you expect anyone else to be?

FIGHT THE GOOD FIGHT

Sometimes no matter what you do, how experienced you are, or how impressive your skills may be, you find yourself in a situation where the men you work with are consistently getting better assignments, faster promotions, and more money than you. Let's not be Pollyannas here: Bias against women in the workplace still exists. It's not everywhere, nor is it usually as overt as it was ten or even five years ago, but it's still an obstacle many of us face. The question is, how do you handle it?

This is a tough one. Before you raise the issue at your company, think hard about how important pursuing justice is to you because you run a real risk of being labeled a troublemaker. I'm not suggesting that you avoid raising the subject because of this risk—fear of being branded is what's kept women from demanding what's fair for too long. But if you forge ahead with a complaint, you should do it with your eyes wide open.

Understand that there are only two possible outcomes: Either your superiors think you are so good at your job and so valuable to the company that they will indeed raise your pay—perhaps not to the level you requested, but close enough to mollify you. Or they'll refuse to budge, in which case you ought to be prepared to leave the company. Staying without more pay shouldn't be an option, as far as I'm concerned. Not only would you be stuck with the same unfair working conditions you had before, but the acrimony and ill will that are bound to develop on both sides would make your daily professional life a nightmare. And pursuing the matter in court would likely take many years and many thousands of dollars—a commitment of time and money that I, for one, probably would not be willing to make. Rather than let bitterness overtake me, I would rather cut my losses and get on with my life.

That's how Ann Henderson, a former director of business development for a Houston oil company, came to see her situation, too. Named to the position in the mid–1990s, Ann shared responsibility for marketing the firm's extensive real estate holdings with three male colleagues. After a couple of years in the job, she came to realize that all three men earned substantially higher salaries than her own base pay of $57,000, even though she brought in more business than they did. Stung by the unfairness of the situation and anxious for more money, Ann, who at the time was a divorced mom with a fourteen-year-old daughter, decided to take the matter up with her boss.

First, though, she did some homework, consulting salary surveys and speaking with local headhunters to find out how similar positions were compensated at other companies. By the time she met with her boss, she had plenty of facts and figures to back up her request for a raise to $87,000. Her boss told her that the company would look into the matter. Nothing happened. Over the course of the next year or so, Ann raised the issue three more times, moving up the chain of command with her grievance until finally she talked with the chairman of the board. Each time she was told that the matter would be investigated and any discrepancies in pay fixed. And each time nothing happened. Eventually she quit and went into business for herself.

Ann has no regrets, either about her initial decision to push for fair pay or her subsequent decision to move on when her complaints went unanswered. "Leaving was the smartest thing I ever did," says Ann, who subsequently opened her own marketing-services business and was earning more than double her old salary within a year. "Success is the best revenge. I feel like I won."

ACTION PLAN

To make sure that you're earning the highest salary that your skills and experience can command, follow these steps:

1. **Do some homework to get an accurate reading of what your skills and experience are worth in the current job market.** Check out salary surveys from professional associations and trade journals. Consult executive recruiters. Talk with friends and colleagues in comparable positions to see how much they earn.

2. **Once you have a good sense of what you're worth, be forthright about what you need.** That holds true whether you're talking with a prospective employer or your current boss. Be equally direct about lobbying for a promotion, if you believe you're qualified for one—and schedule time with your supervisor to discuss exactly what you need to do to get it. Remember: If you don't ask, you don't get.

3. **Network with anyone you know—and anyone *they* know—who can possibly help in your search for higher-paying work.** Join a professional association, attend work-related meetings and trade shows, show up at get-togethers sponsored by your college alumni association. Once at these events, make a point of chatting with as many people as possible, and don't be shy about asking for an introduction or making your pitch. Then keep up with your key contacts even after you've landed a job—you never know when they might come in handy.

4. **Don't downplay your talents and accomplishments—a typically female mistake—either in job interviews or at performance evaluations.** Make a list of your skills and achievements so that when asked about them, they come to mind easily.

5. **When negotiating salary and raises, think in terms of the total compensation package, not just your base pay.** Bonuses, benefits, stock options, and the ability to earn overtime all put more money in your pocket.

6. **Always do more than is expected of you, and do it to the best of your ability.** It's a particularly good idea to volunteer for high-profile or difficult assignments that will increase your visibility to key mmanagers at your company.

Consider Going Solo

*T*here is, of course, one other way that you may boost your earning power substantially: You can go into business for yourself.

Ann Henderson, the marketing manager in chapter 14 who failed to win equal pay in her oil company job, did it. I've done it. And record numbers of women across the country are doing it, too. Whether they are frustrated by the lack of opportunities in the corporate world, yearn for a more flexible work schedule, or have a professional dream they want to pursue, more and more women are choosing to buy or launch their own businesses. Between 1987 and 1996, in fact, the number of U.S. companies owned by women grew 78 percent, outpacing overall business growth by nearly two to one, reports the National Foundation for Women Business Owners. And by the year 2000, according to estimates by the Internal Revenue Service, two-thirds of all businesses in the United States will have a woman in the top slot.

The potential payoff in running your own business can be great: In addition to the satisfaction you feel from putting your own business ideas into action and gaining control over the way you work, studies show that self-employed people are *four times more likely* to become millionaires than people who earn their living working for someone else. In their best-selling book *The Millionaire Next Door*, for example, authors Thomas Stanley and William Danko found that of the millionaires they studied who were still working, fully *two-thirds* were self-employed.

Certainly from my personal standpoint, I've found running my own company to be a terrific way to make a living. I was far happier during my days as CEO of La Prairie than I ever was as an employee of Fabergé or any other company I've ever worked for. I was far better compensated, too—La Prairie made me a millionaire in my own right. And I'm even more content today running my own consulting business, and just as successful financially.

But I have to tell you frankly that not every woman (or man, for that matter) is cut out financially or temperamentally to be an entrepreneur. It's a livelihood fraught with pitfalls and risks (more than half of all new businesses fold before their sixth birthday), and you're as likely to lose a bundle, at least initially, as you are to make one. Unless you have an independent source of income or support, it can take a long, long time before you can eke out a decent living. And if you choose a home-based business (as some 3.5 million of the 8 million women business owners out there do), you may not be comfortable with the isolation involved.

Determining if the advantages of self-employment outweigh these disadvantages is a very personal process. What follows are some guidelines to help you make the decision and, if you do decide to forge ahead, some advice on how to make your venture a success.

THINK IT THROUGH

Whether you're aiming to work on your own as a freelancer or consultant or have an idea for a product or service that will ultimately employ a cast of thousands, the burden of success or failure rests squarely on your own shoulders. To figure out if you are really suited to being an entrepreneur, ask yourself these questions:

- Do you have a product or service that others will actually want to buy? Your odds of success improve dramatically if you have a unique product or service to offer that fills a real need or niche in the marketplace—either a completely new idea or an innovative or dramatically improved approach to an old one. Often these ideas are born of your own frustration, or those of friends and colleagues, at being unable to find some product or service you personally need or want. Former financial journalist Yla Eason, for instance, decided to go into business for herself in 1985 after her search for a black superhero doll for her three-year-old son came up empty, according to an article in Working Woman magazine. Since introducing Sun-Man, the first black action figure, Yla has launched an array of other characters, ranging from the Bronze Bombers (fashioned after black army units) to Imani, an African American princess. And her company, Richmond, Virginia–based Olmec Toys, has grown into an enterprise generating more than $6 million in annual revenues.

Prospective consultants and freelancers can also prosper by tapping into current trends, such as corporate outsourcing, the need for specialized technological know-how, the need to service the nation's increasingly diverse workforce, and the aging of the population. Former systems analyst Sharon Martire, for example, grosses well into six figures teaching global companies like AT&T how to market to women, minorities, and other underserved customers. Physical therapist Sonia Brauerbach left a hospital staff job five years ago to become an independent contractor serving geriatric clients who need rehabilitative care in their homes, and has more than doubled her income in the process.

Most of the time you'll do best if, like Sonia, you stick close to your field. Since you're most familiar with your own industry and profession, you stand the best chance of discovering—and eventually profiting from—its untapped niches. Staying close to your current line of work also enables you to make good use of the skills, knowledge, and contacts you've built up over the years.

In my case, for example, I had had years of experience in consumer sales, marketing, and new-product development before I even considered going into business for myself. So when I made up my mind that I wanted to buy a company, I focused on ones in the cosmetics industry, which, after my years at Fabergé, was the field that I knew best. I understood the market, I knew the players, and I already had credibility. The learning curve was not nearly as steep as if I'd chosen to go into, say, the pet-food business or computer sales.

But I don't want you to think that you can be an entrepreneur only if you've been in the workforce for years building up skills and contacts. Nor do you have to be thinking in terms of a full-fledged enterprise that will command your attention and energy forty, fifty, or more hours a week. The beauty of self-employment is that you can fashion it to *your* needs rather than the other way around. If you're simply looking to pick up some extra money—whether you're a homemaker hoping to supplement the household income or an employee aiming to pad your salary—a sideline business may be the answer.

Often the best way to go about it is to parlay a hobby or some other activity that you love into a money-making proposition. If you're a terrific baker, for instance, you might turn your homemade breads, cookies, and cakes into a dessert-catering business. If you're great at needlepoint, you might create specialty-design pillows that you can sell for holidays and special occasions, such as Christmas or Mother's Day. If you love gardening and have a flair for arranging flowers, you might offer your services as a floral arranger for dinner parties and weddings. Or if you're great with animals, you could launch a home-based pet-grooming business.

If you're not going to be dependent on your business for your entire livelihood, you can skip the following questions and skim the rest of this chapter for the advice that's relevant to you. But if you're looking for this venture to be an integral contribution to your household income—or, indeed, to supply all of it—please read on.

- **Do you have enough money saved to see you through the initial dry period?** When I decided to go into business for myself, I was lucky enough to be in a financially secure marriage, so I didn't have to worry about bringing home a paycheck. And since my husband at that time handled our day-to-day living expenses, I could sink a lot of my savings into my business without running the risk of bankrupting myself or even having to scale back my lifestyle.

  Most women, I know, don't have that luxury. That's why financial planners and small-business experts alike urge anyone starting a business to have enough money saved to cover their living expenses for six months to a year, preferably even longer, before taking the plunge. (For my suggestions on how to put together this kind of emergency fund, check back to chapter 8.) And that's not even counting the capital you'll need for the business itself, which could range from next to nothing to tens of thousands of dollars or more, depending on the type and scale of the business that you're planning.

- **Can you handle the insecurity?** When you work for someone else, you can count on steady assignments, set hours, and a paycheck at regular intervals. When you work for yourself, you spend a lot of time (at least at first) anguishing over where the next project or sale will come from and waiting with bated breath for the mail to arrive to see if someone, *anyone*, has finally sent you a check. And you can kiss the nine-to-five life good-bye. While being your own boss gives you more flexibility over *when* you work than most staff jobs, *how much* you work is another matter. In fact, home entrepreneurs average nine more working hours a week than do corporate managers, according to a study by AT&T and the Bureau of Labor Statistics.

Some people thrive on the unknown, on taking risks, and on throwing themselves totally into projects of their own creation— I know, I happen to be one of them. Others may not exactly like the insecurity but feel confident enough about themselves and the prospects for their new business to cope with it. For still others, living every day with this kind of uncertainty and instability may be a constant source of emotional distress as well as a heavy financial burden. If you fall into that last category, self-employment may not be such a hot idea, after all.

- **If the business you're considering is home-based, can you handle the isolation?** Talk to any gathering of women who run businesses from their own homes, and before long the issue of isolation will come up. Even those who generally love the self-employed life confess to missing the collegiality of working in an office, the support system and, yes, even (or perhaps especially) the gossip. Although there are ways you can and should reduce this perpetual solitude (for example, by scheduling regular face-to-face meetings with clients or getting together occasionally with other home-based entrepreneurs in your area), that's no substitute for working among colleagues on a daily basis—particularly if you're the kind of person who thrives on social interaction.

There are advantages, too: chief among them, a dramatic increase in productivity. Without the endless meetings, the lunches, the collegial interruptions and, yes, the gossip, you'll likely find you get a lot more done in a lot less time than you ever could in an office setting.

- **Do you understand the basic principle of entrepreneurship—that everything that can go wrong will go wrong—and are you prepared to deal with that reality?** Murphy's Law applies to self-run businesses, twenty-four hours a day, fifty-two weeks a year. If you're easily rattled when things go wrong—and go wrong again and again and again—a self-run business is the wrong business for you. If, on the other hand, you thrive on troubleshooting and have a knack for solving problems, you have the final prerequisite nailed.

GIVE YOURSELF A RUNNING START

No matter how gung-ho you are to get going, though, don't quit your day job just yet. In fact, try to hang on to it for as long as possible. That way you can continue to receive a paycheck while you fine-tune your idea, line up customers, secure funding, and investigate insurance options—a process that could take months and eat up lots of cash. You can also volunteer for assignments that will hone the skills you'll need in your new enterprise, expand your contacts, and maybe even help you line up those all-important first customers.

While you're still at your old job, it's also a smart idea, if possible, to take your new venture for a test run. Accept a few freelance projects, if your business lends itself to that sort of thing. Work on a prototype and get feedback from a few potential clients about its feasibility. Anything that you can think of to help you determine if you can really make a go of it, and to solicit and line up customers in advance will help.

Here are some other steps you'll need to take during this warm-up period:

- **Draft a detailed, realistic business plan.** Before you officially launch your product or service, you need a clear vision of what you want your business to be and how you plan to achieve that goal. Among the questions you need to address in a written outline of your new enterprise: who your customers will be and how you plan to reach them; who your competitors will be and how you plan to beat them; how you will handle marketing and distribution; what your start-up costs and continuing overhead will be; and when you expect the business to start generating revenues, along with your projections of what your short- and long-term profits will be. Also include a short description of your product or service, a statement of your business goals, and the results of any market research you have conducted.

This kind of business blueprint is an absolute must if you're planning a sizable venture or if you'll need outside financing of any kind. But it's also an extremely worthwhile exercise even if you're a one-woman show, need relatively little money to get going, and can finance it all yourself. That's because a written plan helps you identify your venture's strengths and weaknesses early on, giving you the opportunity to figure out how best to exploit them and correct them, respectively. What's more, psychologists have found that the very act of writing a plan, rather than just talking or daydreaming about launching a business, will make you more committed to your goals and, as a result, more likely to follow through on them.

- **Shore up the funding.** Your business plan should tell you in as much detail as possible how much money you'll need to start and run your business. Then you actually have to come up with the cash. Many small-business experts advise entrepreneurs to use their own money to the greatest extent possible since it's typically the cheapest source of financing and comes with the fewest strings attached. I prefer to spread my risks by getting others to invest in my businesses with me. Few of us, after all, can afford to let all our assets ride on a single venture, no matter how much money we have or how promising the business may be. Moreover, bringing in backers makes me work that much harder to succeed because I am much more protective of other people's money than I am of my own. It's a point of honor with me.

I'd turn first to family and friends, if they can afford to lend you the money. Toy maven Yla Eason, for example, launched her firm with $60,000 in seed money raised from her family. Just keep it on a businesslike footing, complete with a written contract that spells out the terms of repayment so everyone's clear on the deal.

If you're trying to buy an existing business rather than building one from scratch, you may also be able to work out a creative financing deal with the seller. That's how Kimberly Hastings and Sarah Spray managed to acquire their own textile-design firm at the tender ages of twenty-four and twenty-six, respectively. As Kimberly told *Working Woman* magazine a couple of years ago, she was just one year out of New York's Fashion Institute of Technology when the husband-and-wife team who owned the textile-design firm where she worked decided to sell the business and offered it first to her. At the time Kimberly was neither wealthy enough to buy the business herself nor was she in a position that she could borrow the money from family or friends. But the owners were willing to make a deal. Instead of requiring cash up front, the owners allowed Kimberly and Sarah, a fellow employee who became her partner, to work out a monthly payment schedule based on the company's revenues that would let them take full ownership in four to five years. More than a year into the venture, when the article appeared, the two women had retained the firm's profitability and were already drawing comfortably higher salaries.

If after approaching those who know you well, you still come up dry, you can turn to any one of a number of lenders who specialize in small-business loans, such as the **Small Business Administration's Microloan Program** (1–800–8-ASK-SBA; www.sba.com). Professional organizations for home-based entrepreneurs and small-business owners are a good source of information about these loans (see the Appendix for the lowdown on these groups). You may also get some good leads from an Internet site called, appropriately enough, Moneyhunter (www.moneyhunter.gov), which lists sources of fund-raising information for small business owners.

- **Rethink your personal finances as well.** When you go into business for yourself, your financial life changes almost as dramatically as your work life. Take taxes, for instance. When you're an employee, your company automatically deducts the income taxes you owe from your paycheck each week and picks up the tab for half of your Social Security and Medicare taxes as well (that's the deduction marked FICA on your pay stub). When you're self-employed, however, you have to take responsibility for your own income tax payments to the IRS, and you'll have to pay both the employee *and* employer portions of FICA taxes as well. That amounts to 15.3 percent off the first $68,400 that you earn from your business (that's the amount for 1998, anyway). To help soften the blow, you can claim half of this tax as a deduction. If you earn $50,000 from your business and pay a self-employment tax of $7,065, for example, this deduction will save you nearly $1,000 in income taxes, assuming that you're in the 28 percent bracket.

As a self-employed person, you can claim a number of other deductions as well. For instance, this year you can deduct 45 percent of the cost of your health insurance premiums (that is, if you'll no longer be covered by a company-provided plan), and that figure is due to rise gradually until the full amount is deductible in 2007. (You cannot, however, deduct your premiums for disability or life insurance.) If you work primarily from home, you can also write off part of what you spend to light and heat your home; a share of the rent if you are a tenant or depreciation on your house if you own it; a portion of your homeowner's insurance and part of your maintenance and repair expenses, too. Unfortunately, claiming this deduction can cost you dearly if you sell your home, courtesy of a new tax law enacted in 1997. So you'll want to consult an accountant to determine if the write-off is worth it. An accountant (or a good tax handbook) can also help you tote up the myriad other deductions that may be available to you, such as tax breaks for your office equipment and supplies as well as for your car and business-related travel.

You'll also need to update your insurance policies if you were previously covered under an employer's plan. If you're married and your husband has health insurance through his company, shift to his plan immediately—that's definitely the easiest and cheapest way to acquire coverage. If you don't have this option, you'll have to shop for a new health plan yourself, as well as for a new disability policy and, depending on your circumstances, possibly life insurance, too. Be warned, though, most individual policies are expensive. To get better rates, you may want to join your professional organization or a small business group, such as the **National Association for the Self-Employed** (800–232–6273; www.nase.org) or the **Home Business Institute** (800–342–5424; www.hbiweb.com). (For more of my tips on how to choose the best coverage at the lowest price, see chapter 9.)

Finally, don't neglect to set up a tax-deferred SEP-IRA or Keogh plan for yourself so you can start making contributions for your retirement as soon as the cash from your new business starts rolling in. (See chapter 7 for details on the advantages of these accounts and setting one up.) As a bonus, every dollar that you put into one of these accounts will reduce your taxable income dollar for dollar, typically up to a current annual maximum of $24,000.

- **Get help.** There's an astonishing amount of free and low-cost help out there for anyone thinking about going into business for themselves. While you'll find a more comprehensive list in the resource section at the end of this book, let me mention a couple of standouts here. In addition to the previously discussed Small Business Administration, you can get free counseling from retired business executives through the **Service Corps of Retired Executives** (800–634–0245); www.score.org), known as SCORE for short. And a number of professional women's groups are especially helpful with assistance on small-business basics, financing information, and networking. Among them: the **American Woman's Economic Development Corp.**, or AWED, for short (800–321–6962; www.womenconnect.com/awed); the **National**

Association for Female Executives, also known as NAFE (800–634–6233; www.nafe.com); and the National Association of Women Business Owners, or NAWBO (800–55-NAWBO; www.nawbo.org).

FOLLOW THE PRINCIPLES OF SUCCESS

When you own your own business, the planning process never ends. Once you have the venture up and running, you have to keep it running; then you have to focus on growing it and then growing it some more. Here are a couple of suggestions:

- Operate your business in a professional manner. Sure, one of the benefits of being the boss is the freedom to come to work in sweatpants and sneakers if you're so inclined, especially if you're working out of your home. But you can't be that relaxed in all of your work habits if you expect clients to take you seriously. If you mean business, you have to look and act businesslike, too.

  That means investing in the best equipment you can afford, including (in all likelihood) a fairly powerful computer (they can be had for under $1,000 these days), fax machine, and high-quality printer. You'll also need a separate bank account for the business. If you'll be working from home, even part of the time, you should also install a separate phone line, which will make it easier to track your deductible phone expenses and prevent the kids from picking up while you're talking to a client. Ideally you'll commandeer a separate room to function as your office; if you don't have that much free space, though, simply create a separate and distinct work area in the most underpopulated room your home has to offer.

  If you have young children, plan on hiring a baby-sitter, or arranging for some other kind of child care, at least part of the time. Yes, perhaps one of the reasons you wanted to work from home in the first place was to spend more time with your kids, but it's a rare woman who's able to combine raising children full-time and running a thriving business without any outside help. Can you really expect a three-year-old to amuse himself quietly while you return clients' phone calls? For most working mothers, the answer, resoundingly, is no.

- **Market, market, market.** Whether you're a one-woman operation or a mini-corporation, your business won't ever amount to much unless you get the word out about what you do, entice clients in the door, and devise a strategy to keep 'em coming back for more. When I was CEO of La Prairie, I'd regularly travel around the country, spending a full day at the various stores that sold my cosmetics. I'd work the counter myself, in suit and high heels for eight to ten hours at a stretch, talking to customers, trying to learn what they wanted, and getting their feedback on the product. I'd be exhausted at the end of the day, to be sure, but I'm convinced that personal contact with my customers contributed mightily to my success.

Small-business experts say to spend anywhere from 20 to 50 percent of your time, at least in the early days, on drumming up business. It may just be a matter of working the phones to remind people that you're out there—calling your contacts, calling your contacts' contacts, and cold-calling hot prospects. Depending on the business, you might also send out flyers and brochures and other mass mailings. From time to time you can also cook up creative incentives to bring business in the door.

That's one of the strategies that Millie Szerman used to grow the Redondo, California, public relations and marketing business she launched roughly a decade ago. At the time Millie was an overworked and underpaid regional sales director for a gift-industry trade magazine. Despite longer hours, her salary had been stagnant for four years. When a client asked her if she had ever considered consulting, Millie knew instantly that she was onto something. Ten months later, she launched her New Directions company to sell her expertise to the gift industry. As she told *Money* magazine a couple of years ago, "The beauty was that I had a ready market—people who knew and trusted me."

Nevertheless, the start was slow. Despite a mass mailing to announce her new venture, Millie calculates that for the first two years she worked round the clock for an average of $1.25 an hour. To win new business, she decided to offer free services to some clients in order to win referrals from them. The strategy worked like a charm. By 1996 Millie was paying herself $70,000 a year, and by 1999 expects to earn a cool $100,000.

DO WHAT YOU LOVE

Stories like Millie's are inspiring indeed. But there is one big fat caveat that I must add to this advice I've given you about work, although I know it may seem like heresy in a book like this, which is dedicated to the notion that money should be critically important to every woman and devoted to helping you accumulate more of it. Nevertheless, here it goes: *DO NOT GO INTO BUSINESS FOR YOURSELF, OR INDEED DO ANY JOB ON A LONG-TERM BASIS, PURELY FOR THE MONEY.*

I'm not going to naïvely suggest that simply doing what you love and doing it well will turn you into a rich woman. No, if that were the case, we'd be a nation of millionaires, and you wouldn't need my advice, or anyone else's, on how to make the most of your money. I do strongly believe, however, that when you truly enjoy your work, you are motivated to do your best and that in turn has the potential for tremendous financial as well as psychic rewards.

To see what I mean, consider what happened to attorney Sheryl Draker when she left the confines of a highly competitive Dallas law firm nine years ago. Sheryl was thirty-one at the time, working sixty-hour weeks and earning $55,000 a year as a second-year associate, when a near tragedy prompted her to reevaluate her life. Her doctor discovered a seven-inch tumor in her pancreas that he said was most likely cancerous. When Sheryl arrived at the hospital for surgery three days later, however, the doctors could find absolutely no sign of the tumor on the ultrasound they performed just prior to the operation. "I didn't care whether I'd been miraculously cured or the doctor had made a mistake in his original diagnosis," she says. "I just knew I no longer wanted to spend every minute of my life working, or thinking single-mindedly about billable hours and career advancement."

So Sheryl quit. To pay the bills while she reconsidered her options, she took jobs as a contract lawyer (the attorney equivalent of doing temp work), and she continued to earn her living this way once she decided to return to school to get a master's degree in psychology. Within a year she was earning more than $80,000 a year, or about 45 percent more than she had at her old law firm, although she was working only half as many hours. When she graduated in 1996, she decided to combine her interests in the law and psychology by hanging out a shingle as a legal and communications consultant, preparing witnesses, helping with jury selection, and advising law firms on client development. Again she ended up boosting her pay while cutting her hours: Sheryl now earns a six-figure salary (more than double what she made as an associate), working no more than eighty hours a month (or just one-third as much time as she put in a decade ago). That leaves her plenty of time to spend with family and friends and to do the volunteer work she loves, including cooking dinner once a week for families of pediatric cancer patients at Ronald McDonald House in Austin, where she now lives.

Reflecting on the lessons she's learned through her astounding professional success since her cancer scare, Sheryl says, "There are many different paths to earning a living and there's no reason why you can't look for one that you not only enjoy, but that also pays you well." But, she adds, "nobody is going to make it happen for you. You have to get active and make it happen yourself."

To me that's the ultimate: a career you love and a job that pays a bundle. Maybe we can't all have it, but Sheryl is right. There's no reason why we can't all try.

ACTION PLAN

To determine if you're really suited to being an entrepreneur and to help make a success of your business if you do decide to strike out on your own, follow these steps:

1. **Realistically assess your chances of success.** When you're self-employed, your odds of earning a comfortable living increase dramatically if you have a product or service to offer that fills a real need in the marketplace, especially if it's innovative or otherwise unique. You'll also need to have enough money saved to see you through the initial dry period, which can last a year or more.

2. **Consider whether you're really the type who'll enjoy the entrepreneurial life.** Think hard about whether you'll be able to handle the insecurity of sporadic assignments and income (at least at first) as well as the isolation, if you're going to be working out of your home. And to get the business going, count on putting in longer hours than you did as a staff employee, although you'll have greater flexibility about exactly when you do your time.

3. **Draft a detailed business plan.** Among the issues you'll need to address: who your customers will be; who your competition will be; how you'll approach marketing and distribution; what your start-up and overhead costs will be; when you expect the business to start generating revenues and what you project your short- and long-term profits will be.

4. **Line up financing.** Try to spread the financial risks of your business by bringing in other people as backers. Turn first to family and friends for additional funding, if that option is available to you. If you need more money than you can raise from people you know, look for assistance from a lender that specializes in small-business loans.

5. **Update your insurance coverage.** If you previously got your insurance through an employer's plan, you'll have to make alternate arrangements. If you're married and your husband has a health insurance policy through his work, switch to his plan. If that's not an option, you'll have to shop for a health insurance policy of your own (preferably through a professional organization that qualifies for group rates) as well as for disability and, depending on your circumstance, life insurance.

6. **Claim your fair share of the tax breaks available to you.** As a self-employed person, you'll be able to deduct half of your Social Security and Medicare taxes, a portion of your health insurance premiums; many of your home office expenses; and a host of other business-related costs, from new computer equipment to car mileage. You'll also be able to deduct your contributions to a SEP-IRA or Keogh retirement plan, typically up to a maximum of $24,000 in 1998.

7. **Run your business like a pro.** Get a dedicated phone line and invest in up-to-date computer equipment. Create a separate space for your work if you're operating out of your home—preferably a separate room you can use as your office. And if you have children, arrange for child care for them while you work, at least part of the time.

8. **Market, market, market.** Spend anywhere from 20 to 50 percent of your time at first drumming up business. Work the phones, send out mailings, meet with customers, and consider offering special incentives to bring clients through the door.

9. **Unless you really have no other way to make a living (and that's rarely the case), do not do any job for the money alone.** Life is too short not to get at least *some* enjoyment out of the work that you do. If you dread going to work every day, it's time to look for something else—no matter how much money you're currently making.

Meet Hard Knocks Head-on

*T*o an outside observer (and even to those of us who lived it), it must certainly seem as if the women in my family have had more than our fair share of hard knocks.

The pattern stretches back four generations, starting with my great-grandmother, Pauline Navlan, who emigrated to the United States from Austria as a young woman. Baba, as my siblings and I called her, was only in her thirties when an unstable boarder in my great-grandparents' rooming house shot and killed my great-grandfather during an argument over the boarder's long-overdue rent. Baba, who had stayed home to raise her five young children while my great-grandfather worked, could neither read nor write English and had no professional skills to speak of. So she did what she had to do to keep the family afloat. One day after my great-grandfather died, she went to the pipe factory where he'd worked, pulled his time card, and punched in. And she continued her dual jobs, working the assembly line and running the boardinghouse, until her children were more than old enough to fend for themselves.

One of those children was my grandmother Mary, who was just ten years old when her father was killed. Now, Grandma was a gorgeous redhead who dropped out of school in the seventh grade, working at a local bakery to help Baba support the family. But despite her lack of formal education, she did well enough for herself. She married a dash-ing Irishman named Bill Bell, a mini real estate mogul who owned a valuable office building in Chicago during the go-go years of the 1920s. For a while they were blissfully happy. But when Bill Bell lost all his holdings in the aftermath of the 1929 stock market crash, he seemed to lose himself as well. After that he gave up looking for work, quarreled frequently with Grandma, and wandered off for days at a time, often gambling away what little money the family had left. Eventually enough was enough. In an era when divorce was unthink-able for respectable women, my grandmother, Mary Bell, courageously divorced my grandfather.

Like her mother before her, Grandma did what she had to do to sup-port herself and her two children. Not long after her marriage ended, she got a job working the midnight shift as a train-signal switcher at a local railroad crossing—a traditionally male, physically demanding job that required pumping heavy hydraulic gates by hand to raise or lower them. But Grandma didn't care how demanding the work was. What mattered to her was the fact that the job provided her family with a steady income *and* allowed her to be home with her children during the day (Baba baby-sat during Grandma's shift at the train yard). And Grandma con-tinued to switch trains right up until the day she retired at age sixty-five.

Unfortunately, marital tragedy has continued to mark the modern history of our family. As you know, my mother, Dorothy Paulsin, who was just six when Grandma got divorced, was only twenty-seven when her husband died in a car crash, leaving her with four young children to support. My father had had no life insurance, no savings, and his job didn't offer a pension, either. And my mother, who had married as a teenager and been a full-time homemaker, had only a high school edu-cation and no job skills to fall back on. But she was determined to do whatever she had to do to keep us all together. She took what jobs she could find, and between her salary and her Social Security survivor benefits, we made it through.

Now here I am at fifty, three times divorced, the last time from a man I'd considered my soul mate for each of the fifteen years we'd been together—right up to the day I learned of his betrayal.

It's not a pretty picture.

The saddest part of the stories of the women in my family, however, is not what a rotten run of luck we've had with the men we've loved. No, the saddest part is that our stories—or at least variations on these themes—are all too common. We are not statistical anomalies: Studies show that nine out of every ten women will be on their own one day. We are instead a composite portrait of what most women face every day.

If and when it happens to you, you can spend your time feeling sorry for yourself, or you can get off your rear, confront the prospect of being alone head-on, and take positive steps to ensure that you survive, even thrive.

I choose to thrive.

TAKE THE NECESSARY PRECAUTIONS

In an ideal world, you'd have made your financial preparations long before there's even a hint of illness or trouble in your marriage. And if you follow the advice in earlier chapters, you'll have done exactly that: You'll have participated actively in managing the family's finances, established credit in your own name, kept up some professional skills, maintained an independent network of friends and professional contacts, learned how to save and invest, and, most important, not made your entire life a function of *his* life.

Unfortunately, real life doesn't always work out that way.

Don't worry. If you're already seeing warning signs that you might be living alone in the near future—say, your marriage has been rocky for a while or your spouse has a serious illness—it's not too late to take action to secure your financial future. The key is not to allow the anger, pain, and grief that you're going through to paralyze you or to let hope, and hope alone, guide your steps. By all means, hope for happily ever after, but don't let it stop you from taking measures to protect yourself in case it turns out to be false hope. Let me be blunt here: You're a fool if you don't prepare yourself, emotionally and financially, for the possibility of a different outcome.

....

By all means, hope for happily ever after, but don't let it stop you from taking measures to protect yourself in case it turns out to be false hope

....

I suggest that every woman with a rocky marriage adopt the following strategy: At the very least, you should make a careful list of the household's assets and expenses so you have a good handle on what is rightfully yours if you need to know. Also make copies of any documents that can verify your household's income and investments, including your joint tax returns, records of both your husband's and your retirement plans, insurance policies, bank and brokerage statements, the deed to your house, appraisals conducted for insurance purposes, and any other relevant financial papers you can think of. Then bundle the documents in one big file that you keep in a safe but easily accessible place, like a locked drawer or a safety deposit box. Notes Carol Ann Wilson, founder of Quantum Financial, a pre-divorce financial consulting service in Boulder, Colorado: "If you don't take steps to protect yourself beforehand, assets have a funny habit of disappearing once divorce proceedings get underway."

Ignorance is expensive. In a divorce, as Wilson suggests, it can allow your ex to walk off with assets you never knew you had—or give you a fraction of what they're worth. And if your husband dies, it can leave you without access to cash from life insurance policies, pension plans, and other benefits for months—or longer—depending on how much time it takes you to locate the documents you need.

Here are a few other smart moves to make during this transitional period:

- **Open a savings account in your name only.** If you haven't already established a private stash of cash, do so immediately. In the event of your husband's death, you'll need easy access to money to pay your household and other expenses until his financial affairs are settled. And if your relationship crumbles, a private stash ensures that you won't be left penniless if your soon-to-be ex makes off with the money in your joint accounts—a sad but all too common occurrence, divorce lawyers tell me.

Julie Anderson,* a bank loan officer that I know of in Nashville, Tennessee, learned this lesson the hard way. After two separations and a year of living in separate bedrooms, Julie told her husband of five years that she wanted a divorce. It was a Sunday night, she recalls clearly, and he readily agreed to the split. On Monday afternoon she went to the bank to withdraw some cash, only to find that her husband had cleaned out every last dime from the account that morning. Julie, now thirty-two, was forced to take out a $2,000 loan to support herself and her three-year-old daughter until she and her husband reached an agreement on child support, and later she sold all the jewelry he had given her to make ends meet.

- **Protect your key assets.** If you're headed toward divorce and want to make sure you don't find yourself in a situation like Julie's, inform your bank, in writing, that both signatures are now required on any withdrawals from your joint account. If you maintain accounts with any brokerage or mutual fund companies, let them know that you'll both need to sign any orders to sell jointly held investments as well.

If instead your husband is sick or considerably older than you are, you can protect your assets by making sure you're listed as a joint owner with rights of survivorship on all of your household's key sav-

*This is an assumed name, but the story is real.

ings and investment accounts. *Joint ownership (or tenancy) with rights of survivorship* is a legal way of owning property that gives the surviving account holder immediate access to the assets after the death of the other owner. Otherwise, you'll have to wait until your husband's will has gone through *probate*, the legal process that assures the property covered by a will passes to the people who are supposed to get it. And if your husband doesn't have a will yet, urge him to have one drawn up right away. (You'll find more advice about wills in chapter 10.) You might also ask him at this time to direct a lawyer to appoint you as his *durable power of attorney*, which would authorize you to act legally and financially on his behalf if he becomes too physically or mentally disabled to do so himself.

- **Find out who your true friends are.** I told key people early on that Robert and I were separating so I could find out who was going to be there for me and who wasn't. I didn't want to waste my time on fair-weather friends. I needed a support system and figured I might as well learn sooner rather than later who that support system was going to be. I knew that I hadn't gone through the worst of the crisis yet, and I knew also that when the worst hit, I was going to need all the help I could get.

Understand this: You are going to be disappointed by the behavior of some friends and family members. Unfortunately, that is just the reality of divorce. It's often the reality as well for wives whose husbands are seriously ill and for new widows, whose grief is compounded by the loss of friends who somehow drift away after the funeral. Some people just can't cope with other people's pain; they feel too awkward and helpless to know what to do for you. Or perhaps they can't bear to be reminded of their own similarly painful experiences. Then too, you'll learn, some people may have liked you only for what you brought to the table as part of a couple rather than for yourself.

Either way, if you know early on who you can count on, you can deal with it and move forward.

FACE THE FINANCIAL FACTS

Divorce and widowhood are financial crises as well as emotional ones. As I pointed out in the very first chapter of this book, the average woman can expect to see her income drop anywhere from 27 to 45 percent in the first year following a divorce, and 80 percent of all widows living in poverty weren't poor before their husbands died. Get with the program, ladies: If you see trouble coming in your marriage, do what you can as fast as you can to secure your income.

If you've been a full-time homemaker for a good portion of your marriage, the single most important move you can make during this transitional period is to reestablish a professional identity. In plain English, that means line up work or at least brush up your professional skills so you'll be ready to reenter the job market. It's a good idea, too, to renew contact with old friends and acquaintances who might help you land a decent position.

When Judy Mueller first realized her marriage was foundering, for example, she hadn't worked outside her home for fifteen years. With a stockbroker husband who pulled in $400,000 a year, she hadn't had to; nor had she paid any attention to the family's finances, from how much they paid in taxes to the kind and amount of investments they held. Looking back, she says simply, "I took a real head-in-the-sand approach to money."

Aware that she'd have to change that unconsciously cavalier attitude if she was going to support herself, Judy chose to work on her professional skills first by going to graduate school to earn a degree in psychology. Still married but increasingly convinced that the relationship couldn't be saved, Judy then took an unpaid position on the board of a local-information agency to gain practical experience in the work world. Within that organization she then created a separate nonprofit organization called The Women's Center, specifically designed to help women like her—women going through a divorce or other major transition who had none of the financial or professional or legal knowledge they needed to make a go of a new self-supporting life—and made herself the head of it.

By the time Judy's marriage finally broke down for good, four years had passed since she began positioning herself for the change. Represented by the same attorney her husband used, Judy initially got a lousy settlement, and her income immediately plunged from $400,000 a year to $20,000. But with her new skills and the Center flourishing, she was still able to make a go of it for herself and her two children, then aged eight and eleven. And as the Center grew, so did her income. Eventually she even worked out a fairer settlement with her ex.

Today, nearly eighteen years after her divorce, Judy lives comfortably. At fifty-eight, she's still running The Women's Center and still dispensing advice to women facing the same challenges she did so many years ago. "The irony," she says, "is that I did everything wrong personally, so I know exactly what women who come to the center are going through and what kind of information and help they need." The greatest lesson she passes along from her experiences? "Money is the key," Judy says bluntly. "Without a job that enables you to make money and the self-esteem that comes with earning your own way, you are that much more vulnerable and frightened in an already frightening situation." She adds, "It's all connected: Economic safety and psychological safety are really the same thing."

· ·

Economic safety and psychological safety are really the same thing.

· ·

KEEP A COOL HEAD

(For prospective divorcees only)

The time may come when, despite all your efforts to salvage your relationship, you recognize that the marriage is really, irretrievably over.

In my second marriage, that moment came when my husband G.B. punched me in the face during one of his drunken tirades. G.B. had been abusing me emotionally for years by that point—he'd told me I was stupid and worthless so many times during the course of our relationship that my self-esteem was barely existent—but this was the first time he'd ever hit me. Sadly, ironically, that punch was the catalyst I needed to finally work up the courage to leave him. No matter how much a divorce would cost me financially and professionally, I knew I could no longer endure the abuse.

I understood that my marriage to Robert was irrevocably over when, after a year of all-out effort to save it, nothing worked.

At these moments of truth, when the pain and anger and sadness and depression threaten to overwhelm you, you must reach deep down inside yourself and find a way to keep a cool head. It's critical to handle the financial aspects of the end of your marriage in as businesslike a manner as possible. Tell yourself your financial future is at stake, tell yourself it's what *he's* doing, tell yourself whatever you need to convince yourself, but DO IT!

In the course of her practice, Chicago financial planner Cicely Maton, who specializes in divorce counseling, sees how differently men and women approach divorce proceedings all the time—and how that difference hurts women. "Women are motivated by their emotions, while men treat ending a marriage like dissolving a business and try to negotiate the best deal," she says. "I tell my women clients, 'Get a therapist to deal with the emotions. When it comes to every other aspect of the divorce, get it on paper, run the numbers, and make a deal.'" Her bottom-line advice? "Forget about getting even, forget even about being equal. Just concentrate on finding out how things work and use that knowledge to your best advantage."

This is the one, and perhaps only, time when it's crucial to play by men's rules. I don't want to fool you. I wasn't always able to follow this advice myself, no woman in the midst of a divorce can. At points during my settlement negotiations with Robert, I was so overwhelmed by grief and confusion, so shattered by the pain and sense of loss, that I *wasn't* always rational in my decisions. Everywhere I turned during this period, there seemed to be a memory of Robert waiting for me, the legacy of fifteen years of shared family, friends, and experiences—and those memories tripped me up. In hindsight, I realize the best thing to do during these inevitable moments is to recognize what you're feeling and do absolutely nothing. Let the turmoil subside, and postpone any further decisions until your head clears and you are more in control of your emotions.

Of course, that's not always possible, either. Realize that despite your best efforts, you will make mistakes in your grief-stricken state. I know I did. Rather than beat yourself up about those mistakes, consult a lawyer to determine if there's any way to revisit your agreement. If there isn't, accept the truth and move on. If there is, however, do whatever you need to do to rectify the situation.

Fairness is important—on both sides. A divorce agreement shouldn't be about getting everything you can, but about understanding what your needs and rights are and taking the necessary steps to protect them under the circumstances. It's about understanding your role and responsibilities in the relationship—including the financial value of your unpaid role as household manager, chief child-care provider, and professional helpmate to your husband.

It is to your advantage to keep relations friendly between you and your husband for as long as you can. Being bitter and angry doesn't get you anywhere. You'll just be that much more miserable, and he'll be that much less willing to grant you what you ask for. Through all the pain, you've got to be smart. It pays—literally and figuratively, in this case—to be practical.

. . . .

> ## *In the end, the only justice you get is the justice you make yourself.*

. . . .

Friendly-to-the-end divorces are rare, however, and I must admit that mine was no exception. Robert and I had some very tense moments in the eleventh hour. When the going gets tough, as it inevitably will, keeping your cool becomes even more important; be open to compromise while you continue to press for fair treatment.

In the end, the only justice you get is the justice you make yourself.

REMEMBER: CASH IS KING

Although the nitty-gritty details of a divorce settlement differ from couple to couple, there is one cardinal rule, applicable to every woman, that you must understand as you enter full-blown settlement negotiations. And it's a rule that widows stand to benefit from greatly, too.

The Number One Rule: *CASH IS KING!*

You know the old proverb about a bird in the hand being worth two in the bush? Well, the same concept applies here. Given a choice between cash (or some other liquid asset, such as stocks or bonds) and a hard asset (such as a car or house) or a future asset (like stock options or a share in your husband's retirement plan), *it's almost always wiser to pick cash*. The car will depreciate in value; the house may be too expensive to maintain; the stock options and the retirement plan could turn out to be worth a lot less than you think. But a dollar in your hand today is a dollar you can put to work for you immediately, either to help pay your current living expenses or to invest for the future.

In short, take the money and run.

There is no single area in which this rule is more important than in the disposition of the house, which in many marriages is the single largest asset a couple have. Many women insist on keeping the house, especially if children are involved, and willingly yield other valuable assets to do so. Big mistake. "Mothers want Johnny and Mary to live the same life as they did before the break-up, but the truth is it can never be the same life again," says Kathleen Miller, a Bellevue, Washington, accountant who specializes in divorce issues. "Then after a while they find they can't afford to keep the house and are often forced to sell anyway, after the house has drained away much of their financial resources." Rather than struggling to keep up with the mortgage payments, property taxes, insurance, maintenance, and the cost of repairing the occasional leaky roof or burst water pipe, Miller and other divorce counselors urge women to agree to sell the house, split the proceeds with their ex, and then buy or rent a smaller, more manageable place.

This advice, by the way, often holds true for widows, too. While it's wise to postpone any big financial decisions until the first wave of grief has passed, with time you too are likely to find that the financial drain of the house and the physical upkeep (mowing the lawn, shoveling the snow, fixing the myriad things that break down) are more of a burden than a comfort.

After a house, retirement benefits—for instance, a pension, 401(k) plan, or IRA—are typically a couple's largest asset. Under federal law, divorcing spouses are usually entitled to a portion of the benefits earned during the marriage, but you may have to jump through hoops to claim your fair share. You'll need a lawyer (preferably one experienced with matrimonial issues) to petition a state court for something called *a qualified domestic relations order*, which spells out how a specific retirement plan will be divided, to whom it will be paid, and when. Again, remember the cash-is-king rule, and try your best to get your money up front, in a lump sum. Then immediately transfer that money to an IRA so that you don't pay taxes on the balance and your money will continue to grow tax-free until you withdraw it.

Fortunately, it's a lot easier for widows to claim their rightful share of their late husband's retirement assets. Simply contact the person that handles employee benefits at his company (as well as at any companies he'd worked for in the past for at least five years), explain the situation, then ask for information on widow's benefits and how to claim them. Pension benefits usually come in the form of a so-called *joint-and-survivor annuity*, which means that the payments continue to be sent to the surviving spouse of a former employee after that employee has died. On the other hand, 401(k) benefits are usually paid out in a single lump sum. Just as for divorcing wives, your best strategy with any lump-sum payments you receive is to transfer the money directly to a roll-over IRA so that your money will continue to grow tax-free until you're ready to retire.

GET DOWN TO BUSINESS

Here are some other practical steps that both divorcing wives and new widows need to take:

- **Use a team approach.** Most women know that an experienced, knowledgeable lawyer is critical to their ability to negotiate a fair divorce settlement. And an estate attorney can be of invaluable help with all the legal questions that arise following the death of a spouse. But in addition to legal counsel, it's also smart to consult a financial planner to help you work through the money issues. "A lawyer can't evaluate whether you should keep or sell the house or help you figure out which assets to keep or fill you in on the tax implications of the decisions you make," notes Miller. You might also want to touch base with an accountant on those tax questions, particularly if there's a lot of money involved. And, of course, if you can afford it, a good therapist at this point in your life would probably be worthwhile, too.

  To find the professionals you need to help you, your best bet is to ask friends, relatives, and colleagues who have been through similar circumstances to recommend the advisers and counselors whom they found most helpful. Reputations, after all, have to be earned, and I'd rather go with a known quantity than place my faith in a name randomly plucked from the yellow pages. If you have no luck with referrals, you can call professional associations for a list of specialists in your area. (You'll find information on these organizations in the resource section in the appendix of this book.) Whichever route you take to find someone, though, be sure to interview at least three candidates to get a sense of their style and smarts before you decide which ones are right for you in your present situation.

- **Take care of the paperwork.** Remove your husband's name from all joint bank, investment, and credit-card accounts, or close these accounts completely and open new ones in your name alone. You'll also need to change the beneficiary designations on any life insurance policies and retirement plans in your name. And you'll need to revise your will, naming new heirs and perhaps a new guardian for your children.

  You'll also need to update your insurance coverage. If you were covered under your husband's health insurance plan, for instance, your best bet is to switch to your own company's plan, if that option is available to you. If not, you can either shop for your own policy or continue coverage under your husband's plan for up to three years under the so-called COBRA rules (these federal rules, however, apply only if your husband's company has at least twenty employees). The main drawback: You'll have to pick up the full cost of the premiums, which is likely to run you a lot more money than was the case when the company was subsidizing the policy. (For more tips on how to find cost-effective insurance coverage, see chapter 9.)

  If you're widowed and have children in college or younger, you should also give some thought to beefing up your life insurance coverage, since you're now likely to be their only means of support. If you're getting a divorce and will be receiving alimony or child support, take out an inexpensive term life insurance policy on your ex, with your name duly noted as the beneficiary, for as long as those support payments are scheduled to continue.

- **Hang on—if it's to your advantage.** Legally, ten years is a magic number for the length of a marriage. As long as you've been married for at least that long and don't remarry, you can qualify for Social Security benefits based on an ex-spouse's earnings when you both reach age sixty-two, even if he has remarried or hasn't yet retired and begun to receive benefits himself. So if you're thinking of splitting after, say, nine and a half years, try to stick it out for a few more months.

Unless your husband died shortly after your honeymoon, widows really needn't concern themselves with any length-of-marriage requirements: You must have been married for a minimum of just nine months before his death to qualify for his Social Security benefits. And if he died as a result of an accident or in the course of military duty, that minimum is waived entirely. If you have children under age sixteen who live with you, you can begin collecting benefits as soon as you've notified the Social Security Administration (800–772–1213) and the paperwork is completed. Otherwise, you must be at least sixty to collect. But it pays to wait if you can. The longer you wait, the higher those payments will be.

LET IT GO

Let me share one more thought with those of you who are in the throes of a divorce.

There comes a point in many of these negotiations, particularly protracted ones, when you are paying a higher price emotionally for continuing to haggle than any additional money or other assets could possibly be worth. Don't confuse your need to get even with your soon-to-be ex with what you need from him financially. Don't be so bent on punishing him financially that you end up punishing yourself even more psychologically. If you're focused on getting even, your actions are still all about him when they should now be all about you. Don't get caught up in a game you can't possibly win.

Think about how many people you know who seem able to talk only about their divorce or their ex-husband or how they were wronged. Maybe it's the circles I run around in, but I've known plenty. And I can tell you they're not fun people to be around. Keep that attitude up, and you'll start to lose your friends as well as your husband. If you think you're depressed now, imagine how you'll feel then.

Sometimes it's better to compromise a little on the money in order to put this chapter of your life behind you and get on with the rest of your life—even when your lawyer, your mother, and your best friend are all urging you to push for more. Remember, the lawyer works for you, and Mother doesn't always know best.

Only your inner voice can determine for you when enough is enough. Listen to it above all other voices.

GET ON WITH YOUR LIFE

There is life after divorce. There is even life after a beloved spouse has died. But no one can or will or should make that new life for you. That's your job—and yours alone.

In the course of researching this book, I have come across dozens of inspiring women who have forged wonderful new lives for themselves after being widowed or divorced. There's Judy Mueller, the divorcee you met earlier in this chapter who founded a nonprofit legal and financial educational center for women so that others wouldn't make the mistakes she had. There's Frances Weaver, a homemaker for most of her life who was happily married to a prominent surgeon for thirty-five years but always felt "second-rate" herself, compared with his achievements. Since his death in 1979, she's become a prominent essayist, penning three books and traveling the world giving speeches. Says Frances, now seventy-three, "My big goal was to make my family proud of me, and along the way, I've become proud of myself, too."

Then there's Rosemary Garbett, a high school graduate who got married when she was only eighteen and left every financial decision up to her husband—that is, until the day he accidentally shot himself with a loaded gun he'd carelessly tossed onto the front seat of his car. Restaurateur Tom Garbett died on the spot, and for Rosemary his death signaled the end of more than twenty years of physical and emotional abuse that she'd silently suffered at his hands. She was forty at the time, and left with four teenage children, $20,000 in life insurance, three struggling Tex-Mex restaurants, and more than a quarter of a million dollars in debt. Rosemary tried to sell the restaurants to raise cash. But when she was offered only half the $800,000 at which they were appraised, she decided to hang on to the business and run it herself instead. Today, at sixty-two, she owns five flourishing restaurants, valued at over $5 million, and is far, far happier than she ever was during her years with Tom.

I've also come across dozens of women who are still trying to put the pieces of their new life together. Oneida Clark is one of them. At age forty-nine, Oneida's life fell apart when her husband died unexpectedly from a short, swift bout with cancer, and she was dismissed from her job as a manager at a janitorial-services company shortly thereafter. "At first I was depressed and just petrified out of mind," she confesses. Unfortunately, things got a lot worse before they got better. Oneida quickly learned that her husband had left little in the way of savings or insurance. And after months of looking for new a job, she found that no local employer wanted to hire her.

But Oneida didn't give up. "The hardest part was getting rid of the bitterness," she says. "But I soon realized that a pity party is no fun." So Oneida signed up for computer and other professional courses offered by a local agency that helps displaced homemakers, and is preparing herself mentally as well as educationally for another job search. "I've realized that the mother role that I've played for most of my life has given me a lot of skills I can transfer to the workplace, such as discipline, compassion, and dedication to the organization," she notes. "I take a lot of pride in my work, which I believe comes with age, and I can focus entirely on my job now, in a way that many younger wives and mothers can't." She adds, "I'm convinced that there will be a good job and a good life out there for me."

Oneida's advice to women in similar straits is simple: "Never put yourself down. Focus on your strong points and build on them. Realize that if you put your mind to a goal, nothing can stop you."

Like Oneida, I refuse to give in to self-pity or bitterness. Of course, it's scary to be alone again. I may always have approached life with a lot of zest and nerve, but that doesn't mean that I wasn't scared to death in the days and months following my break-up with Robert. I'm still scared sometimes. After all, a lot of things have changed in the fifteen-odd years since I was last single. I'm not twenty-five years old anymore; I'm not even thirty-five; I'm fifty years old and the thought of dating again is terrifying.

You have to say to yourself, as I do virtually every day, that it's going to be okay—maybe not today, or next week, but soon. There *is* another life out there for me, and with time I will find it.

Cultivating this attitude is, in fact, essential for overcoming any of the hard knocks life hands you—not just the kind that stem from relationships with men. Whether you've just lost a job, been turned down for a promotion, had your home damaged by a natural disaster, or otherwise hit hard times, say to yourself, "I may not know at this very moment how I'm going to overcome the obstacle that has been thrown in front of me, but I will find a way. I may have been knocked off the path to my goal temporarily, but I'll get back on and *I will still achieve it.*"

My goal for many years was to spend the rest of my life happily married to Robert Mosbacher, and that goal has been shattered. What hasn't been shattered is the greater goal: to share my life with someone who values me and whom I value in return. I don't know who that someone is right now. But I'm not going to sit here feeling sorry for myself and allow my failed marriage to defeat me or make me believe there isn't someone else out there for me.

There's still a lot of life to be lived, people and places to experience, joy and fun to be had. I won't let fear or lack of self-esteem stop me from experiencing that adventure. I've been to the base of the mountain before and climbed it, and I'll climb it again.

In short, I'm not going to quit.

Don't you quit, either.

ACTION PLAN
Studies show that nine out of every ten women are likely to find themselves on their own one day. Events like divorce or the death of a spouse can wreak financial as well as emotional devastation if you don't take steps to protect yourself. Here's what you've got to do to minimize the damage:

1. **Don't live on false hope**. If your marriage is troubled or your

spouse's health is poor, take action to safeguard your financial future now. At the very least, take a complete inventory of your family's income and assets, locate and copy the household's most important financial papers, and keep them filed together in a safe place. That way you'll have easy access to the financial information you need if you need it.

2. **If you don't have a liquid savings account in your name only, open one immediately.** If your husband passes away, you'll need access to cash quickly to pay your household and other expenses until his financial affairs are settled. And in the event of a break-up, a private account will ensure that you won't be left in a financial hole if your soon-to-be ex drains your joint accounts.

3. **Protect your key assets.** If you're headed toward divorce, inform your bank and any investment companies where you maintain joint accounts that both signatures will now be required on any withdrawals. If your husband is ill or considerably older than you are, make sure you're listed as a joint owner on all of your household's key savings and investment accounts. And have your husband appoint you as his durable power of attorney, which enables you to act legally and financially on his behalf if he becomes incapacitated.

4. **Figure out who your support system will be.** At a time like this, you'll need all the help from friends and loved ones you can get. Also, line up a team of professionals who can advise you on your best moves: an experienced divorce or estate attorney, a financial planner (and perhaps an accountant as well), and a good therapist, if you can afford one.

5. **Brush up on your professional skills if you've been out of the workforce for any length of time.** Renew contact with old friends and former colleagues who may be able to help you land a good job if you need one.

6. **Handle divorce negotiations in as businesslike a manner as possible.** Don't be consumed by getting even or any other emotion that can blind you to what is best for you financially. Hire the savviest matrimonial lawyer you can afford, consult a financial planner to help you run the numbers, think through the issues and options, and then cut your best deal.

7. **Remember the cardinal rule of divorce negotiations as you work out a settlement: Cash is king.** Nine times out of ten, when faced with the option of taking a hard asset, such as the house or a car, or accepting cash and other liquid assets instead, take the money and run. This rule, by the way, often turns out to be smart advice for widows, too.

8. **Don't neglect the paperwork.** Close all of your joint bank and investment accounts, change the beneficiaries on your insurance and retirement plans, and rewrite your will. You'll also need to update your life insurance policy, and your health coverage as well if you were covered by your husband's plan.

9. **Know when enough is enough.** No matter what anyone else urges you to do, heed the inner voice during divorce proceedings that tells you when whatever additional money you might get by continuing to negotiate is not worth the emotional price you'll pay.

10. **Let it go.** Once you've reached a final divorce settlement, once the sharpest wave of grief has passed, take concrete steps to forge a new life for yourself. Every morning when you wake up and every evening before you go to bed, tell yourself, "It's going to be okay—maybe not today or tomorrow but soon. There *is* another life out there for me—filled with fun and joy and adventures—and with time *I will find it!*"

Step 17:

Be Good to Yourself

Most women I know, myself included, spend the better part of their lives caring for others, routinely placing other people's interests before their own. We do it for our husbands, we do it for our children and, as we get older, we do it for our parents and often our spouse's parents, too. We're so busy looking after the many loved ones who depend on us, in fact, that we typically neglect the one person who truly needs us the most.

That person is you.

Think about it: We tend not to spend money on ourselves, unless we feel the item in question is truly a necessity. We defer to our family's tastes in just about everything—what to eat for dinner, which program to watch on TV, where to go on vacation, even, and especially, how much to save and where to invest our money. We rarely carve out time for ourselves to do what *we* want to do—see a friend, take a course, read a book, or simply be alone for an hour or two with our thoughts. Most important, we put our dreams on the back burner until our obligations to everyone else in our lives have been met.

By then, all too frequently, the flame has burned out.

In the long run, I'm convinced, this overdeveloped sense of selflessness—some might call it martyrdom—doesn't do anyone any good. Not your husband and not your kids, who as a result fail to learn the life skills they need to take care of themselves. And certainly not you, who will find your resentment building and your spirit slowly and painfully withering away. Without prized possessions and interests and experiences and goals of your very own, you become a less vibrant and, ultimately, less interesting person—to yourself and to everyone around you. You end up either bitter or faded, which are both, as far as I'm concerned, thoroughly unattractive and unacceptable outcomes.

You also, by the way, give up all hope for true financial security. You cannot achieve that all-important goal—or true fulfillment in anything else in this life, for that matter—without putting yourself and your needs first, at least part of the time. If you do not have skills of your own, friends of your own, possessions of your own, and money of your own, you are by definition dependent on someone else to provide those things for you. Now, that's what I call financial insecurity, with a great big capital I.

....

You cannot achieve financial security without putting yourself and your needs first, at least part of the time.

....

If you can't, at least some of the time, put yourself and your needs first for the right reason (because you deserve it!), do so for the most pragmatic reason of all: If you don't take care of yourself now, someone else will be forced to do it later. That, of course, assumes that there will be someone else around later, which we know is an assumption we cannot count on.

So get with the program, my friends: The time to start paying attention to your own needs is *now*!

GET RID OF THE GUILT

The root of the problem is guilt, I'm sure of it.

Maybe it's our natural maternal instincts (whether we have children or not), maybe it's the way we were raised, but we women typically feel guilty about wanting anything for ourselves. It's okay to want for our family, it's admirable to want for our children, it's understandable to want for our mothers and our husbands and even our best friends. But somehow we're not good people if we want something for ourselves and ourselves alone. It's not in our job description as nurturers and caregivers—and we pride ourselves on a job well done.

Well, that may be the way we feel, but it's simply not right. Everyone is entitled to something of their own—possessions, time, dreams.

To keep your dreams and your soul alive, you must schedule space for yourself in your life, the way you would schedule any other important activity, from a key business meeting to an appointment at the hair salon. At least once a month (for a full day) or once a week (for an entire morning or afternoon) or once a day (for an hour, at minimum), block out time for yourself to read, shop, take a course, visit your mom, write a few pages of the novel you've always dreamed of penning, or simply be alone, with no husband or kids or bosses around to demand anything of you. Then, just as you did earlier in this book when you were putting together an action plan to achieve your financial goals, mark the hour and day down in your date book and follow through.

No excuses. As the time approaches, remind yourself by saying out loud, "I deserve this. I am entitled to it. This moment in time belongs to me."

I also think it's a good idea to force yourself to spend money on yourself from time to time—not on something you really *need*, but on something you truly *want*. In other words, indulge yourself. Money shouldn't always be earmarked for serious and grand purposes, such as your retirement, your kids' college education, or a new house. Sometimes it should just be for fun. What good is working so hard to amass money if you never get to enjoy the fruits of your labor?

So take yourself out to lunch at that new restaurant you've been dying to try. Sign up for a half day of treatments at a nearby spa. Buy that cute little purse you saw in a shop window or the earrings or the sweater. Treat yourself to a new lipstick or book or CD. Take yourself to the movies or the theater or the ballet or some other activity that no one else in your family enjoys but you.

You deserve it.

Private space, private time, private stuff. They're all food for the soul. And you *do* deserve them. You *are* entitled to them. Everyone is.

LOOK FOR ENCOURAGEMENT

It's a lot easier to follow through with this plan if you share it with someone who will support your efforts. Better yet, find a partner. Maybe you have a girlfriend who's dying to break away occasionally, too. She might sign up for a course with you or be your once-a-month lunch date. It's certainly worth asking.

Moral support is just as crucial when it comes to taking the larger steps necessary to achieve your financial dreams. You need to surround yourself with the kind of friends, family members, and colleagues who will say yes, you can, no matter what the goal in question is or how overcome with self-doubt you become.

Just as important as knowing who to trust with your dreams is knowing who not to trust. I'm not just talking about the obvious candidates—those few people in your life who, for whatever reason, don't want you to succeed. I also mean the many good folks who might discourage you, seemingly for the best of reasons.

Brenda Lauderback, a sales and marketing executive who has achieved great success in her field, is a perfect case in point. When asked by *Executive Female* magazine to name the most important turning point in her career, Brenda, who at the time was group president of a leading shoe manufacturer, recalled a moment early in her working life when she was working for a different company and had just been promoted to be a buyer in women's sportswear. The kindly owner of a company with whom she regularly did business congratulated her on her new position. In turn, Brenda , who is African-American confided to him her ultimate career goal, which was to become a vice president and general merchandise manager at her firm. In his fatherly way, the man gently discouraged her from setting her sights too high, saying, "You will probably be disappointed. In the history of your company, there has never been a Jewish or female, much less black, vice president and GMM."

Far from discouraging Brenda, however, the man's comments spurred her to work even harder toward her goal. And she succeeded, becoming the first female, first African American, and youngest person ever to become a vice president and merchandise manager at that company. She holds no ill will toward the man who discouraged her because he meant her no harm and ended up teaching her a great lesson. "I learned that no matter what the intention, never let anyone put limits on you," Brenda told *Executive Female*. "The only limitations you have are in your mind."

TUNE OUT THE NAYSAYERS

How many times have *you* been gently discouraged by a colleague or your boss from pursuing a project or goal that seemed to them beyond your reach? How often has your best friend or your parents or your husband said, "Honey, you can't do that"? Or "That's impossible." Or even "Are you crazy?" They all mean well (or so they say) in their attempts to shield you from hurt and disappointment. But they'll do you harm with their defeatist attitude, nibbling away at your self-esteem and crushing your dreams before you've even positioned them for takeoff.

Don't let them.

When I get that kind of negative response, I discourage the conversation from the outset. No matter what the particular task is, if someone says to me, "Don't you find that hard?", my answer is no. "It's a challenge," I say, "and it'll be fun and exciting. I can't wait." That's my mantra, no matter what the "it" in question is.

Most recently, the "it" was an invitation from Lou Dobbs, producer of CNN's *Moneyline* program and head of that network's business coverage, to tape a pilot for a new talk show. Now, I've appeared as a guest on several television programs, but I've never done my own show, nor is TV the field in which I've been trained. And if you mess up on television, you're not exactly messing up anonymously. So I was nervous, to put it mildly. But I also knew that whether the show turned out to be successful or not, the opportunity was probably too good to pass up. And it could genuinely turn out to be exciting and fun.

. So I said yes. When I told friends about the upcoming pilot, some couldn't have been more supportive. "You're a natural," they'd tell me, or "You'll be great, don't worry" or variations on those themes. I think they genuinely meant what they were saying but, frankly, I didn't really care. Because even if they didn't mean it, those words were what I needed to hear at the time. And those were the friends I continued to turn to for counsel and encouragement at those odd moments when my skittishness about the project got the upper hand.

Other friends, however, couldn't help sharing their misgivings with me. They'd ask, "Won't it be hard, Georgette?" "Won't you be nervous?" "Have you ever *done* anything like this before?" They were particularly concerned because I'd be preparing for the pilot around the same time that I'd be finalizing my divorce from Robert. They'd ask, "Do you really need more stress at this time in your life, Georgette?" I have to tell you, I cut those conversations right off at the pass. I knew that if I let them continue, I'd find it too easy to use their negative comments as an excuse to back out rather than just getting on with the task at hand.

Because that's another mistake that women routinely make: We tend to seek out advice that will reinforce our unconscious desire to travel the easy route in life. It's easier for us to hear that we're crazy to want whatever it is that we want because then we don't have to take action. And if you don't take action, you don't have to be afraid of failing or goofing up or subjecting yourself to ridicule.

FORGIVE YOUR MISTAKES

What you must understand, though, is that you *will* make mistakes—mistakes are inevitable, they're a part of living. But mistakes don't have to be lethal. Regard them merely as road signs that say "Take a Detour Here" or "Warning: Change Direction."

Making mistakes doesn't mean that you're stupid or even that you're wrong; they're usually just lapses in judgment. And you know what? Big deal. Learn from those mistakes and move on.

Sometimes a mistake can even turn out to be positive if it causes you to move in a different direction, which in turn takes you where you want to go, perhaps even faster.

....

There is only one really and truly bad mistake you can make with your money, and that is entrusting your financial well-being to someone else.

....

As far as I'm concerned, there is only one really and truly bad mistake you can make with your money, and that is entrusting your financial well-being to someone else. Even that, however, isn't irrevocable. As you know, I've done it twice in my life, during my first and second marriages, and each time I had to rebuild my finances virtually from scratch again. But I recovered (emotionally *and* financially); I learned from my mistakes; and ultimately I triumphed (again, emotionally *and* financially).

Don't beat yourself up about a dismal outcome. Don't say to yourself, "See, I shouldn't have tried that, because I failed." That's a trap, a cop-out even. Instead say to yourself, "Okay, that didn't work, so let me try another way."

I'm not saying it's easy. You have to cultivate a bit of fearlessness, strengthen your inner voice, build your self-esteem. But you *can* do it if you put your mind to it.

LEARN FROM MEN

In this respect, I'd like to see women take their cues from men. Men typically don't internalize mistakes or wallow in self-blame the way that women so often do. As young boys, on the soccer field and the baseball diamond and all the other sports arenas in which they play, they learn that mistakes and even occasional failures are just part of the game. And they carry that ability to shrug off defeat and carry on with the task at hand well into their adult lives.

Here are a few other pointers I'd like to see women pick up from men:

- Men understand from a young age that money represents power and the freedom to do what they want. Women don't see it that way—and should.

- Men typically regard money as a sport, when it comes to both making it and spending it. Women don't—and should (at least up to a point). We seem unable to get real joy from money, to use it for pure fun. In other words, we take it too seriously. We hoard our money, even after we've achieved financial security, the very time we should be enjoying it the most.

- Men understand that you must take some risks in order to make your money grow. Women don't—and should. I'm not advocating rushing to act on every hot tip you hear, but rather taking carefully calculated, carefully researched risks when it's appropriate. As the saying goes: No guts, no glory.

Of course, there's plenty about the way men view money that we should reject as well. Topping my list is the way that men use money as a way to keep score in life, as if it's some kind of benchmark you can use to determine who's a winner and who's a loser. Following close behind is the way that men use money as a means of punishing or rewarding others, lavishing the green stuff on those who please them and withholding it from those who don't. That sort of behavior is mean and petty, plain and simple. And those are two qualities that I don't want any part of.

No, I wouldn't trade *our* attitude toward money for *theirs*, but I would like to incorporate a few feminized versions of these male traits in our mix.

Most of all, though, I'd like women to share the confidence that men have about their ability to manage money. As with so many things in life, men just assume that they can handle money well (even if they can't), while women assume that they can't (even if they can). Believing you can do it and do it well is really half the battle.

....

Men just assume that they can handle money well (even if they can't), while women assume that they can't (even if they can).

....

SPREAD THE WORD

If I could, I'd also pass that confidence on to the youngest generation of girls so that they don't grow up with the same hang-ups about money that so many of their moms and grandmas and sisters and aunts have.

You have to start young—really young. By the time they're teenagers, girls already feel far less confident and knowledgeable about managing their money than boys. Those are the findings of a new study of kids in the ninth, tenth, and eleventh grades by Girls Inc., a nonprofit group dedicated to helping girls become strong, smart, and bold. Girls are also far more reticent than boys about learning how to make money in the stock market (64 to 48 percent, according to the study), less likely to say they'd invest any money they earn, and when they *are* willing to invest, they say they'd put away much smaller amounts.

From whom do they learn all this stuff? From their moms, of course. Half the girls in the study said that their mother is the one person who has taught them the most about money, making it far and away the top response. (Dads, by the way, were a distant second, named by just 27 percent of the girls.)

As mothers (and sisters and grandmas and aunts and godmothers and friends), we owe it to our girls to do better. We owe it to our daughters to teach them the principles of financial planning as early as possible. We cannot pat them on the head and tell them not to worry. As mothers, we have a responsibility to tell them that they cannot rely on Daddy or Prince Charming or any other man to provide for them. We must tell them to depend only on themselves, so they will always be free to make the choices in their lives that they want.

If I had a daughter, this is the specific financial advice I'd pass along:

- First and foremost, get yourself the best education you can because it is crucial to have skills to make a good living.

- Always save some of the money you earn and do it in some automatic way so it doesn't require discipline from the outset.

- It's never too early to save. Start by putting aside a portion of the money you get on birthdays, continue with the dollars you get from baby-sitting, supplement your savings with cash earned from doing extra chores around the house or after-school jobs. Then keep up the savings habit for the rest of your life.

- Respect money. That means living within your means, shopping around for the best values, and never, ever abusing credit cards to finance a lifestyle you can't afford.

- Understand the importance of money in your life. Don't get caught up in that silly notion that money isn't everything and that we shouldn't be driven by money. Well, money *is* everything if you're hungry. In the real world, you need money. I'd tell my daughter not to listen to the people who tell her that money doesn't buy happiness—you just try being happy without it!

GET ON WITH IT

There is one more piece of advice that I'd pass along to my daughter—and I pass it along now to you, too, as we near the end of this book: *DO NOT WAIT A LIFETIME TO PAY ATTENTION TO YOUR NEEDS AND WANTS. THE TIME TO SEE TO YOUR OWN NEEDS IS NOW!*

Women constantly put their lives on hold, waiting for exactly the right time to do whatever it is they really want to do. We figure we'll start to save money after we get our next raise or pay off our credit cards or take that long-overdue vacation or renovate the kitchen. We tell ourselves that we'll pursue our dreams after our husbands are more settled in their careers or our kids have started school or when they're all grown up and don't need us around all the time anymore. Somehow, though, that ideal moment never comes, and we are left financially and spiritually bankrupt.

It is in your power to change that outcome.

Even small changes have the power to change your life dramatically for the better. Just ask Robin Steinner, fifty-six, a Chicago school nurse who made a single purchase for herself a few years back that ultimately led to her changing careers, husbands, and lifestyles. A self-described "helper type" who never had any burning career ambitions, Robin centered most of her adult life around her three kids, who were four, eight, and nine when her marriage to an artist broke up. Money was not particularly plentiful in the single-parent household that the split created, but there was enough to go around, as a result of steady child-support payments and various jobs that Robin took. Her longest stint (five and a half years) was as a travel agent. "I thought it would be my dream job because it seemed so glamorous and I loved to travel," she says. "But mostly what you do as an agent is sit by a computer and plan other people's trips. I didn't find that particularly fulfilling."

··

Don't listen to the people who tell you money doesn't buy happiness. You just try being happy without it!

··

Then, shortly after her forty-eighth birthday, Robin took a little trip of her own, to visit her sister, who owned a vacation cottage in the tiny town of Salt Haven on Lake Michigan, a two-hour drive from Chicago. While Robin was there, she fell in love with a tiny rundown cottage that was on the market for $25,000. Robin wanted it—badly. And so, after half a lifetime of working hard to make ends meet, of looking after her children's needs first, of being the ultimately pragmatic single parent, Robin did the thing she felt compelled to do. She bought the cottage, despite all the work that she'd have to do to make it habitable, despite the fact that her full-time job in Chicago would leave her little time to use it, and despite the fact that she could have come up with a thousand more practical uses for the money.

As it turned out, the decision to buy the cottage set off a chain reaction in the rest of Robin's life. Once she began using her vacation getaway, she realized how much she loved the little lakeside community and the life she lived there and how unwilling she was to use it only on weekends and the two weeks' annual vacation she got from the travel agency. So she quit her job, began substituting in Chicago's public school system, and soon landed a job as a school nurse at a suburban elementary school. (She had completed most of the course work for a nursing degree several years earlier.) The job turned out to be the fulfilling career that had eluded her when she was younger. She says, "It's like being a mother again, only now I've got six hundred kids instead of three."

The following year she also decided to marry the man she'd been involved with for seventeen years. And she's never been happier, spending her summers and weekends at the cottage and the rest of the year building a new life with her husband and students. "I feel like I'm living in paradise," she says, adding that she never consciously set out to change her life so completely. "Maybe it was the fact that I was approaching my fiftieth birthday, but somewhere along the line I realized that I'd been living my whole life for others and now it was my turn," she notes. "I realized I had only so many years left to enjoy my life in good health, and I wanted to get on with it. My feeling was—and still is—if not now, when?"

Indeed.

Robin's got it right. Whether you're twenty-five or eighty-five or anywhere in between, *now* is the right time to take control of your financial future. *Now* is the moment to take the steps necessary to put your goals and dreams into action. *Now, right now!*, is the point at which you should start to live the life you want and deserve.

As I told you at the very outset of this book: All it takes is money, honey—and the resolve to make it happen.

I've shown you how to get the first. Now the rest is up to you.

ACTION PLAN

To achieve true financial security, you have to learn to put your own interests first, at least some of the time. Women also need to take money a little less seriously, have fun with it. Here's how:

1. **Stop feeling guilty!** Everyone is entitled to want something for themselves and to pursue those wants, whether you're talking about money, possessions, time, or dreams. Carve out time by

making regular weekly or monthly appointments with yourself, put them in your day planner, and keep the date. Repeat to yourself when the time comes, "I deserve this. I am entitled to this. This moment in time belongs to me."

2. **Force yourself to spend money on yourself from time to time.** You don't have to drop a bundle (you shouldn't, in fact, if you can't afford it), but there's no reason you can't pamper yourself from time to time with some small treat—lunch out with a friend, a new book, a new tube of lipstick. Anything that will bring a smile to your face will do.

3. **Surround yourself with friends, colleagues, and family members who will support you in your goals.** To stay on track, everyone needs moral support and to hear the words "you can do it!" from time to time.

4. **Tune out the doubting Thomases and Thomasinas—even those who seem to have your best interests at heart.** Anyone who says "that's too hard" or "you're crazy to try" is not someone you want to hear from. Head them off with a positive comeback—something along the lines of "It's a challenge, yes, but I'm sure it will turn out great!"—and steer the conversation firmly in another direction.

5. **Forgive yourself for your mistakes and quickly move on.** Figure out what went wrong and use your newfound knowledge to point you back in the direction you want to go.

6. **Explain the financial facts of life to your daughters and nieces and little sisters while they are still young.** Let them know that Prince Charming isn't coming. Tell them they must depend on no one other than themselves to support them when they are grown.

Then help them learn the specific financial skills they need to make that outcome a reality.

7. **Get with the program—*now*!** No more excuses, no more putting it off until tomorrow. Start taking control of your financial life today and build a tomorrow of dreams come true.

Appendix

Resources to Help You On Your Way

*B*efore I leave you, I'd like to share some of the resources that I've found most helpful when it comes to managing my money and furthering my dreams. Here they are:

Good General Sources

American Association of Retired Persons
6011 E Street, NW
Washington, DC 20049
Phone: 202–434–2277
Website: www.aarp.org

Consumer Federation of America
1424 16th Street, NW, Suite 604
Washington, DC 20036
Phone: 202–387–6121
Website: under construction at this writing

National Center for Financial Education
P.O. Box 34070
San Diego, CA 92163–4070
Phone: 619–239–1401
Website: www.ncfe.org

National Center for Women and Retirement Research
Southampton College, Long Island University
239 Montauk Highway
Southampton, NY 11968
Phone: 800–426–7386
Website: www.southampton.liunet.edu/ncwrr

National Institute for Consumer Education
559 Gary M. Owen Building
300 W. Michigan Avenue
Ypsilanti, MI 48197
Phone: 734–487–2292
Website: www.emich.edu/public/coe/nice

Education Information

American Association of University Women
1111 16th Street, NW
Washington, DC 20036
Phone: 800–326–2289
Website: www.aauw.org

Business and Professional Women's Foundation
2012 Massachusetts Avenue, NW
Washington, DC 20036
Phone: 202–293–1100, ext. 169
Website: www.bpwusa.com

Council for Adult and Experiential Learning
243 South Mahash, Suite 800
Chicago, IL 60604
Phone: 312–922–5090
Website: www.cael.org

Directory of Financial Aids for Women
Reference Service Press
5000 Windplay Drive, Suite 4
El Dorado Hills, CA 95762
Phone: 916–939–9626
Website: www.rspfunding.com

Distance Education and Training Council
161 18th Street, NW
Washington, DC 20009
Phone: 202–234–5100
Website: www.detc.org

The Financial Aid Information Page
(sponsored by the **National Association of Student Financial Aid Administrators**)
Website only: www.finaid.org

United States Distance Learning Association
P.O. Box 5129
San Ramon, CA 94583
Phone: 510–820–5845
Website: www.usdla.org

Women Work! The National Network for Women's Employment
1625 K Street, NW
Washington, DC 20006
Phone: 202–467–6346
Website: www.womenwork.org

Investment Resources

American Association of Individual Investors
625 North Michigan Avenue, Suite 1900
Chicago, IL 60611
Phone: 312–280–0170
Website: www.aaii.com

Morningstar
225 West Wacker Avenue
Chicago, IL 60606
Phone: 800–735–0700
Website: www.morningstar.net

Mutual Fund Education Alliance
1900 Erie Street, Suite 120
Kansas City, MO 64116
Phone: 816–471–1454
Website: www/mfea.com

National Association of Investors Corp.
P.O. Box 220
Royal Oak, MI 48068–0220
Phone: 248–583–6242
Website: www.better-investing.org

Value Line Investment Survey
220 East 42nd Street
New York, NY 10017
Phone: 800–577–4566
Website: www.valueline.com

Other On-line Investment Resources

Charles Schwab: www.schwab.com
Hoover's: www.hoovers.com
Invest-o-rama: www.investorama.com
MarketPlayer: www.marketplayer.com
Money Magazine: www.money.com
Quicken: www.quicken.com
Vanguard: www.vanguard.com
Yahoo! Finance: www.yahoo.com

On-line Money-Management Resources Specifically for Women

Money Minded: www.moneyminded.com
WomenConnect: www.womenconnect.com/info/finance
Women's Wire: www.womenswire.com/money

Counsel and Advice: Financial Advisers

American Institute of Certified Public Accountants
1211 Avenue of the Americas
New York, NY 10036
Phone: 800–862–4272
Website: www.aicpa.org

American Society of CLU & ChFC
(insurance agents)
270 South Bryn Mawr Avenue
Bryn Mawr, PA 19010–2195
Phone: 888–243–2258
Website: www.agents-online.com

Institute of Certified Financial Planners
3801 E. Florida Avenue, Suite 708
Denver, CO 80210
Phone: 800–282–PLAN
Website: www.icfp.org

National Association of Personal Financial Advisors
355 West Dundee Road, Suite 200
Buffalo Grove, IL 60089
Phone: 888–FEE–ONLY
Website: www.napfa.org

Other Advisers

American Academy of Matrimonial Lawyers
150 North Michigan Avenue, Suite 2040
Chicago, IL 60601
Phone: 312–263–6477
Website: www.aaml.org

American Association for Marriage and Family Therapy
1133 15th Street, NW, Suite 300
Washington, DC 20005
Phone: 202–452–0109

National Child Support Enforcement Association
Hall of the States
400 No. Capitol Street, NW, Suite 370
Washington, DC 20001–1512
Phone: 202–624–8180

National Council on Child Abuse and Family Violence
1155 Connecticut Avenue, NW, Suite 400
Washington, DC 20036
Phone: 800–222–2000

Work/Entrepeneurs

American Women's Economic Development Corporation
71 Vanderbilt Avenue, Suite 320
New York, NY 10169
Phone: 212–692–9100
Website: www.womenconnect.com/awed

American Society of Women Entrepreneurs
2121 Precinct Road, Suite 240
Hurst, TX 76054
Phone: 888–669–2793
Website: www.aswe.org

National Association for Female Executives
30 Irving Place
New York, NY 10003
Phone: 800–634–6233
Website: www.nafe.com

National Association for the Self-Employed
P.O. Box 612067
DFW Airport
Dallas, TX 75261–2067
Phone: 800–232–6273
Website: www.nase.org

National Association of Women Business Owners
1100 Wayne Avenue, Suite 830
Silver Spring, MD 20910
Phone: 301–608–2590
Website: www.nawbo.org

Online Women's Business Center
Website only: www.onlinewbc.org

Service Corps of Retired Executives (SCORE)
409 3 Street, SW
Washington, DC 20024
Phone: 800–634–0245
Website: www.score.org

Small Business Administration's
Office of Women's Business Ownership
409 3 Street, SW
Washington, DC 20416
Phone: 800–827–5722
Website: www.sbaonline.sba.gov/womeninbusiness

Debt and Credit Card Resources

Bank Rate Monitor
11811 U.S. Highway 1
North Palm Beach, FL 33408
Phone: 561–627–7330
Web address: www.bankrate.com

CardTrak
RAM Research
P.O. Box 1700
Frederick, MD 21702
Phone: 800–344–7714
Web Address: www.cardtrak.com

National Foundation for Consumer Credit
8611 Second Avenue, Suite 100
Silver Spring, MD 20910
Phone: 800–388–2227
Website: www.nfcc.org

Insurance Resources

Ameritas
5900 "O" Street
P.O. Box 81889
Lincoln, NE 68501–1889
Phone: 800–552–3553
Website: www.ameritas.com

Insurance Information Network
110 William Street
New York, NY 10038
Phone: 212–669-9200
Website: www.iii.org

Insurance Shopping Network
6909 S. Holly Circle, Suite 240
Englewood, CO 80112
Phone: 800–467–8736
Website: www.insureme.com

MasterQuote
221 N. LaSalle Street, 27 floor
Chicago, IL 60601
Phone: 800–337–5433
Website: www.masterquote.com

Quotesmith
8205 South Cass Avenue, Suite 102
Darien, IL 60561
Phone: 800–556–9393
Website: www.quotesmith.com

USAA
9800 Frederiscksburg Road
San Antonio, TX 78288
Phone: 800–531–8000
Website: www.usaa.com

Index

Education (cont.)
    programs for women returning to
        school, 46–47, 51
    resources, 256–57
    see also Job skills
Emergency fund, building an, 92–94
Emotional roadblocks, *see* Mental traps
Employers:
    disability insurance, 111, 112
    401(k) plans, *see* 401(k) plans
    homework before an interview, 193
    maximizing your earning power
        with, *see* Maximizing your
        earning power
    on-the-job training, 51–52
    reimbursement for education
        expenses, 50–51
    retirement plans, *see* Retirement
        plans
    stock-purchase plans, 179
Employment, *see* Career
Entertainment expenses, 72, 79
Executive Female, 242, 243
Exercise, physical, 61
Exercises:
    goal-setting, 25–26
    mental, 23–24
Expenses:
    budget, developing a, 76–77
    figuring out your, 70–73

Failure, fear of, 27, 36
Family Money, 80, 117, 139
Ferguson, Charlotte, 52
Ferrarini, Elizabeth, 139–40
Fidelity Investments, 170
Financial IQ Test, xiii–xv
Financial planners, 231, 258–59
Financial safety net, *see* Safety net,
    having a
Financial security:
    Action Plan for independent, 14–15
    depending on someone else for,
        xviii, 4–6, 245
    false sense of, 124–25
    taking control of, 249–51
Financing a small business, 209–10,
    260–61
Flight insurance, 118
Floater, insurance policy, 114
Forbes, 172
401(k) plans, 84–87
    automatic deductions for, 84

borrowing against, 86–87, 144
divorce settlements and, 230
matching funds from employer, 84,
    85
payment to the widow, 230–31
penalties for early withdrawals, 86
taxes and, 84–85
Freelancers, *see* Self-employment
Friendships, 11, 13, 224, 225, 233,
    242–44
    see also Support network

Gap, the, 178
Garbett, Rosemary, 234–35
Garbett, Tom, 234
General Nutrition Company, 184
Georgette Mosbacher Enterprises, 11,
    203
Gifts, spending on, 73
Girls Inc., 248
Goals:
    Action Plan, 40
    baby steps first, 37–38
    breaking it down into do-able
        chunks, 35
    commitment to your, 35
    doing what you have to, 35
    emotional roadblocks, getting past,
        36–37
    initial lack of success, 36–37
    prioritizing, 26
    setting, 24–26
    step-by-step strategy to make it
        happen, 33–35
    tenacity in reaching, 38–39
    tools to achieve your, *see* Education;
        Job skills
Good Housekeeping, 52
Greenwood, Melissa, 139
Grooming, 62
Guilt, getting rid of, 241–42

Hanes, 177
Happiness and money, xviii
Hastings, Kimberly, 210
Health care expenses, 72
Health insurance, 106–108, 211, 212,
    232
Health maintenance organizations
    (HMOs), 106, 107
Henderson, Ann, 199, 202
Hidden costs, looking for, 140–43
Hoffman, Sharon, 148